The

Gigantic

Book of Games

for Youth Ministry,

Volume 1

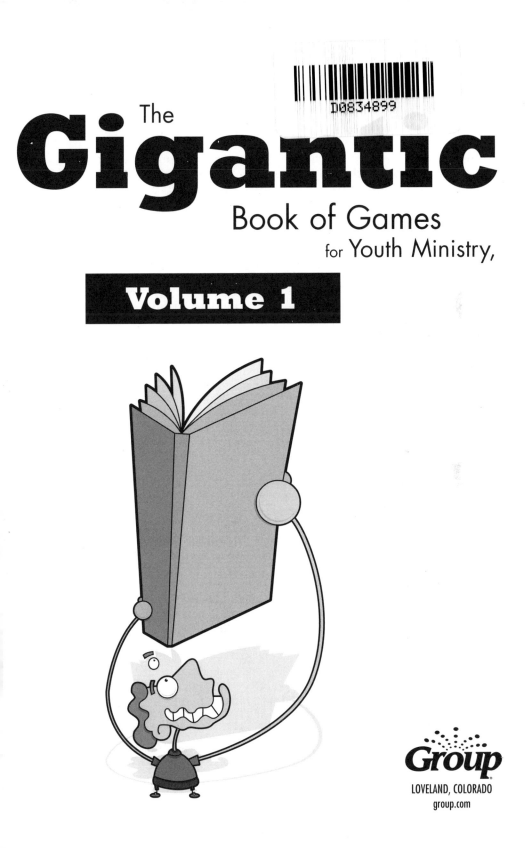

Group

LOVELAND, COLORADO

group.com

The **Gigantic** Book of Games for Youth Ministry, **Volume 1**
Copyright © 1999 Group Publishing, Inc.

Visit our website: **group.com**

Credits
Contributing Authors: Michelle Anthony, Tom Aron, Michael W. Capps, Karen Dockrey, Mike Gillespie, Monica K. Glenn, Michele Howe, Bill Hughes, Mikal Keefer, Pamela Ann Malloy, Erin McKay, Christina Medina, Julie Meiklejohn, Erika Moss, Lori Haynes Niles, Todd Outcalt, Siv M. Ricketts, Dave Thornton, and Helen Turnbull
Book Acquisitions Editor: Amy Simpson
Editor: Dennis R. McLaughlin
Creative Development Editor: Dave Thornton
Chief Creative Officer: Joani Schultz
Copy Editor: Julie Meiklejohn
Art Director: Ray Tollison
Cover Art Director: Jeff Storm
Cover Designer: Becky Hawley
Computer Graphic Artist: Eris Klein
Illustrators: Ray Tollison and Eris Klein
Production Manager: Peggy Naylor

Library of Congress Cataloging-in-Publication Data
The gigantic book of games for youth ministry/ [contributing authors,
   Michelle Anthony...et al.; editor, Dennis R. McLaughlin].
        p.   cm.
      Includes indexes.
      ISBN 978-0-7644-2113-6 (v. 1 : alk. paper)
      1. Church group work with teenagers.   2. Games in Christian
education.   I. Anthony, Michelle.   II. McLauglin, Dennis R.
BV4447.G54   1998
259' .23--dc21   98-29467
                                                       CIP

20 19 18 17 16   16 15 14 13 12

Printed in the United States of America.

Contents

Introduction 9

Bible-Learning Games 13

Team-Building Games 141

Introduction

Consider for a moment the life of Edith McLaughlin. When she was a child, she sat on her father's shoulders to hear a speech delivered by Ulysses S. Grant off the back of a train caboose. Not only did she go on and witness Edison's invention of the phonograph, but she was alive during the Industrial Revolution, the invention of the first automobile, and the Wright Brothers' invention of the flying machine. She lived through both World Wars, was around for the birth of the first computer, and then finally, from her television, watched the Apollo moon landing in 1969.

All the change that occurred from the time of Ulysses S. Grant to the time of Neil Armstrong is certainly amazing, but it moves into the category of perplexing when you consider that during our time the world changes that much every two years.

With such a rapidly changing society, it's little wonder that today's teenagers are being overwhelmed with an amazing array of pressures and challenges. The choices available to young people today, from the food they eat and the clothes they wear to the gods they worship, are greater than those of any previous period in human history. In his book *Right From Wrong,* Josh McDowell suggests that "today's youth are being…bombarded with thousands of hours of sounds and images that glamorize immorality and mock biblical values."

With so many choices competing for their time, it should not be surprising to hear many teenagers say, "I'm just too busy to come to another meeting!" As a result, the church is experiencing fewer and fewer opportunities to impact the lives of today's youth. While it is often clearly a matter of priorities, one can hardly deny that society's demands on teenagers have pushed them into such a frantic pace and hurried lifestyle that there is often little time left for them to build a solid faith relationship with Jesus Christ.

Consequently, the time teenagers do spend engaged in a

Christian group experience must be of substantial quality. It must be a time of healing and renewal; it must be a time when teenagers can share together, play together, and study God's Word together; and it must be a time they can laugh together.

In his recently released book, *The Second Coming of the Church,* George Barna claims that "to remain relevant and influential, we must be current in our understanding of cultural changes and their implications." One of our primary objectives at Group Publishing is to do just that. We recognize the tremendous pressures you face as you minister to teenagers in this quickly evolving society. We know your job isn't easy and your time is valuable. That's why we've developed this *easy-to-use* book with you in mind.

After perusing the pages of *The Gigantic Book of Games for Youth Ministry, Volume 1,* you will quickly discover that each game has been specifically included to help you enhance your group experience in one of three categories: (1) Bible-Learning; (2) Team-Building; and (3) Energy-Burning. We believe these three activity areas form the backbone of any successful group-ministry program for teenagers.

Bible-Learning Games will insightfully challenge your kids to develop a deeper Christian faith by strengthening their knowledge of the Bible.

Team-Building Games will encourage participants to work together and deepen friendships while teaching them a positive sense of sportsmanship.

Energy-Burning Games will help your kids unwind and get rid of excess built-up energy and stress.

You'll quickly discover that some of these games will turn into moments of laughter and will teach the kids not to take themselves too seriously. Others will challenge them to think deeply about their relationships with others, with their church, and with God.

As they experience each game, kids will enjoy being together while learning to be gracious winners. They'll receive the benefit of strengthening their self-image as a group and as individuals. In addition, these activities will motivate your teenagers to want to make their group meeting a high priority in their lives.

Not only does this book include three hundred exciting games, it also provides variations which will increase the ways in which you can use many of them. And if all these benefits aren't enough, the games are very easy-to-use as well.

Each game includes several quick *at-a-glance* references. Each one provides an overview that includes a list of the supplies you'll need and simple easy-to-understand directions to get you ready to roll. It also recommends an appropriate group size and tells you the time it will take to play.

Christian adults often express that some of their most memorable faith-building experiences are the result of youth group activities when they were teenagers. Thus, *The Gigantic Book of Games for Youth Ministry, Volume 1* promises to give you the tools necessary to make many lasting memories. But more importantly, it will provide opportunities to make life-changing differences in the fast-paced lives of your teenagers.

Bible-Learning Games

The Gigantic

Book of Games
for Youth Ministry,

Volume 1

Animals in Action

Overview: Kids will combine imagination and teamwork with their knowledge of Bible stories involving animals.

Supplies: You'll need a Bible and an index card for each team and a marker.

Preparation: Prepare the cards ahead of time so each one has a Bible reference and a brief description of the animal story written on it. Appropriate verses include: Jonah 1:17 (the great fish that swallowed Jonah); Matthew 13:47 (a net full of fish); Mark 5:11-13 (pigs with evil spirits); Luke 15:4-7 (a lost sheep); and John 12:14 (the donkey for Jesus' entry into Jerusalem). You can easily find others as well.

Time Involved: 20 minutes to 1 hour

Begin by selecting two or more "animal" teams made up of four to twelve players each. (Having more than ten animal teams will make it difficult to finish the game in one hour.) Next, instruct the teams to go to different parts of the activity area and prepare to make their animals. Give each team one card, and tell the teams to keep their animals' identities a secret. The object will be for the other teams to guess each animal correctly.

Instruct the kids on each team to assemble themselves so that their team can imitate the animal described on the card. No props should be used unless there are enough available for everyone. Once assembly is complete, each animal will be asked to move six to eight feet during the team's presentation. Allow teams ten to fifteen minutes to prepare.

Reassemble everyone, and call the teams forward one at a time. Allow the animal to move for about a minute. Ask everyone else to try to identify the animal. If a guess is correct, ask the guesser to decide which Bible story the animal is associated with. Then ask someone from the animal's team to read the Bible story. Be sure to have everyone applaud at the end of each animal presentation.

Conclude with a brief discussion about the importance of animals in the Bible. Ask:

● **How do the animals of the Bible better help us understand God's message?**

● **How can we use animals to show God's presence in our lives?**

Assemble the Message

Overview: Kids will meet each other as they match up words or phrases to form an important Bible message.

Supplies: You'll need a Bible, one index card for each player (two-inch squares of paper will work just as well), a marker, and a basket or a small box.

Preparation: Preparation is the key to success. Choose Bible verses that each have a total word count of at least double the number of kids you expect. (For example, if you expect forty kids, use verses with a total word count of at least eighty.)

Next, clearly write the first two or three words of the first Bible verse on a card and the next two or three words on a second card. Continue in this way to the end of the verse. Write the same letter on each card in each verse group so the kids will recognize more quickly which verse group is theirs. (The cards for the first Bible verse will each have an (a), the cards for the second Bible verse will each have a (b), and so on.) For example, Matthew 7:7 is a long verse, so it could be used for nine cards. On Card 1 write, "(a) Ask and"; on Card 2 write, "(a) it will be"; on Card 3 write, "(a) given to you;"; on Card 4 write, "(a) seek and"; on Card 5 write, "(a) you will find;"; on Card 6 write, "(a) knock and"; on Card 7 write, "(a) the door"; on Card 8 write, "(a) will be"; and on Card 9 write, "(a) opened to you".

Time Involved: 10 to 30 minutes

Put all the cards in the basket, and have kids each draw one as they arrive. Instruct them to find all the other kids with the same verse (indicated by the letters), and introduce themselves. Next, ask kids to arrange themselves in the correct order of the verse. Once everyone is in order, have each participant read off his or her part of the verse. Also have the groups include the Bible references for their verses.

Blind Eskimos

Overview: Kids will laugh their way into an important Bible lesson in this fun game.

Supplies: You'll need a Bible and several bandannas or strips of cloth to use as blindfolds.

Preparation: None is needed.

Time Involved: 10 to 15 minutes

Divide the group into male-female pairs, or randomly select partners. Instruct partners to stand about two feet apart and face each other. Then announce that they are going to practice the ancient Eskimo art of kissing by lightly rubbing their noses together. However, to make it interesting, one of the partners in each pair will be blindfolded. That person will move forward slowly and try to touch his or her nose to the tip of his or her partner's nose. The partner who is not blindfolded must not talk and cannot move or assist the blindfolded partner. If the participants are having difficulty, the partner in each pair who is not blindfolded may growl or make some other peculiar noise to guide his or her partner.

Leader TIP

If time allows, let both partners in each pair wear blindfolds.

After a few tries, have the partners switch roles. The misses and near misses are sure to generate laughs.

To simplify the game, have one partner in each pair close his or her eyes, eliminating the need for blindfolds.

After the game, read 1 John 4:20 and lead a brief discussion about love as mentioned in the Bible by asking the following questions:

● **What other kinds of love exist besides the one that exists between romantic partners?**

● **What does the Bible say about love?**

One appropriate verse about love and not seeing is 1 John 4:20b ("Anyone who does not love his brother, whom he has seen, cannot love God, whom he has not seen."). Any of the following Bible passages will help the group focus: Psalm 136; Matthew 3:17; Matthew 5:44; Matthew 19:19; John 13:34; or 1 John 4:16.

Choose Yes or No

Overview: Kids will learn to make choices quickly, based upon their knowledge of the Bible. They will also learn that God allows them to make choices.

Supplies: You'll need a Bible, masking tape (optional on floors or other hard surfaces), paper, and a pen or pencil.

Preparation: Make four parallel lines in the dirt (or use masking tape on a floor or another hard surface). The intervals between the lines should be fifteen feet, three feet, and fifteen feet. The length of the lines should be somewhat longer than necessary for all members of the group to stand side by side.

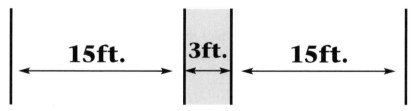

Next, make a list of simple Bible questions with "yes" or "no" answers. Use the following questions to get you started:

● Did Peter deny three times that he knew Jesus? (yes)

- Did Jesus bring a dead man back to life? (yes)
- Did Judas kiss Jesus because he loved him? (no)
- Does the first of the Ten Commandments say: "You shall not murder"? (no)
- Did John the Baptist die on a cross? (no)
- Were Noah and the others on the ark the only survivors of the great flood? (yes)
- Did it take God seven days to create the world? (a tricky "no"—it was created in six days and God rested on the seventh day)

Time Involved: 10 to 30 minutes

Randomly divide the group into two equal teams, and have the teams stand on the center two lines (three feet apart), facing each other. Designate one team "Blue" and the other team "Red."

Tell the group that you'll read a Bible question aloud. If the answer to the question is "yes," the members of the Red team should turn and run to the line fifteen feet behind them. The Blue team should try to tag the Red team players before they get to the line. If the answer to the question is "no," the members of the Blue team should turn and run to the line fifteen feet behind them. As they run, the Red team should try to tag them before they get to the line. Every player that gets tagged joins the opposing team. Kids tagged several times will change teams every time they are tagged. Expect some exciting confusion, as the kids will occasionally run the wrong way.

The first team to tag all the other team's members wins. If a winning team has not surfaced within the allotted time, stop the game and declare the team with the most members the winner.

After the game, ask the group to assemble in a circle for a brief discussion about choices. Ask:

- **During the game, did you have a choice about which way to run or did you have to follow your teammates?**
- **In life, what kinds of choices do we have to make?**

- **Why does God let us make choices in our lives?**
- **What is the biggest choice he lets us make?**

Reading and discussing Deuteronomy 30:19 will help show the group that God does not force anyone to choose his way of doing things. Rather, God hopes that we will choose him (life).

Leader TIP

If you have more than thirty minutes, groups larger than forty can play this game and also have a meaningful experience.

Clobber the Cliché

Overview: Kids will gain awareness of the importance of words in this fun, noncompetitive game. They'll also see that the slightest change in a saying can cause a significant change in meaning.

Supplies: You'll need a Bible, index cards or small sheets of paper, pens or pencils, and a dictionary (optional).

Preparation: Make a list of clichés and other popular sayings to get the game started. (Do this only if you think your group may need help.)

Time Involved: 15 to 30 minutes

If there are more than nine or ten kids in the group, divide them into teams of two or three kids each. Give each player (or team) an index card or a small sheet of paper and a pen or a pencil. Every player (or team) should select a cliché or saying and write a parody on it. (Note: A parody is a weak or humorous imitation.) Changing one or two words in a saying will create a funny takeoff on the original. Here are a few examples:

- "If at first you don't succeed, *cry, cry* (try, try) again."
- "A bird in the hand *usually pecks you* (is worth two in the bush)."

- "A fool and his money *will get a lot of dates* (are soon parted)."
- "You can lead a horse to water, but you can't make him *brush his teeth* (drink)."

After each team has written a parody, have someone on the team read it out loud. You may choose to give special recognition to the most clever and funniest ones.

After the game, lead a brief discussion about the importance of words in understanding and using the Bible. Ask:

- **How important were the individual words to the overall meaning of each saying?**
- **Why should we be careful with the words we use?**
- **What does the Bible say about using words carefully?**

Helpful Bible references include Proverbs 4:20-22; Isaiah 55:11; Jeremiah 1:12; Romans 10:8-10; and, especially, James 1:26.

Don't Laugh

Overview: Kids will experience the difficulty of trying not to laugh in inappropriate moments as well as learning an underlying spiritual lesson.

Supplies: You'll need a Bible.

Preparation: None is needed.

Time Involved: 10 to 30 minutes

Begin by instructing kids to say the word "Ha!" without laughing and with solemn looks on their faces. Have the first person begin the game by saying, "Ha!" Have the second person say, "Ha! Ha!" and so on. If there are twenty-five kids in the group, the last person will say "Ha!" twenty-five times.

It's unlikely that you'll get all the way around the group before someone laughs and sparks the entire group's laughter. When this occurs, start over again by having the next person begin with one "Ha!" and continue around the group.

At the end, have a brief discussion using the following questions:

● **Were you uncomfortable with the rule against laughing? Explain.**

● **How did you feel when others laughed and you tried not to?**

● **Do you think that God wants us to be happy and enjoys our laughing? Why or why not?**

Refer to Psalm 118:24. See also Genesis 17:19 and note that God told Abraham to name his son Isaac (meaning "he laughs" in Hebrew). Refer also to Genesis 21:6 where Sarah (Isaac's mother) says, "God has brought me laughter."

> ## Variation
> When traveling in a bus, kids can play this game by staying in their seats and facing the aisle. It will definitely be a happy bus!

Feed the Hungry

Overview: Kids will experience feeding their teammates and being fed by them in a competitive game that has biblical significance.

Supplies: You'll need a Bible, chairs, toothpicks, paper cupcake-pan liners, and four pieces of candy corn for each person.

Preparation: None is needed.

Time Involved: 10 to 30 minutes

Randomly divide the group into three or four equal teams. Arrange the chairs in single file lines, and have members of each team sit in the chairs in one line. Give each person a toothpick and a paper cupcake-pan liner with four pieces of candy corn in it. Tell kids that no one is allowed to touch the candy with his or her hands, and no one may eat directly out of his or her cup. Everyone must feed and be fed by another team member.

To begin, have the first person in line on each team feed all four pieces of candy to the player immediately behind him or her. (The candy should be pierced and lifted with the toothpick and placed in the other person's mouth.) When the first person finishes feeding the second person, that person should then feed the next team member in line. Continue this process until the last person on the team has been fed. The last person should then jump up and run to the front of the line and feed the first person. The first team that finishes feeding all of its members is declared the winner. A prize for the winning team is optional.

After the game, ask kids to form a circle for a brief discussion. Ask:

● **What did it feel like to feed someone in this manner? To be fed?**

● **What would it be like to feed someone who was really starving?**

● **Name some Bible stories about feeding the hungry.**

A few Scriptural references that will be helpful include Exodus 16; Matthew 14:13-21; and Matthew 15:29-39.

If time allows, a second important discussion may be started with the following questions:

● **What did Jesus say in Matthew 6:2 about giving to the needy?**

● **What did he say about our own hunger in Matthew 6:25-26?**

● **What did Jesus mean in John 21:15-17 when he said, "feed my lambs" and "take care of my sheep"?**

Find the Lost Riches

Overview: Kids will experience a faith lesson by finding lost treasures.

Supplies: You'll need a Bible; index cards; several small items such as a coin, a candy bar, a peanut in its shell, a pencil, a small toy, a book, a hand tool, or a kitchen utensil (at least one item per person); a pen; paper; a battery-operated CD or cassette player; an inspiring, somewhat loud musical selection; and a watch with a second hand.

Preparation: Write the name of each item on a separate card. Hide the items around the activity area, and make a note of the locations on a piece of paper for use during the game.

Time Involved: 20 to 40 minutes

Give each person an index card, and say: **The item on the card is your lost treasure. It is lost somewhere in the activity area; you'll need to use all your senses to find it. You are not allowed to help each other.**

Variation

If your group exceeds twelve kids, randomly divide kids into teams of two or three each to keep the game within the expected time range.

Send kids out one at a time, and keep track of each person's time. Kids may ask questions about how they are to find the items. Repeat the instruction that they are to use all their senses. The person who finds his or her lost treasure the most quickly wins.

At the beginning of the game, begin to play the CD or cassette player at a moderate volume. As the first person moves near the hiding place for his or her lost treasure, gradually increase the volume. As he or she moves away from the hiding place, gradually decrease the volume. When the player is very close to the hiding place, turn the volume of the CD or cassette player up to its maximum level. Continue in this way with all of the other group members. Give no indication before the game that this is the purpose of the music; kids will quickly figure it out on their own.

Assemble everyone in a circle after the game. Begin a brief discussion focused on faith and believing. Ask:

● **Before you started your search, did you really believe your hidden item was out there? How about after you searched for a while? Explain.**

● **In your life, do you have to see something before you believe in it or do you believe in it before you see it?**

Helpful references include Matthew 7:7-8; Luke 18:40-42; and 2 Corinthians 5:7.

If time allows, discuss a related and important biblical idea, using the following question:

● **What are the lost treasures, or riches, in our lives?**

Refer the group to Matthew 13:44; Luke 15:8-10; and Philippians 4:19.

Finish the Quote

Overview: Kids will gain knowledge of parts of the Bible in this fun contest.

Supplies: You'll need a Bible, paper, a pencil, and a watch with a second hand.

Preparation: Make a list of famous Bible quotes, including the appropriate references along with the people who said them. Include one quote for each person in your group. The following are some suggested Bible quotes and answers:

1. "The Lord is my shepherd,..." ("I shall not be in want.")
—Psalm 23; David

2. "So God created man..." ("in his own image.")
—Genesis 1:27; Moses

3. "Blessed are the poor in spirit..." ("for theirs is the kingdom of heaven.")—Matthew 5:3; Jesus during the Sermon on the Mount

4. "Do not be afraid. I bring you..." ("good news of great joy.")—Luke 2:10; an angel of the Lord announcing Jesus' birth

5. "You shall have no other gods..." ("before me.")—Exodus 20:3; Moses in the Ten Commandments given to him by God

6. "In my Father's house are many rooms; if it were not so, I would have told you. I am going there to..." ("prepare a place for you.")—John 14:2; Jesus

7. "I tell you the truth, anyone who will not receive the kingdom of God like a little child..." ("will never enter it.")—Mark 10:15; Jesus

8. "Therefore everyone who hears these words of mine and puts them into practice is like a wise man who built his house..."

("on the rock.")—Matthew 7:24; Jesus

9. "Give to Caesar what is Caesar's, and..." ("to God what is God's.")—Matthew 22:21 and Luke 20:25; Jesus

10. "Surely this man was..." ("the Son of God!")—Mark 15:39b; an unnamed Roman soldier at Jesus' crucifixion

11. "So in everything, do to others what..." ("you would have them do to you.")—Matthew 7:12; Jesus

12. "Seven days from now I will send rain on the earth for..." ("forty days and forty nights.")—Genesis 7:4; God talking to Noah

Time Involved: 20 to 30 minutes

Randomly divide the group into two teams. Tell them that each person will be given the first part of a famous Bible quote. That person will then be allowed ten seconds to finish the quote. If he or she does so correctly, the person's team gets five points. If he or she fails to finish the quote correctly within the allotted time, the opposing team will be allowed five seconds to offer one answer. The members of the second team may confer quickly for their answer. If the opposing team members give the correct answer, they will get the five points. If no one gives the correct answer, move to the next quote. The teams should take turns trying to complete each Bible quote.

If the first person correctly finishes the quote, his or her entire team can be given a bonus question. Allow team members to confer on the bonus question. They have ten seconds to offer one answer that identifies either the person who said the quote or the book of the Bible the quote is found in. This also applies to the opposing team that correctly finishes the quote if the first player fails to do so. A correct and timely answer to a bonus question should be awarded twenty points. There is no penalty for an incorrect answer. After all the players on both teams have had an opportunity to finish a quote, the team totals should be added and the winning team congratulated.

Conclude with a brief discussion on the Bible quotes or the bonus questions that both teams missed. You can also use the

26

following questions to encourage further discussion:
- **What does this quote mean to you?**
- **How can the meaning of the quote help you in your life now?**

The Happy Bible Quiz

Overview: Kids will love this fun Bible quiz that promotes laughter and joy with its unusual questions and offbeat answers. There are no losers in this contest! This game will refresh kids' memories about some Bible passages, but primarily it will be an exercise in lighthearted fun. All the answers are silly, and some effort may be required to read them for the maximum laughs.

Supplies: You'll need a Bible, "The Happy Bible Quiz" handout (pp. 28-30), scissors, and small candies or other treats to use as prizes.

Preparation: Cut the "Happy Bible Quiz" handout into cards ahead of time. You might also want to consider saving the cards for later use with another group. Have sufficient prizes so that everyone gets one. See the list of suggested questions and answers on the handout that follows the game description.

Time Involved: 30 minutes to 1 hour

After explaining the game, read one card as an example.

Let each person read at least one card by first asking the question and then allowing the group one minute to guess the answer. After an appropriate pause, encourage the Reader to give the answer. The fun begins when the answers are read. The group should be encouraged to indicate their approval of the answers by laughing or clapping or their disapproval with a loud "argh!" Feel free to lead kids in applause or an "argh!" especially at the beginning of the game. Remind the group that an "argh!" (or disapproval) is directed at the answer and not at the Reader.

In the rare event that someone correctly guesses an answer, give him or her a prize. Remember to keep the competition lighthearted.

After completing the questions and answers, hand out prizes to everyone. Then lead a brief discussion about joy and laughter using the following questions:

- **What made us laugh during the game?**
- **What benefit is there to being joyful?**
- **Does the Bible suggest that God wants us to be joyful?**

Helpful Bible references are Luke 1:44, 57-58; Luke 2:10; 2 Corinthians 9:7; and Philippians 4:4.

THE HAPPY BIBLE QUIZ

Q: When was money first mentioned in the Bible?

A: When the dove brought the *green back* to Noah's ark.

....

Q: When was making money first mentioned in the Bible?

A: When Pharaoh's daughter got a little *prophet* (profit) from the bulrushes.

....

Q: How did God prevent Adam and Eve from gambling?

A: He took away their *paradise* (pair of dice).

....

Q: Why couldn't Noah play cards on the ark?

A: Because some of the animals sat on the *deck*.

....

Q: Who was the greatest financial genius in the Bible?

A: Noah—he *floated his stock* while the whole world was *in liquidation*.

....

Q: Who took the most stuff onto Noah's ark?

A: The elephant. He took his whole *trunk*.

....

Q: Who took the least stuff onto Noah's ark?

A: The rooster. All he took was his *comb*.

....

Q: (Argh! Not another Noah question!) What did the tomcat say just before the ark landed?

A: Is that *Ararat* (a rat)?

Q: Was Adam born in the a.m. or the p.m.?

A: p.m.— just shortly before *Eve*.

....

Q: Why didn't Eve catch the chickenpox?

A: Because she'd already *Adam* (had 'em).

....

Q: How do we know that Adam and Eve were rowdy?

A: Because they *raised Cain.*

....

Q: What man in the Bible had no parents?

A: Joshua—he was the *son of Nun.*

....

Q: The world's shortest man was mentioned in the book of Job. Who is he?

A: Bildad the *Shuhite* (shoe height).

....

Q: Who was the straightest man in the Bible?

A: Joseph—the pharaoh made a *ruler* out of him.

....

Q: Who was the most popular actor in the Bible?

A: Samson—he *brought down the house.*

....

Q: What was the minor physical problem that actually killed Samson?

A: *Fallen arches.*

....

Q: Who was the most successful doctor in the Bible?

A: Job—he had the most *patience* (patients).

....

Q: Why should we be encouraged by the story of Jonah?

A: He was *down in the mouth,* but he came out OK.

Q: When were there five people sleeping in Moses' bed?

A: When Moses slept with his *forefathers*.

....

Q: Eve really wasn't the first woman in the Bible. Who was?

A: It was *Genesis* (Jenny Sis).

....

Q: Baseball was popular in the Bible. The first "World Series" was held in the Valley of Elah. The Israelites won. Who was their "star pitcher," and who did he beat?

A: David—he was the "rookie of the year" and he struck out the giants *(Giants)*.

....

Q: The Israelites' "general manager" was the first to use "baseball scouts." Who was he and what did he do?

A: Saul—he told his attendants, *"Find someone who plays well and bring him to me."*

....

Q: Who was the first woman mentioned in Bible baseball?

A: Rebekah—she went to the well with the *pitcher*.

....

Q: Who was the first person to score in Bible baseball?

A: The Prodigal Son—he made a *home run*.

....

Q: Jesus was asleep when the storm came up on the lake. The scared disciples awakened him, and he calmed the waters. After they got to shore, ten of the disciples formed a great basketball team. What were they called?

A: The *lakers* (Lakers)

....

Q: The other two disciples joined up with a different basketball team. What were these guys called?

A: The *parables* (pair of Bulls).

....

Q: What did Noah have to keep repeating to the rabbits?

A: Only two! Only two!

Keep It Up!

Overview: Kids will develop teamwork and learn Bible verses that call for unity.

Supplies: You'll need a Bible, large feathers or medium-sized party balloons, and a CD or cassette player with music appropriate for the game.

Preparation: If balloons are used, be sure to inflate them first.

Time Involved: 15 to 45 minutes

Divide the group randomly into equal-sized teams. Each team should have at least three kids, with a maximum of ten. Mix boys and girls. Instruct members of each team to hold hands in a small circle and not let go during the game. The object of the game is to keep a balloon or feather in the air by blowing on it. Touching it in any way will be considered the same as letting it hit the floor.

The team that keeps the feather or balloon in the air the longest wins the game. Declare a tie if more than one team keeps its balloon up in the air continuously until the end of the game. The maximum length of play should be ten or fifteen minutes.

If a team allows its feather or balloon to hit the floor, toss it up again and resume play. Everyone should keep playing until either a winner is declared or the time runs out.

Active and age-appropriate music will add to the fun if it is played during the game. The players often will move to the rhythm as they try to "keep it up!"

After the game, assemble everyone and lead a brief discussion about teamwork and the Bible. The following questions will be helpful:

● **What was the main reason for holding hands?**

Leader TIP

If your group is large, you will need more assistants to help monitor all the teams' efforts to "keep it up."

● **What was the primary reason for success in "keeping it up"?**

● **How are teamwork and unity of purpose encouraged in the Bible?**

You may choose to read part of Paul's letter to the Romans (15:5-6). Refer also to Psalm 133:1 and Colossians 3:13-14.

The Magic Mirror

Overview: Kids will get a chance to use their imaginations in this brain-teaser game as they test their memories of Bible names.

Supplies: You'll need Bibles, a large mirror, poster board, markers, paper, and pencils.

Preparation: Use the poster board and the marker to make a sign that says "Mirror, mirror on the wall—just show me!" and tape it to the mirror.

Time Involved: 10 to 20 minutes

Place the mirror before the group, and instruct kids to write as many names of people in the Bible as possible using the letters on the sign on the mirror. Encourage kids to use their Bibles, and let them know there is a potential for many names. Here are a few of the obvious ones: Jesus, James, John, Lot, Matthew, Miriam, Naomi, Noah, and Thomas. After about ten minutes, declare the player with the most names the winner.

As time allows, lead a brief discussion about the people named in the game.

Variation

If you have more than ten kids, divide them into teams of two or three each. Everyone will have fun "brainstorming" name ideas with their teammates.

Run With the Angels

Overview: Kids will get an opportunity to use teamwork while they experience safety and protection similar to that promised in the Bible.

Supplies: You'll need a Bible, two baseball bats, and tape.

Preparation: None is needed.

Time Involved: 20 to 40 minutes

Randomly divide the group into two equal-sized teams, and have the teams stand about twenty feet apart. Have teams form trios, and have the trios line up single file behind a starting line (use tape for this if necessary). Have members of each trio stand side by side.

Leader TIP

If the group isn't divisible by three, select a person to go twice.

The middle person in each trio will be designated the Leader for the first run. Each trio will run three times with a different player as the Leader each time. When the game is finished, everyone will have had the opportunity to be a Leader once and an accompanying person (an Angel) twice.

Establish a turnaround point for each team about thirty feet from the starting line. At each team's turnaround point, put a baseball bat on the ground. When the game begins, the first trio on each team should be instructed to run to the turnaround point. Have each Leader place the bat upright on the floor or the ground and put his or her forehead on the upper end. While in this position, the Leader should quickly run around the bat three times and then run back to the starting line. His or her two teammates (Angels) should run back with the Leader, staying close at hand to keep the Leader from falling or straying because of dizziness.

As soon as the first trio gets back to the starting line, the next trio should repeat the same process. After the members of each trio complete a turn, they'll go to the end of their team's line. One of the Angels in the finishing trio will become the Leader for the trio's next run. This rotation should continue until every person on the team has run as a Leader. The first team to complete a full rotation is declared the winner.

When the game is finished, assemble the group and lead a discussion about the experience. Ask the following questions to help everyone focus on the significance of the Bible to the experience.

● **Did the dizziness make anyone afraid of falling?**

● **How did you feel about your two Angels when you were dizzy and trying to run?**

● **What events in your life can make you feel off-balance?**

● **How does God give you protection in life like you had in this game?**

Continue the focus on God's protection by referring to Psalm 91:11-12, 14-15. Refer also to Psalm 23; 103:20; and Ephesians 6:10-11. Remind kids that according to Matthew 7:7-8, they can ask God for his protection in their lives.

The Bear in Heaven

Overview: Players will be inspired to consider the numerous Bible references to heaven while playing this fun, noncompetitive game.

Supplies: You'll need Bibles, a double-sized blanket, and a large teddy bear.

Preparation: None is needed.

Time Involved: 10 to 20 minutes

Spread the blanket on the ground, and have kids stand around it. Have them slightly roll up the blanket's edges and get a good grip on it. Place the teddy bear in the center of the blanket, and announce that kids are going to try to toss the bear high enough to go to heaven.

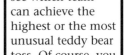

After having the whole group yell "one, two, three—go to heaven!" have everyone pull back on the blanket at the same time to toss the teddy bear in the air. Encourage kids to repeat this several times, trying to achieve higher and higher tosses. As kids become better at tossing the teddy bear into the air, encourage them to try to catch the falling teddy bear in the blanket for an instantaneous re-toss or to try other tricks.

Variation

If you have ten or more kids, consider dividing the group into teams of four or five each and see which team can achieve the highest or the most unusual teddy bear toss. Of course, you should give the teddy bear a nickname!

Conclude the game with a discussion about the common Bible references to heaven being "up" or "above us." These questions may help start the discussion:

● **How do we regard heaven when we think about going there?**

● **If heaven isn't above us, where is it?**

● **What Bible passages suggest that heaven is above us?**

Leader TIP

If younger kids are involved, one or two may be tempted to get on the blanket and be tossed like the teddy bear. Discourage this for safety reasons.

The following references will help inspire kids to look through their Bibles: Matthew 28:2 ("for an angel of the Lord came *down* from heaven."); Matthew 28:6 ("He is not here; he has *risen*."); and Mark 16:19 ("After the Lord Jesus had spoken to them, he was *taken up* into heaven.).

Lions and Snakes

Overview: Kids will get a fun lesson about God's protection as they play this noncompetitive game.

Supplies: You'll need a Bible, clothesline rope, scissors, tape, and plenty of balloons.

Preparation: Cut the rope into five-foot lengths, one for each player. Then blow up the balloons and tie one to one end of each rope length. Blow up a few extra balloons in case some get popped during the game.

Time Involved: 15 to 30 minutes

Have kids form pairs, and designate one partner in each pair a Lion. Give the Lion in each pair a length of rope, and have him or her tuck the rope in the back of his or her pants as a tail. The balloon end should drag on the floor. Designate the other partner in each pair a Snake, and give each Snake a length of rope. Have each Snake loosely tie his or her rope length around one wrist or hand so that his or her balloon also drags on the floor.

Mark off a starting line and a finish line about twenty yards apart, and line up all the pairs at the starting line. Tell kids that when you shout "Lion!" the Snakes should run to the finish line, dragging their balloons behind them. The Lions should chase their partners, trying to step on the balloons. When the Lions chase the Snakes, they should be encouraged to roar loudly. The chasing stops when each Snake crosses the finish line.

Next tell kids that when you shout "Snake!" the Lions will run back to the starting line. The Snakes will chase them, trying to step on the balloons tied on the Lions' "tails." When the Snakes chase the Lions, they should hiss loudly. The chasing stops when the Lions all cross the starting line.

If a balloon gets stepped on or pops from being dragged, tie on an extra balloon and resume play. Continue the game until it appears that kids are starting to lose their excitement or a predetermined time limit has been reached.

After the game, let kids "cool down" by

Leader TIP

Check the heights of your kids to make sure that five-foot lengths of rope will be long enough to allow the balloons to drag safely on the floor. If a length of rope is too short, the balloon will be too close to the runner and he or she might get kicked accidentally by his or her partner trying to step on the balloon.

sitting in a circle while you lead a discussion about lions and snakes in the Bible. Begin by asking the following questions:

● **How did you like chasing your partner? How did you like being chased?**

● **What do snakes and lions usually represent in Bible stories?**

● **What does God want us to know about protection from lions and snakes?**

Review Genesis 3:1-4, 13-15 (the serpent tempted Eve); Psalm 91:13-14 (God promised his protection); Daniel 6:16-23 (God protected Daniel); and Matthew 12:34 (Jesus called evil men "vipers").

Hidden Path

Overview: Kids will compete in a game that helps them discover God's path for their lives.

Supplies: You'll need a Bible, two 12x3-foot strips of newsprint, masking tape, a yardstick, a marker, a small sheet of paper, and a pen.

Preparation: Tape the two strips of heavy paper side by side on the floor to make a paper runway that's twelve feet long and six feet wide. Mark one end "Start" and the other end "Finish." Use the yardstick and the marker to mark off the runway in one-foot intervals lengthwise and widthwise, creating seventy-two squares. Then randomly print a letter or a symbol in each of the squares. On the small sheet of paper, hand-draw a key showing the runway and mark a pathway from Start to Finish. For an example, see the illustration following this game.

Time Involved: 20 to 30 minutes

Divide the group into two teams, and line them up at Start. Have kids all remove their shoes and play in their socks. Announce that there is a hidden path down the runway to Finish and the team which first gets one of its members to Finish wins.

Leader TIP

Preparation for this game may take thirty minutes and is easiest to do before the kids arrive. Be sure to make the hidden path more straightforward for younger kids and more difficult or erratic for older ones. An example of a more straightforward path is included below.

Tell kids that only one person at a time will be allowed on the runway. He or she will be allowed to proceed by stepping from one square to another until he or she steps onto a square that isn't in the hidden path. When a misstep occurs, yell "off!" and have the person go to the back of his or her team's line. A member of the other team will then take a turn. Members of each team will continue to alternate until one person reaches Finish without stepping off the hidden path.

Remind everyone to pay attention to which squares kids stepped on during previous turns and to avoid the ones that made kids get called "off!" Also tell kids that once the game begins, nodding, pointing, and gesturing are OK, but talking is not allowed. Randomly select one team to begin by sending its first person down the runway. Lead cheers and applause when someone reaches the Finish!

Afterward, ask the group to sit down around the runway. Lead a brief discussion about staying on the right path in life. The following questions will be helpful:

A Completed Runway

	K	V	C	O	D	N	B	U	I	A	
S	J	B	X	I	L	M	V	Y	O	S	F
T	H	Z	N	U	K	A	C	T	D	D	I
A	G	M	D	Y	J	S	X	R	L	F	N
R	F	A	W	T	H	D	N	E	K	G	I
T	D	S	E	R	G	F	D	M	J	H	S H

• **How do the runway and its squares symbolize real life?**

• **What does the hidden path represent in your life?**

• **What does the Bible say about your walk, or your path through life?**

Review with kids 2 Samuel 22:31; Psalm 1:1; Psalm 23:1-4; Psalm 37:5-6; and John 14:6.

A Key Showing the Hidden Path

Team Time

Overview: Kids will learn to lean on each other and stay together in a tight spot.

Supplies: You'll need a Bible, masking tape, and a few packs of gum.

Preparation: Make a 3x4-foot rectangle on the floor with masking tape.

Time Involved: 20 minutes

Divide your kids into groups of ten to twelve. Say: **We're going to find out how well you can work together and how close you can be in a tight situation.** Point to the rectangle on the floor, and tell kids that you want them to fit as many people in the rectangle as possible.

Let each group try separately. Keep track of how many kids each group manages to fit into the rectangle and how long kids stay in the rectangle without falling. Award members of the winning group each a stick of gum for "sticking together."

When you are done, combine the groups and let them try to break the winning group's record.

Use this game to set up a brief talk on friendship and how we can encourage and build each other up. Begin by reading 1 Thessalonians 5:11 aloud and then ask:

● **What are some ways we can encourage each other?**

● **What types of behavior or actions would divide us as a youth group?**

● **How can we grow closer as a group?**

Kite-Flying Frenzy

Overview: Kids will build their own kites and learn just how important instructions are. This game works best on a breezy or slightly windy day.

Supplies: You'll need heavy-duty plastic trash bags, scissors, transparent tape, 3/16-inch dowels, light-gauge wire clothes-hangers, kite string, large snap swivels, and the "Kite Instructions" handout (p. 42).

Preparation: Cut the dowels into enough fourteen-inch lengths for each group to have one, and make enough photo-copies of the "Kite Instructions" handout (p. 42) for each of half of the groups.

Time Involved: 30 to 45 minutes

Divide the kids into groups of three to four. Give each group the materials needed to make a kite: a dowel piece, two trash bags, scissors, transparent tape, kite string, and a large snap swivel. Give only half the groups the "Kite Instructions" handout (p. 42). Tell the other half that they need to figure out how to make the kites on their own.

Leader TIP
Instruct the groups to work on differ-ent sides of the room, so they can't copy each other.

When each group has assembled its kite, have groups try to fly their kites. Take note of which groups get their kites to fly most easily (if at all).

After groups have finished trying to get their kites into the air, gather them together and ask the following questions of the groups who had no instructions:

Variation

This game can be modified so that kids make paper airplanes instead.

● **Was it difficult to put a kite together without instructions? Why or why not?**

● **Would it have been easier to put the kite together with the instructions? Why or why not?**

Ask the groups who had the instructions:

● **How easy or difficult was it to put the kite together?**

Ask the whole group:

● **How did the instructions or lack of instructions affect your kites' ability to fly?**

Say: **Going through life is kind of like putting the kite together. We can either make decisions or do things based on what we think is right without directions or guidance, or we can read God's instruction book, the Bible.**

Discuss how the Bible gives us instructions and guidance and helps us to make wise decisions so we can "soar like a kite" through life.

Kite Instructions

1. Begin by taking apart the hanger and forming the wire into a circle.

2. Place a trash bag over the wire circle and cut the trash bag around the circle, leaving a one-inch overlap.

3. Fold the trash bag around the back of the wire circle and tape it onto the wire. Keep the trash bag pulled as tight as possible.

4. Place the dowel across the center line of the back of the kite. Allow equal lengths to extend on either side of the wire circle. Tape the dowel in place.

5. Use cord to tie the swivel to the middle of the dowel (near the center point of the kite). Use tape to help secure the cord and keep it from slipping. Thread the string through the swivel and tie it securely.

6. For the tail, cut four three-inch plastic strips and tape them to the bottom of the kite.

In All Fairness

Overview: Kids will learn how it feels to be treated unequally.

Supplies: You'll need a Bible and five large bags of candy.

Preparation: None is needed.

Time Involved: 20 minutes

Take five students away from the rest of the group, and explain to them how the game works. Be sure that the other kids cannot hear your instructions to the five. Tell each of them you are going to give them bags of candy to share with the other students. There's only one catch: They can give candy only to the boys, or only to the girls, or only to kids with black tennis shoes. (The idea is to pick something that will eliminate at least half of the kids.) Remind kids not to tell the others why some kids are getting candy and others aren't. Warn kids to only give candy to those in the designated group, even if the other kids beg.

After giving the first five their instructions, tell the rest of the group: **In a moment, I'm going to let the five kids back into the room. When they come in, they'll have some candy to share. You can ask, bribe, and beg them for it, but do not take it from them. You may or may not get some candy. If you figure out what the criteria is for getting candy, you'll be entitled to a double portion.**

Call the first five kids back into the room. Allow them time to circulate through the group handing out candy to the chosen few. When they have completed their task, play the game again, picking five new kids to pass out candy. During this round, pick a different category of kids to give candy to. For example, you may choose those who have buttons on their shirts, those who are wearing white T-shirts, or those with long sleeves.

Leader TIP

If the kids haven't already figured out the game, be sure to explain how it was supposed to work.

Once you have completed this phase of the game, ask:

● **What was it like to be one who received candy?**

● **What was it like to be left out or passed over?**

● **Did anyone figure out why he or she did not get candy?**

● **Are you nicer to some people because of the way they look, or do you ignore others because they appear to be different?**

● **What makes you treat some people differently than others?**

Near the end of the discussion, say: **The Bible instructs us to treat each other fairly and equally. God loves us all the same. No one is more or less special in the eyes of God, and we are instructed to treat each other the same way.**

Close by reading James 2:1-10 aloud and then pass out candy to everyone!

Light Up the Dark

Overview: Kids will learn that walking in God's light will help them lead others to Jesus.

Supplies: You'll need a Bible, one flashlight for each person, paper, and a pen or pencil.

Preparation: Hide the flashlights in inconspicuous places. Be sure to write the hiding places down so you won't lose any of the flashlights.

Time Involved: 10 to 15 minutes

Say: **I've hidden some flashlights, and it's your job to find them.**

There are enough flashlights for everyone to find one. When you find a flashlight, turn it on and then help someone else find one. Continue to help others

find flashlights until each person has one. The game is complete when everyone has found a flashlight.

Upon completion, gather the group into a large circle and have kids point their lighted flashlights into the middle.

Read Matthew 5:14, 16 aloud and then ask:

● **Why did Jesus call us the light of the world?**

● **How can we share our light to show others the way to Jesus?**

Say: **When we ask Jesus into our hearts, he becomes the light that shines within us. Just as we used our lights to help others find theirs, the Bible instructs us to use the light within us to help others find Jesus.**

End in a prayer asking God to help kids share Jesus' message with others as they let their light shine.

The Straight and Narrow vs. the Crooked and Wide

Overview: Kids will learn that walking God's straight and narrow path is better than choosing their own way.

Supplies: You'll need items to create an obstacle course (such as tables, chairs, trash cans), a stopwatch or a watch with a second hand, paper, and a pen or pencil.

Preparation: Set up two identical obstacle courses, one with a straight path and one with a crooked or winding path. If everything goes well, it will take less time to go through the straight course than the crooked one.

Time Involved: 10 to 15 minutes

Divide your group up into two equal teams. Have members of each team line up behind the starting line of their obstacle course. Instruct teams that when you say "go!" they are to go through their obstacle courses as quickly as possible. Remind them that they are being timed.

As each team completes its course, note its time. Then have the teams switch places so that each team gets to try both courses.

Ask:

● **Which course was more difficult to get through? Why?**

● **Which course would you rather do if you had the choice? Explain.**

Say: **Much like these two obstacle courses, God has set a path before us. God wants us to choose his way to live rather than following our own crooked ways.** Read Matthew 7:7 aloud and then say: **As we seek God in prayer, he will lead and direct us in the way we should go.**

A Quick Change

Overview: Kids will change in and out of dress up clothes to symbolize that they are new creations in Christ.

Supplies: You'll need a Bible, robes, dress up clothes, and large plastic trash bags.

Preparation: Have your kids each wear old robes over their clothes to this activity. (Robes can be borrowed from family members or friends.) Put four sets of clothing (hats, shirts, vests, shorts or pants, socks, and so on) in a large plastic trash bag. Have one trash bag for every group of four kids.

Time Involved: 10 minutes

Divide your group up into teams of four. Have members of each team stand in a straight line. About twenty feet in front of each group, place a trash bag full of clothes.

Say: **When I say "go," I want the first person in line**

to run to the bag and grab something out of it. **Whatever it is, take off your robe and put it on over the clothes you already have on. When you are done, run back and tag the next person in line. That person is then to run to the bag and do the same thing. Continue until the bag is empty. There is, however, one catch. If you pull a shirt out and you had already pulled one out on a previous turn, you lose your turn and it becomes the next person's turn.** The first team who outfits its members with the all of the items you placed in its bag wins.

When the game is finished, read 2 Corinthians 5:17 aloud and discuss what it means to be a new creation in Christ.

At the end of the discussion, say: **Just as you took off the robe to put on your first piece of clothing, Jesus changes your heart and makes you a new person when you believe in him. It's an immediate change. However, that doesn't mean you will be perfect or that you won't make mistakes. Just as you kept adding clothes to your outfits until the game was complete, during your life you'll keep growing in your knowledge of God until someday you will be complete.**

Bouncers

Overview: Kids will better understand patience and endurance by bouncing various objects around a room.

Supplies: You'll need tape, chair, a basketball, a foam ball, a beach ball, three or four eleven-inch balloons, paper, a pen or pencil, and a watch with a second hand.

Preparation: Inflate and tie off the balloons, and mark a starting line with tape.

Time Involved: 10 minutes or more (depending on group size)

At one end of the room, arrange the group in a single file line. Place a chair about five feet from the first person in line, and hand a basketball to that player.

Explain that you are going to see how long it takes the group to bounce the basketball around the chair. One person will start by bouncing the ball to the chair, around the chair, and back to the starting line. The first person will then tag the second person, give him or her the ball, and go to the end of the line.

Continue playing until everyone has bounced the basketball around the chair. Note the time and then repeat the activity with the foam ball, the beach ball, and finally, the balloon. Be sure to note the time it takes to complete each round.

After all four rounds, gather the group and discuss the following:

● **Which relay was easiest? Which was most difficult? Explain.**

● **In what ways are the objects we bounced like problems we face every day?**

Say: **While some problems are easy to solve, others require extra time and special care.** Ask kids to give you examples of problems like this.

Ask:

● **In what ways are the objects we bounced like people we meet?**

Say: **While some people are easy to relate to, others require extra time and special care.** Ask kids to give you examples of people like this.

Ask:

● **What does it take to face tough problems and deal with difficult people?**

Say: **God asks that we show patience and endurance in our everyday lives. Much like running in a race, we are to pace ourselves and "hang in there" until the end. Just like others who were offering encouragement during the relays, God encourages us to hang in there.**

Lighthouse

Overview: Kids will experience faith and trust by trying to reach the "lighthouse" before time runs out.

Supplies: You'll need a Bible and blindfolds (optional).

Preparation: None is needed.

Time Involved: 5 to 10 minutes

Gather kids to explain the game and then select a person to be the Lighthouse for the group. This person will stand somewhere in a large dark room while others try to make contact with him or her. The job of the Lighthouse is to remain mo-

> **Leader TIP**
> For safety, remind players to move slowly around a room that's completely dark.

tionless while whispering the words of Proverbs 3:5-6 over and over. Explain that everyone will have three minutes to reach the Lighthouse before time runs out, leaving them "treading water." Once a person reaches the Lighthouse, he or she is to lock arms with that person. All connected players should join in whispering Proverbs 3:5-6.

At the beginning of the game, take everyone out of the room except the Lighthouse. As you give last-minute instructions, have the Lighthouse take his or her place in the darkened room. This game will work best if the Lighthouse picks the spot farthest from the door to stand.

Turn off the lights, and let the group enter. After kids are inside, give a signal to begin. After three minutes, announce the game is over and see who has been successful and who is left "treading water."

Gather the group in a seated circle, and ask:

● **What was challenging about this activity?**

Ask those who reached the Lighthouse:

● **How did you feel once you reached the Lighthouse?**

● **Did hearing more and more voices make it easier to locate the Lighthouse?**

Ask those who were left "treading water":

● **How did it feel to know you didn't reach the Lighthouse before time ran out?**

Say: **God often asks us to go somewhere or do something by faith which may not make sense. Many times we all feel alone in our journey. But God provides encouragement through other people, and his desire for us becomes clearer as we go. God asks that we trust his direction, walking in faith until we reach the goal.**

For one reason or another, we sometimes fail to meet our goals. One who believes in God sees this as an opportunity to trust God more. The one who does not believe in God views the failure as if it were a "sinking weight in an ocean of worry."

Quick Switch!

Overview: Kids will describe how objects in their possession might have been used in Bible times. This activity can be used in almost any setting and with any Bible story. It is especially effective in casual Bible study or retreat settings.

Supplies: You'll need a Bible, paper, and a pencil (optional).

Preparation: None is needed.

Time Involved: 10 minutes; longer if working with a large group

Start by selecting a Bible story, such as David and Goliath (1 Samuel 17). Share the story out loud, emphasizing its key elements. For example, you might highlight such things as the sling, the smooth stones, the spear, and so on. If it will be helpful, you may want to make a list on paper.

After each item has been presented, ask:

● **In what ways does this item represent an element of the story?**

After highlighting the key elements of the story, ask the kids to produce personal objects such as a comb, a wallet, a ring, a photograph, or a hairbrush. Again using the story of David and Goliath, be creative and have them relate their personal items to the Bible items in ways such as these: elastic hair-band and sling, coins and stones, and hairbrush and spear.

Afterward, tell or read the story again. This time substitute shared objects with story elements. For example, a paraphrase of the story of David and Goliath might read: "David took his trusty **hair-band** and five **coins** to defeat Goliath. Though the giant had a large **hairbrush**, David knocked him down with just a **nickel**."

Most often, the revised story will sound silly. However, serious discussion may surface by asking questions which give the story a modern-day application. Questions from the David and Goliath story might include these:

● **If this story appeared on the evening news, do you think people would believe it? Why or why not?**

● **Can you think of a modern-day David who has faced a Goliath? Explain.**

● **Are there giants in your own life that need defeating? Explain.**

● **What tools does God provide to help you win the battle?**

Signs of the Times

Overview: Kids will create modern-day parables by replacing biblical objects with things found while traveling.

Supplies: You'll need a Bible.

Preparation: None is needed.

Time Involved: 15 to 20 minutes

The beauty of this storytelling game is that it will never be

> **Variation**
>
> An alternate method calls for the leader to read the parable, stopping whenever a word or a phrase is to be exchanged. Using a single leader to read the passage helps keep the story flowing.

played the same way twice. Changing road signs and routes will insure some added fun while traveling.

Start by selecting a Bible parable, such as the prodigal son (Luke 15:11-32). You may read the story from a Bible or simply paraphrase it.

Explain that the group is going to retell the story by substituting objects on road signs and billboards for objects in the story. Players can use both sides of the road while traveling.

Start with the person at the front of the vehicle. Have him or her take the first verse and restate it by substituting an object on a sign or billboard for an object in the story. If using a Bible, simply pass it person-to-person so everyone can have a turn to read out loud.

Toss and Tell

> **Variation**
>
> Another way to play this game is to test one's general Bible knowledge. It may be used to review lists such as Bible books, the Ten Commandments, and the fruit of the Spirit or while recalling a time line of events, such as in the Creation story.

Overview: Kids will test their Bible knowledge by tossing an object back and forth. This activity works well as a Bible study or as a test of general Bible knowledge. It may be played in any casual setting, such as a Sunday school classroom or on a retreat.

Supplies: You'll need a Bible and a piece of old cloth such as a hand towel, a pillowcase, or an old sock.

Preparation: None is needed.

Time Involved: 5 minutes

After reading a Bible passage or conducting a Bible study, explain to the group that you are going to make a statement from the lesson. Next, toss the piece of cloth to one of the kids. Whoever the piece of cloth is thrown to should catch it, and based on his or her recall of the lesson, answer "true" or "false."

Leader TIP
This game should never be used to embarrass someone or to put someone on the spot.

After answering either correctly or incorrectly, the person should toss the piece of cloth back to the leader. Continue playing until everyone in the group has had a chance to try answering a question. If an incorrect answer is given, students should take a moment to discuss or research the correct answer from a Bible or lesson material.

Tools and Talents

Overview: Kids will identify which tools are best for particular jobs and begin to understand that God gives each of us special tools and talents to accomplish our life's work.

Supplies: You'll need a Bible and a large paper bag filled with common kitchen gadgets such as a whisk, a potato peeler, a wooden spoon, an egg slicer, a garlic press, a spatula, a cheese grater, and a baster (at least one item for each person).

Preparation: Fill the paper bag with the kitchen gadgets.

Time Involved: 10 to 20 minutes

Have kids sit in a circle, and pass the paper bag around. Have each person take one gadget from the bag without looking.

Begin a discussion by asking each person to first identify his or her kitchen gadget and then to tell a story about how it's used. Be prepared for silliness, but try to gently keep the group on task!

Emphasize that each gadget has a specific purpose, and although it may be used in different ways, it was best created for one unique job.

When all the objects have been identified and a story has been told about each, spend a few minutes discussing the tools and talents God gives each of us to do his special work. Begin by reviewing Bible passages such as the parable of the talents (Matthew 25:14-28). Then ask:

● **Do you think everyone has a unique talent or ability that God has given him or her?**

● **Name some talents, and explain how they might be used to work for the Lord.**

● **What are the talents and abilities that God has given you?**

Scramble and Swap

Overview: Kids will experience the difficulty of trying to be like someone else as they are asked to scramble and swap their coats and shoes.

Supplies: You'll need a Bible.

Preparation: None is needed.

Time Involved: 5 to 10 minutes

It's important that this game be played in cold weather so students will arrive wearing coats and additional outerwear. As kids enter the room, ask them to put their shoes, coats, hats, mittens, scarves, and any other items of outerwear they may be wearing in a pile in the middle of the floor. Then ask everyone to line up side by side on one side of the room.

Explain that on your command, you want everyone to scramble to the pile and put on two pieces of clothing and one pair of shoes belonging to someone else. Give kids approximately one minute.

At the end of the minute, ask:

● **How many of you are more comfortable wearing someone else's clothing**

> **Variation**
>
> As an additional activity relating to the same lesson, you might want to organize a running relay and emphasize the difficulty in wearing shoes which don't quite fit.

rather than your own? Explain.

Use this game to start a discussion about how "cool" we may think it would be to be like someone else, only to find out that his or her style doesn't quite fit. You might also remind kids that we are all unique individuals created in God's image and not in the image of others.

This game works well to introduce discussions on Bible passages such as Ephesians 5:1 instructing us to be imitators and followers of God. To continue the discussion, you may want to ask questions like these:

● **What qualities in others do you admire?**

● **If you could be anyone who has ever lived, who you would choose?**

● **What are some areas of your life in which you would like to be a better follower and imitator of God?**

Bible-Rap Memory

Overview: Kids will memorize Revelation 21:4 by setting it to a rap rhythm and learn how to apply its message to their lives when times are rough.

Supplies: You'll need Bibles.

Preparation: None is needed.

Time Involved: 10 to 15 minutes

To avoid "Ninety-Nine Bottles of Beer on the Wall" boredom, challenge youth to create their own songs. They will combine the fun of singing with the delight of Scripture by putting Bible verses to music. The easiest tunes to use are rap rhythms, but don't rule out commercial tunes or contemporary Christian tunes (kids can even use the "Ninety-Nine Bottles of Beer on the Wall" rhythm).

For this rap, invite one or two kids to start the rhythm, complete with knee slapping and lip smacking.

As the rapping person (or people) repeats the rhythm, lead the others in matching the words of Revelation 21:4 to that rhythm. An example of this might be:

"He will wipe ev-ry tear fro-o-om their eyes.

There will be no-o-o more death or mourning

Or crying or pain, for the old order...

For the old order of things has passed away."

Keep repeating the verse with the rhythm until the group says it smoothly several times. Then call for volunteers to repeat the verse from memory. After kids finish, begin a discussion by asking:

● **How can the truth of our rap help you make it through tough times in your life?**

● **What other verses would be good to say when the going gets rough?**

Hall of Fame of the Faithful

Overview: Kids will guess Bible characters in Hebrews 11 by asking yes and no questions.

Supplies: You'll need Bibles.

Preparation: None is needed.

Time Involved: 10 to 30 minutes

Say: **We're going to play Twenty Questions to discover what choices can make a person more faithful. Each of us will choose a person in Hebrews 11, answer "yes" or "no" to questions the group asks, and then explain why we like that person. In the process, we'll study several faithful actions we can choose to show our loyalty to God.**

Ask kids to turn to Hebrews 11 and scan it for names. Direct them to notice details about each person and check the bottom or center of their Bible pages to see if cross-references for the name are listed. Explain that not all Bibles will include these, but some will.

Variation

You can use this game for any Bible passage that mentions several names. Avoid playing Twenty Questions with the entire Bible, since this tends to make kids feel they can't learn the Bible.

Ask the person with the birthday furthest from the day's date to choose a person in Hebrews 11 and not tell anyone who it is. Guide the rest of the group to ask questions that can be answered "yes" or "no." Caution the person being asked questions to give no answers besides "yes" or "no."

For example, if the person chose Abel, questions the group could ask might include: "Is this a woman?" "Is this a man?" "Does he have four letters in his name?" "Did he offer a better sacrifice?" "Is it Abel?"

If the group is unable to guess the character's name in twenty questions, let kids ask more questions that can be answered with single words, such as, "In what verse will I find this name?" or "What's one action this character did?"

Leader TIP

Encourage kids to ask questions that name the person's faithful action rather than immediately asking: "Is it (person's name)?"

After each successful guess, comment further about the faithful action, perhaps discussing related Bible passages. For example, if the character is Abel, you might guide youth to scan Genesis 4 for ways Abel showed faithfulness and Cain did not.

Other faithful persons listed in Hebrews 11 include: Enoch, Noah, Abraham, Isaac, Jacob, Sarah, Joseph, Moses, Rahab, Gideon, Barak, Samson, Jephthah, David, and Samuel.

Slap That Card

Overview: Kids will create a card game and learn to distinguish the fruit of the Spirit from acts of the sinful nature (from Galatians 5).

Supplies: You'll need Bibles, index cards, and markers.

Preparation: None is needed.

Time Involved: 20 minutes

Leader TIP

If kids don't remember the game or have never heard of it, take a moment to explain the rules to them.

Have kids form teams of two to four, and have members of each team sit in a circle. Give each team several index cards and markers.

Remind kids of the game they played as children called Slapjack. Invite them to tell you the rules they remember.

Then say: **We're going to play by the same rules except we'll slap fruit of the Spirit instead of Jack. The rules of the game are: (1) One person deals the cards face down into equal piles for each person; (2) The person to the right of the dealer turns one card face up in the center; (3) If the card names a fruit of the Spirit, everyone tries to slap it. The first person to slap the card takes the whole center pile; (4) If the card names an act of the sinful nature, avoid touching it. Anyone who slaps the card by accident must give up two cards by placing them on the center pile. The game ends when one person runs out of cards.**

Guide teams to read Galatians 5:19-23 and then write every act of the sinful nature and every fruit of the Spirit on a separate index card. (The acts of the sinful nature are sexual immorality, impurity, debauchery, idolatry, witchcraft, hatred, discord, jealousy, fits of rage, selfish ambition, dissensions, factions, envy, drunkenness, orgies. The fruit of the Spirit is love, joy, peace, patience, kindness, goodness, faithfulness, gentleness, and self-control.) In this way, each team will create its own deck of cards.

Have each team turn its cards face down, shuffle them, and play the game according to the rules. After several rounds, invite each player to name four fruit of the Spirit and four acts of the sinful nature.

Begin a discussion by asking:

- **Why do you want the fruit of the Spirit in your life?**
- **What actions can you take to cultivate this fruit?**
- **What things make you drawn to the acts of the sinful nature?**
- **How can you weed those things out of your life?**

Guess the Letter

Overview: Kids will focus on key phrases by discovering them one letter at a time (a variation of Hangman).

Supplies: You'll need Bibles and a chalkboard and chalk, or a dry-erase board and a dry-erase marker, or paper and a pencil.

Preparation: Pick key phrases from whichever Bible passage you're studying.

Time Involved: 10 to 60 minutes

To help kids focus on key phrases in the Bible passage you're studying, guide them in discovering the phrases letter by letter. Choose the phrases you want the kids to focus on, and draw a line on the chalkboard, dry-erase board, or paper for each letter. If your phrase is "restore him gently" from Galatians 6:1, you would write:

— — — — — — —   — — — —   — — — — — — —

Invite kids to take turns naming letters that might fit the phrase. Start with the person who was born closest to the first day of the month and continue in this manner until everyone has had a turn. If a person chooses a correct letter, write it in every

60

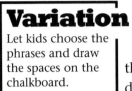

Variation

Let kids choose the phrases and draw the spaces on the chalkboard.

blank where it belongs. If the letter chosen isn't in the phrase, write that letter out to the side. For example, in the sample phrase, the letter "e" fits in three blanks, whereas "u" does not fit anywhere.

A person may name the phrase only when it is his or her turn to guess a letter. Hopefully many kids will discover the phrase and will be eager to name it. Having to wait their turn makes kids repeat the phrase in their heads over and over, thus helping them memorize it.

Pencil Charades

Overview: Kids will draw key phrases of Scripture and begin to better understand them.

Supplies: You'll need Bibles, index cards, paper, and pencils.

Preparation: Divide a chosen Bible passage into phrases that are each between three and seven words long, and write each phrase on a different index card. For example, if you use Romans 12:1-2, your phrases might be:

- Therefore, I urge you, brothers,
- in view of God's mercy,
- to offer your bodies
- as living sacrifices,
- holy and pleasing to God–
- this is your spiritual act of worship.
- Do not conform any longer
- to the pattern of this world,
- but be transformed
- by the renewing of your mind.
- Then you will be able
- to test and approve
- what God's will is–
- his good, pleasing, and perfect will.

Shuffle the index cards so the phrases aren't in the correct order.

Time Involved: 10 to 20 minutes

Divide kids into teams of between two and six players each, and give each team paper and pencils. Have one player from each team come forward, silently read the phrase on the first card, and then run back to draw the phrase for his or her team. Team members should keep their Bibles open so they can identify the phrase. The first team to guess the phrase should stand and shout the phrase. Continue in this manner until you've finished the Bible passage, having teams choose a different person to draw each time.

Comment briefly on each phrase to prompt youth to apply it to life. For example, if the phrase is "as living sacrifices," you might say: **You have a choice to offer yourself to God as a living and active person.** Then ask:

● **What words or actions would show you have offered your life to God?**

Bible Crossword

Overview: Kids will create crossword puzzles that show the meaning of Bible phrases.

Supplies: You'll need Bibles, graph paper, pencils, and copies of a printed Bible study or commentary.

Preparation: None is needed.

Time Involved: 30 minutes

Digesting a block of a printed Bible commentary is not usually an activity kids enjoy. Kids do, however, want solutions to their struggles, and a commentary or study can often help point them in the right direction.

Give kids each a copy of the commentary or Bible study, a pencil, and two pieces of graph paper. Challenge them each to underline ten Bible truths that they think will best address the issue you're studying. For example, for a study about conflict, kids might use the verse "Do not be overcome by evil, but over- come evil with good" (Romans 12:21). From the commentary or study, you might have kids each choose ten actions that stop evil before it starts.

Have kids use the following steps to make their own cross- word puzzles using the facts they've chosen:

Variation

If a guest speaker is coming, explain prior to his or her arrival that you want kids to jot down ten fascinat- ing facts from the speaker's speech that will be used in the crossword puz- zles. After the speaker has fin- ished speaking, have kids each make a puzzle.

1. For each fact, pick one word to fit in your puzzle.

2. Write a clue that helps identify the word.

3. Arrange the words on graph paper, and number them.

4. List the clues to match the Across and Down numbers.

5. Draw a blank grid by putting a second piece of graph paper over your first grid and tracing it.

6. Trade puzzles with each other, and have fun solving them.

7. Find the words in the original com- mentary or study, and learn more about them.

Prop Pontification

Overview: Kids will use props to explain the meaning of a Bible passage.

Supplies: You'll need Bibles and several wearable props, such as hats or sunglasses.

Preparation: After choosing your passage, find props to go along with it.

Time Involved: 45 to 60 minutes

As you begin a Bible study, give each person a prop to wear

or hold, such as sunglasses, a hat, a wristwatch, a walking stick, or a ring. Tell kids they'll be making statements by using their props in creative ways.

For example, for a study about John 10:1-10, offer kids a pair of sunglasses and a walking stick. The discussion might go something like this: The person wearing the sunglasses might say," Because I can **see** with Jesus' eyes, he helps me **see** the difference between what's true fun and what will steal my life from me." The person holding the walking stick might then say, "Yes, and so I **walk** in God's truth by choosing to have parties that don't put people down." The person holding the sunglasses could say, "Yes, and my parties don't need alcohol because we don't want our memories stolen from us. We want to see them the next day." The person with the walking stick might say, "And if I **walk** behind Jesus like a sheep follows its master, I will get into the right gates—meaning I'll go to the right houses to party." The person with the sunglasses might say, "And if I **see** a party is deteriorating into people being hurt or fun being stolen, I can walk back out the gate I came in."

Other examples of props and passages that go together are:

● a ring and Genesis 3. Kids can talk about how the **ring** symbolizes loyalty to God, how sin **rings** your neck, and how we can't pass off our **ring** of responsibility to someone else.

● a wristwatch and Ephesians 5:15. In addition to speaking of making **minutes** count, kids can speak of keeping an eye on what they do with their **time,** using it for good purposes rather than participating in foolish talk.

Crossed and Uncrossed

Overview: Kids will pass a pair of scissors around and decide whether they are crossed as they learn about things that may distract them from their faith. This game is not what it appears to be on the surface.

Supplies: You'll need a pair of children's scissors.

Preparation: None is needed.

Time Involved: 10 to 15 minutes

Have kids sit in a circle, and pass the pair of scissors around the circle. Say: **The object of this game is to decide whether the scissors are crossed or uncrossed. When you receive the scissors, you may change them by either crossing or uncrossing them.**

Once you determine what makes the scissors crossed or uncrossed, keep the secret to yourself and keep playing. Remember: This game may not be what it appears to be on the surface.

Have kids change the scissors each time they pass them—sometimes opening them, sometimes closing them, and sometimes flipping them over. It will be your job as the leader to tell the person who receives the scissors whether they are crossed. It has nothing to do with the actual scissors, but is determined by whether the person receiving the scissors has his or her legs crossed. If the person's legs are crossed, announce that the scissors are crossed. If the person's legs are uncrossed, the scissors are uncrossed.

Keep playing until almost everyone has caught on. After the game is over, explain that it takes some people a long time to study something in order to make sure it's correct. This can be very good.

After the game, lead a simple discussion with the following questions:

● **Whether or not I said the scissors were crossed had nothing to do with the scissors but everything to do with the person's legs. What do we set up as measures of biblical faith that have nothing to do with faith?** (Kids may say things such as feelings, the opinions of others, or non-Christian religions.)

● **What are the true measures of faith?**

● **Watching the scissors distracted many of us from discovering the real answer. What often distracts our**

attention and keeps us from what's important in faith?
● How can we demonstrate that we value what's really important?

Out of the Mouths of Lions

Overview: Kids will write Bible events from the viewpoint of an animal, another person, or an object.

Supplies: You'll need Bibles, paper, and pencils.

Preparation: Choose a Bible passage to have kids study.

Time Involved: 20 minutes

Add fun to your Bible study by guiding kids to imagine themselves involved in Bible events. Direct kids each to choose a character in the passage and tell about the events from that character's viewpoint. For example, if the passage is Daniel 6, the lion could speak of how hungry he was and tell why he didn't eat Daniel. Or the king could speak about how much he regretted letting others trick him into sentencing Daniel to death. Or the walls of Daniel's upstairs room could even start their story by saying, "People often want walls to speak, so today I'm speaking. I'm the walls of Daniel's upstairs room, and here's what I know..."

Urge your students to start with the facts that the characters would have been most aware of and go on to tell the entire Bible passage from their characters' viewpoints. They could use phrases such as, "I heard that..."

To help keep kids focused on the actual Bible story, have them each quote from the passage at least three times. In addition, urge kids to include feelings as well as events, and prompt them to interpret rather than just read the passage.

Invite kids to read or dramatize their monologues.

Generously applaud each story and highlight how it helped you understand the passage more completely.

Table-Top Football Discussion

Overview: Kids will play table-top football as they discuss a Bible passage.

Supplies: You'll need Bibles, paper, and a long table.

Preparation: Choose a Bible passage and write down questions to guide kids in discussing it.

Time Involved: 30 to 60 minutes

Give kids each a piece of paper, and show them how to make table-top footballs using these instructions: (1) Fold the paper in half lengthwise, and crease it well; (2) Fold the paper in half lengthwise a second time, and crease it; (3) Starting at one end, fold one corner to the side to make a triangle. Keep folding this triangle over until you can tuck the other end of the paper into it.

As you explain the instructions, be sure to urge excellence in folding to assure kids that doing their best in anything glorifies God.

When the footballs are folded, direct kids to take a place along one end of the table and open their Bibles to the passage you've chosen. They'll probably all be wanting to "kick" their footballs across the table. But ask them to wait until you're done explaining the game. Say: **Before you kick your football, you must say something about the**

Variation

● Have kids form pairs, and have each pair interpret a part of the passage for the group. After a pair interprets its part of the passage, have both partners kick their footballs.

● After the study, allow kids to personalize their footballs with initials and logos. Then guide them to write the words from Philippians 4:19 on their footballs, and have them keep them as a reminder that God will meet their needs.

Bible passage or add to what someone else said about it. After you make your comment, kick your football and we'll all cheer for your play.

Have kids take turns making comments and "kicking" their footballs across the table with finger flicks. Urge the players to make comments about the Bible passage by utilizing their experiences and other things they may have learned in the Bible study. As the leader, you'll probably want to ask questions to help move the process along. For example, for a study of Philippians 4:19, you might ask, "When and how has God met one of your needs?"

Have kids flick their footballs along the table as they try to get them to the other side without falling off. If a person's football falls off the other side, he or she must start over again. Stand ready to retrieve and return footballs so the kids aren't under the table looking for them. The person whose football is closest to the far edge of the table without falling off, wins the game.

Bible Limbo

Overview: Teams will answer Bible questions as they compete to get a limbo stick to its lowest point.

Supplies: You'll need a Bible, a limbo stick (a yardstick or a three-foot dowel), masking tape, and a marker.

Preparation: Tear off a piece of masking tape that's several feet long, and place it vertically on a wall or a piece of furniture in your room. Mark points on the masking tape at intervals of a few inches. For example, you might measure twelve inches off the ground and mark that spot, and then measure up three inches and mark that spot, and so on.

Write out several Bible questions to test kids' knowledge. Here are some suggestions to help you create Bible questions:

- Focus on everything that happened in one book of the Bible.
- Focus on people of the Bible.
- Ask questions about Jesus' life.

● Use major Bible events as questions.

Time Involved: 20 to 60 minutes

Divide the group into two or more teams and have teams scatter around your meeting area. Have two volunteers hold up the limbo stick with one end next to the masking tape line on the wall.

Say: **The goal of this game is for your team to answer as many Bible questions as possible and get the limbo stick to the lowest possible point. Each time a team gets a correct answer, it gets to send someone under the limbo stick. If that person passes under the limbo stick successfully, the limbo stick will be moved down a notch. Team members must take turns going under the stick, and a team must get one player under each notch of the stick before it can be moved down to the next level. The first team to get the stick all the way to the bottom wins that round. If a team member hits the stick when he or she is attempting to go under it, another team member can try again at that same level when the first team member gets a correct answer.**

Variation

When a team gives a wrong answer, raise the limbo stick up one notch from where that team had it.

Begin the game by asking a Bible question. The first team to have a member raise his or her hand and correctly answer the Bible question gets to send a team member under the limbo stick. (If a team gives an incorrect answer, go on to the team that had a member raise his or her hand second.) Start a new round when a team gets the limbo stick to the lowest set level. (Make sure you keep track of which notch the limbo stick is on for each team.)

Bible Oscars

Overview: Kids will pantomime Bible events in a race against the clock.

Supplies: You'll need the "Events From Jesus' Life" handout (p. 70); scissors; a container such as a box, basket, or bag; and a small hourglass timer (available in many board games).

Preparation: Cut apart the cards on the "Events From Jesus' Life" handout (p. 70). Fold the cards and place them in the container.

Time Involved: 20 to 60 minutes

Divide the group into two or more teams. Tell teams they're going to pantomime events from Jesus' life. Have one person on the first team go to the container and take out a slip. He or she will pantomime that event for the team. The team will have the time allotted by the timer to guess the event that is being pantomimed. If the team guesses the correct answer before the time runs out, another member of the same team will take another slip and play again. The first team's turn is over when team members can't guess an answer in their allotted time. The next team will start the timer over when its turn begins.

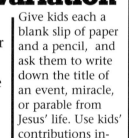

Variation

Give kids each a blank slip of paper and a pencil, and ask them to write down the title of an event, miracle, or parable from Jesus' life. Use kids' contributions instead of the handout.

Announce these two basic rules for pantomiming before beginning the game. (You may add other rules of your own as you choose.)

● No sounds can be used.

● Fingers can be used to show the number of words, the number of the word a person is working on, or the number of syllables in a word.

Give teams each one hundred points when they get a correct answer.

Events From Jesus' Life

▲ *Jesus is born in a stable.*

▲ *Jesus visits the temple when he is twelve.*

▲ *Jesus calls some fishermen to be his disciples.*

▲ *Jesus heals a blind man.*

▲ *Jesus brings a dead girl back to life.*

▲ *Jesus calms a bad storm at sea.*

▲ *Jesus clears out the money-changers in the temple.*

▲ *Jesus is beaten.*

▲ *Jesus feeds 5,000 people.*

▲ *Jesus is crucified.*

▲ *Jesus is raised from the dead.*

Bible *Jeopardy!*

Overview: Kids will make up *Jeopardy!* game statements based on a particular book or passage of the Bible.

Supplies: You'll need Bibles, paper, and pencils.

Preparation: None is needed.

Time Involved: 20 to 60 minutes

Divide the group into two teams. Give each team Bibles, pencils, and paper. Tell each team to divide itself into two groups–one will be the Question group and one will be the Answer group.

Assign a particular Bible book or passage to each team. For example, you might focus on the first eleven chapters of Genesis or five chapters in the gospel of Mark. Instruct the Question groups to go through the assigned Scriptures and come up with *Jeopardy!*-type statements using events and information in their Scriptures. For example, if kids are using the first eleven chapters of Genesis, some of the statements might be:

- He was the man God asked to build a big boat.
  - He named all the animals.
  - He murdered his brother.
  - She was Adam's partner.

Give kids a specific number of statements to create.

Instruct the Answer groups to read and study the assigned Scriptures so they will be able to give answers to the other team's statements. Both halves of each team must work independently of each other, although their goal is the same (helping the team). Half of each team is trying to make up statements the other team will not be able to answer. The other half is studying so it

Variation

- Assign the two teams a specific area to study, and make up the statements for them.
- Have team halves switch roles in the middle of the game.
- Get your junior and senior high groups to compete against each other.
- Use this game for a parent night, and have parents and kids compete against each other.

can answer whatever the other team asks.

Begin the game by having one team give a statement. The opposing team will then try to answer it. If the second team answers the question correctly, it's given another question. The team continues until it misses an answer. When a question is missed, the Answer half of the asking team gets to try to answer the question. Set a time limit to allow the team to give the answer. Also, allow the Answer group to use its Bibles. It's then the other team's turn to ask questions. Continue in this manner until kids run out of questions. Give each team points for correct answers.

Bible Fill-Up

Overview: Teams will answer Bible questions to see which team can fill up its chairs first.

Supplies: You'll need Bibles, chairs, paper, and a pencil.

Preparation: Write out Bible questions in advance. Set up a single file line of five chairs for each team. Scatter the lines of chairs around the meeting area.

Time Involved: 30 to 60 minutes

Divide kids into two or more teams, and have each team stand near one line of chairs. Give each team five Bibles. Tell kids you are going to ask them questions from the Bible. The first team member that raises his or her hand and answers the question correctly gets to place a Bible on the first chair in the team's row of chairs. For each additional correct answer, the team will place a Bible in the next empty chair. The first team to place Bibles in all five chairs wins the round. When a team gives a wrong answer, it must remove

Variation

For large groups, have teams send people to sit in the chairs instead of placing Bibles in the chairs. When a team answers a question incorrectly, one of the team members occupying chairs must return to the team.
● Rather than having them raise hands, give each team a bell to ring.
● Give each team a place in the room to run to once it knows the answer.

one of the Bibles from its line of chairs.

Teams are allowed to use the Bibles that are still in their possession to try to find the correct answers to the questions.

Real Treasure

Overview: Kids will search for pennies hidden around a room in the church and learn about spiritual treasures.

Supplies: You'll need a Bible and 100 pennies.

Preparation: Hide the pennies around the meeting room.

Time Involved: 20 to 30 minutes

Tell kids that you have hidden pennies around the room. On your signal to start, have kids begin searching for the pennies. After three minutes, stop the game and have the kids form a circle. Ask them each to name one thing they are thankful for, either physical or spiritual, for every penny they have found.

After kids have shared what they're thankful for, read Matthew 6:19-24 aloud and begin a discussion regarding spiritual and physical treasures. Ask:

● **Why did you want to accumulate the most pennies?**

● **What are some examples of spiritual treasures?**

● **Which is worth more in life: physical treasure or spiritual treasure? Why?**

Clothed in Compassion

Overview: Kids will guess professions by asking questions about the clothes worn in those professions.

Supplies: You'll need a Bible, paper, markers, and tape.

Preparation: Write the names of various professions on sheets of paper, one per person in your group. Professions might include such things as a nurse, a firefighter, a lawyer, a minister, an Olympic ice skater, or any other professions that you choose.

Time Involved: 30 to 45 minutes

Tape one sheet to each person's back without letting him or her know the profession that's written on it. Have kids circulate, asking each other yes or no questions about the kind of clothing worn in the professions. (The object is for each person to guess what profession is taped on his or her back.) Allow the game to continue until each person has guessed the correct profession.

After everyone has guessed correctly, have kids gather and sit down for a discussion. Read Colossians 3:12 aloud. Begin a discussion about how both our physical and spiritual clothes tell others about ourselves. Continue by asking:

● **How can you have compassion for someone who is hurting?**

● **How can you extend a helping hand to those who are hurting?**

● **How does God care for the hurting?**

Discuss ways to help victims, both those that kids know personally and those far away such as victims of war or famine.

The Bible Pyramid Race

Overview: Kids will compete in a relay race in which Bible knowledge is important.

Supplies: You'll need a Bible, boxes, newsprint, scissors, tape, markers, and the "Instructions for Building Pyramids" handout (p. 76).

Preparation: Find ten identical empty boxes with the tops intact for each relay team. The size of the boxes is not important. Drugstores and grocery stores can be good sources of boxes. Wrap each of the boxes with white paper. On each of the six sides of each box, write a different item that will fit into one of the following categories (make sure all categories are represented on each box):

- the first ten books of the Old Testament,
- the last ten books of the Old Testament,
- the first ten books of the New Testament,
- the last ten books of the New Testament,
- the Ten Commandments (without the numbers), and
- any ten of the twelve disciples.

For example, one box might say "Exodus," "Haggai," "Acts," "1 Peter," "You shall not steal," and "Andrew." The boxes should look similar to dice with words on the sides instead of numbers. Scatter the sets of boxes around the room. Make enough copies of the "Instructions for Building Pyramids" handout for each team to have one.

Time Involved: 15 to 20 minutes

Divide the group into teams of four to ten, and have each team stand several feet away from one of the piles of boxes. Have the first person on each team run to the boxes and follow the first set of instructions

Variation

Allow kids to work on the pyramids in pairs.

on the "Instructions for Building Pyramids" handout (p. 76). He or she must build a pyramid using the correct sides of each box in addition to getting the boxes in the correct order.

Check to make sure the pyramids are correct before the team members run back to their teams. The next person on each team should then run to the boxes and build a pyramid following the next set of instructions on the handout. Continue in this manner until everyone has had a chance to build one pyramid, even if some kids have to take more than one turn.

Leader TIP

For the disciples category, any order is fine.

Instructions for Building Pyramids

Instruction 1

Build a pyramid using the ten boxes. The front side should show the first ten books of the Old Testament in their correct order. The bottom left box should be the first book and the top box should be the tenth book.

Instruction 2

Build a pyramid using the ten boxes. The front side should show the first ten books found in the New Testament in their correct order. The bottom left box should be the first book in the New Testament and the top box should be the tenth book.

Instruction 3

Build a pyramid using the ten boxes. The front side should show the last ten books found in the Old Testament, books number twenty-nine through thirty-nine in order. The bottom left should be book number twenty-nine, which is Amos. The rest of the books should be in order with the top box being the last book of the Old Testament.

Instruction 4

Build a pyramid using the ten boxes. The front side should show the last ten books of the New Testament, books number seventeen through twenty-seven in order. The bottom left box should be book number seventeen, which is Philemon. The top box should be the last book in the New Testament.

Instruction 5

Build a pyramid using the ten boxes. The front side should show the names of disciples. You may place these names in any order.

Instruction 6

Build a pyramid using the ten boxes. The front side should show the Ten Commandments in correct order. The bottom left box should be the first commandment and the top box should be the tenth commandment.

Real-Life Basketball

Overview: Kids will play basketball as they learn about both teamwork and the future.

Supplies: You'll need a Bible, basketball goals, a basketball, and the "Real-Life Basketball Instructions" handout (p. 79).

Preparation: Make two photocopies of the "Real-Life Basketball Instructions" handout (p. 79).

Time Involved: 1 hour

Divide the group into two teams with nine or more players each, and give each team a copy of the "Real-Life Basketball Instructions" handout (p. 79).

Allow kids to manage the teams as they see fit, rather than having adults make substitutions. Play the first three quarters just as the rules suggest, awarding bonus points according to the instructions.

> **Leader TIP**
>
> This game is much more effective when there are plenty of kids on each team.

At the beginning of the fourth quarter, shout: **Sorry, the game is over! Jesus has just returned!**

Award twenty bonus points to any team whose players have all taken a shot during the first three quarters. After adding up the points, discuss the importance of teamwork. Read 1 Corinthians 12:1-11 aloud. Ask:

● **Why is it important that in the church we let everyone have a chance to participate?**

● **Did you find it hard to pass up a shot and allow someone else to take it?**

● **What can we learn about including everyone from playing this game?**

Have someone read aloud Matthew 24:36-51. Point out:

1. No one knows just when or how Jesus will return (Matthew 24:36).

2. We must live every day ready for Jesus' return (Matthew 24:44).

3. Even if Jesus doesn't return while we are alive, we won't have the opportunity to replay our life to make it work out the way we want (Matthew 24:45-51).

Conclude the discussion by asking:

● **How do you think you would feel if you were waiting to do something, like taking a basketball shot, and before you had a chance to do it, you either died or Jesus came back? Explain.**

REAL-LiFE BASKETBALL

I N S T R U C T I O N S

You are going to play basketball, but the rules will be changed slightly. The scoring system will be totally different. The game will be played in four ten-minute quarters. All baskets will score either two or three points just as in regulation basketball. Each time a person scores, your team gets an extra two points if the person scoring has not yet scored in that quarter. At the end of the quarter, your team will receive five bonus points if at least five different people on your team attempted a shot during that quarter. At the end of the game, your team will receive an extra twenty points if everyone on your team attempted a shot sometime during the game.

Roadside Scripture Hunt

Variation

You can play one van against another van, girls against guys, pairs against pairs, or kids against adults.

Overview: Kids will learn Bible verses while they are traveling.

Supplies: You'll need a Bible, paper, and pencils.

Preparation: Write out the words of several Bible verses on a sheet of paper and make one copy for each person. Realistically, the game will probably only hold interest for about an hour, so don't use too many verses.

Time Involved: 30 to 60 minutes

Leader TIP

This game can become somewhat confusing on a bus; divide kids into teams or sections to keep from having forty teenagers screaming words all over the bus.

When a group trip is under way, give each person a Bible-verse sheet and a pencil. Direct kids to search the billboards along the road looking for any word found in the Bible verses. When a person finds a word, he or she is to yell out the word, claim it, and underline it on his or her sheet. The winner is the first person to find all the words on his or her sheet. A word on a sign may only be used by the first person who sees the sign and calls the word out.

Fictitious Bible Stories

Overview: Kids will learn about the Bible as they make up stories containing false facts.

Supplies: You'll need Bibles, pencils, and paper.

Preparation: None is needed.

Time Involved: 30 to 40 minutes

This game works best when kids are studying a particular Bible story in a class or retreat setting. Divide the group into teams of three to five players each. Assign the teams to each rewrite the Bible story adding five to ten false facts invented by the team. For example, if kids are studying about the birth of Jesus, they could fictitiously write "On the night of his birth, wise men came to see him." After teams have written out their false Bible stories, have a member of each team read the team's story aloud. The other teams are then to try to guess which facts are false. The winning team is the one who has the most false facts to go undetected.

The object of the game is to try to make up facts that are false but seem to be true without being too ridiculous.

Following the game, you may want to discuss just how easy it is to add things to what the Bible really says by asking:

● **In what ways do we try to add things to what the Bible says?**

● **How do we sometimes take away from what the Bible says?**

Bible Bingo

Overview: Kids will play Bingo and learn where various Bible stories are located.

Supplies: You'll need a Bible, paper, index cards, pencils, and a box or bag.

Preparation: This activity is a matching game involving fifty Scripture references and fifty matching Bible stories. (For example: Luke 15:11-32 matches the parable of the prodigal son.) Create several cards with Scripture references in five columns down and five rows across for a total of twenty-five references per card. (Use the illustration on page 82 as an example.) Make at least five or six different patterns (more if possible), using each of the fifty Scriptures at least once. Then make several copies of each pattern. Write the corresponding Bible stories on index cards, and put them in a box or bag.

Time Involved: 15 to 30 minutes

Begin by giving each person one Bingo card and a pencil. Draw one of the fifty stories from the box or bag. Before you read the index card, announce: **Story number 1**, and write a "1" on the index card. Instruct kids to each write "1" above the corresponding Scripture passage on their Bingo cards. (For example, if the fifth call is the parable of the prodigal son, kids should write "5" on top of Luke 15:11-32 if it appears on their Bingo cards.)

When a person matches five stories in a row in any direction, he or she yells out "Bingo!" or "Amen!"

If someone comes up with a Bingo, check his or her card against the numbers you have written on the index cards. You can continue the game by playing for first, second, and third place.

When the game has concluded, review all the passages and their corresponding Bible stories. Use the remaining cards to play the game again a few weeks later. You'll be amazed at how much the kids have remembered.

Sample Bible Bingo Card

(This is a sample with only two rows. Develop your cards with five rows.)

MATTHEW 7:24-27	MATTHEW 13:1-23	EXODUS 3:1-14	1 KINGS 17:1-6	JOHN 2:1-11
MATTHEW 8:22-27	MATTHEW 14:15-21	JONAH 2:10	JOSHUA 6:1-20	LUKE 15:11-32

(Answers left to right: wise builders; the sower; the burning bush; Elijah and the ravens; Jesus turning water into wine; calming the storm; feeding of the 5,000; Jonah in the whale; the fall of Jericho, the prodigal son)

Just Desserts

Overview: Kids will compete for a prize and end up learning about God's love.

Supplies: You'll need a Bible, paper, pencils, and a delicious treat for each player.

Preparation: Before you play the game, create a list of tasks for the kids to perform. Examples of tasks might be: (1) Find a partner and sing "Row, Row, Row Your Boat" together; (2) Move three chairs from one side of the room to the other side; and (3) Stand on one foot, and call out the names of the last five U.S. presidents. Have at least twenty tasks or enough to last 15 to 30 minutes.

Make one copy of the list for each person.

Time Involved: 15 to 30 minutes

Give kids each a list of tasks and a pencil. Set a time limit, and announce it to the group. Explain that there will be rewards at the end of the game. However, don't say that only those finishing their task lists will receive the reward.

When a person performs a task, have him or her get a witness to check-mark his or her list to verify that the task was actually completed. When a few people have finished their tasks, declare that time is up. Reassemble everyone and ask for those who have completed their lists to raise their hands. Then without comment, give everyone the same treat.

Next, ask the kids who actually finished the task lists how they feel about everyone receiving the same treat. After they've answered the question, read Matthew 20:1-16 aloud. Ask kids what they believe to be the meaning of the parable. Be sure to emphasize the following points from Scripture:

● God is more concerned with our faithfulness than he is with the actual results of our efforts.

● God's love is freely given to all who respond to him, regardless of when they respond.

● God is a just God, and his decisions are always fair.

Conclude by asking:

● **How does it make you feel to serve a God who is so loving?**

● **How can we let others know that God loves them in this manner?**

Bible Baseball

Overview: Kids will review Bible facts in a simulated baseball game.

Supplies: You'll need a Bible, chairs, paper, and pencils.

Preparation: In the middle of the room, arrange four chairs like a baseball diamond and set up one chair in the middle for the pitcher. Set up one row of chairs on either side of the room to serve as "dugouts," and set a piece of paper and a pencil near each dugout.

Write out several Bible fact questions. Choose some questions that are easy to be the "singles," some harder ones to be "doubles," more difficult ones to be "triples," and the most difficult questions to be "home runs." Be sure there are plenty of questions in each category (preferably about twenty-five of each for a thirty-minute game)

Time Involved: 20 to 45 minutes

Begin the game by dividing the group into two teams and having them sit on opposite sides of the room. You'll sit in a chair in the middle of the diamond.

The game is played by having a person from one team move to the chair at "home plate" and select a question level from one of the categories: single, double, triple, or home run. Next, ask the person sitting in the chair a question in the category he or she selected. If he or she answers correctly, have him or her move to the base that corresponds to the category of the question.

If the person answers incorrectly, have him or her return to the dugout and record an "out" for that team. A team continues to "bat" until it makes three outs, and then it's the other team's turn at bat.

For each correct answer, a person sitting on a "base" should advance the same number of bases as the "batter." For example, a person at second base will go "home" and score if the batter hits a double, but he or she will only go to third base if the batter hits a single.

Play the game for as long as time allows or until your questions run out.

Musical Bible Facts

Overview: Kids will learn Bible facts as they play Musical Chairs.

Supplies: You'll need a Bible, chairs, a tape player, a cassette or CD of instrumental music, a cassette or CD player, slips of paper, a pencil, and envelopes.

Preparation: Arrange the chairs in a circle, and set up the cassette or CD player. Write one question on each slip of paper based on a Bible story you will be studying or have already studied. Then place the questions in envelopes. Have at least one question for each person you expect to be present.

Time Involved: 20 to 30 minutes

Begin by having kids sit in the circle of chairs. Make sure every chair is occupied. Start the music on the cassette or CD player, and instruct kids to pass one of the envelopes around the circle. After a few seconds, stop the music. The person caught holding the envelope has two options; he or she may either pass it to the next person in the circle or attempt to answer the question in the envelope. If the person chooses to answer the question, he or she must leave the game if his or her answer is incorrect. However, the person remains in the circle if his or her answer is correct. If the player passes the question, the next person gets an opportunity to answer it. If a correct answer is given, the person who passed the envelope has to leave the game.

Remember, the person must choose to either pass or play before the envelope can be opened and read. Once a person leaves the game, he or she must also take the chair he or she was sitting on. Continue the game until there is only one person left.

Egg-Drop Soup

Overview: Kids will create delivery packages that can protect free-falling eggs.

Supplies: You'll need a Bible; eggs; various packing materials such as pieces of cardboard, cloth squares, foam pellets, and newspaper; scissors; small cardboard boxes; duct tape; string; a small bag of flour; and water and other cleanup supplies.

Preparation: Create a "landing zone" by poking a hole in a bag of flour and then walking around with the bag to create a medium-size circular line.

Time Involved: 20 to 30 minutes

Tell kids to think of this as a physics and engineering dilemma. They should ask themselves how they can quickly and effectively protect an egg from gravity.

Have kids form teams of three, and give each team an egg, a small cardboard box, some packing materials, scissors, duct tape, and string.

Announce that teams have twelve minutes to create packages that will protect eggs when the eggs are dropped from an open second-story window. Add that the packages must land in the designated landing zone.

After approximately twelve minutes, ask a

Leader TIP

This is an opportunity to empty your garage of the old packing materials you've been saving for years!

representative from each team to take the team's package upstairs and toss it out the window.

Applaud all efforts enthusiastically...*especially* if they work! Clean up the mess, pick up package materials, and use generous amounts of water to wash away broken eggs and spilled flour.

Ask kids to gather in their groups and discuss the following questions:

● **On a scale of 1 to 10, with 10 being the most difficult, how difficult was this challenge?**

● **What would have made the challenge easier?**

Next, read aloud Matthew 28:19-20, and ask the groups to discuss the following questions:

● **On the same scale of 1-to-10 difficulty, how difficult is this Bible challenge? Why?**

● **In what ways are the two challenges alike? Different?**

Ask trios to share their conclusions with the larger group. Then ask each group to close with a prayer of commitment to faithfully obey God.

Shadowlands

Overview: Kids will team up and provide shadow skits for familiar Bible stories.

Supplies: You'll need a Bible, a sheet, a clothesline, clothespins, masking tape, and a powerful light source.

Preparation: Prepare a stage area by hanging the sheet on the clothesline and placing a powerful light source behind it.

Time Involved: 20 to 60 minutes

Form groups of up to four people. Announce that you are going to narrate some familiar Bible stories and the groups will act them out as shadow skits. Demonstrate for the teams how shadows appear on the sheet.

Variation

If space is limited, place the sheet in front of a table and ask kids to use only their hands to tell the stories. This can be easily accomplished by having the kids sit on the floor and stick only their hands above the backlit stage area. This variation combines both hand-puppet shows and shadow plays.

Position the first group behind the sheet and then ask:

● **Did I mention that you'll have to make up the actions as I read?**

Read the first passage and have the first group act it out. After the first group finishes, give each of the other groups a turn. Be sure to applaud all kids' efforts.

You may want to choose from among the following passages:

● Genesis 7:6-16
● 1 Kings 3:1-28
● Jonah 1:1-5, 15-17
● Matthew 14:22-33
● Matthew 27:1-5

Close by saying: **Here's one last passage to act out.** Read aloud Jesus' words found in John 13:34-35.

Have everyone look at the blank screen and reflect on the passage for a few moments. Then lead a short discussion by asking:

● **What would it look like if we shared love with others in our group? With our families? In dating relationships?**

Bible Relay

Overview: Kids will learn to quickly find and remember Scripture references.

Supplies: You'll need Bibles, chairs, paper, and pencils.

Preparation: Line up five chairs in a single file row for each team. Write five Scripture references on a piece of paper, and make a copy of the list for each team.

Time Involved: 10 minutes

Divide kids into teams of five, and have each team sit down in a row of chairs. Give the first person in each row a Bible and a list of Scripture references. On the command to begin, have that person look up the first reference and memorize the first five words. Once this has been accomplished, have the first person hand the Bible and the reference list over his or her head to the next team member. The second person should do the same thing with the second listed passage and then pass the items on to the third person, and so on. The winning team is the one who finishes first and can recite the first five words of all five verses.

Bible Object Match

Overview: Kids will be able to match a modern-day object to the biblical story or character that it represents.

Supplies: You'll need Bibles, a selection of items from those listed below, paper, and pencils.

Preparation: Place items around the room.

Time Involved: 10 minutes

Give each person a piece of paper and a pencil. Have kids wander around the room looking at the items you have scattered. Tell them to try to equate each item to a Bible story or character.

Some items and the Bible stories they might represent are as follows:

● a roll of gauze—the parable of the good Samaritan
● a birth certificate—Jacob and Esau
● small animals—Noah
● a piece of purple cloth—Lydia
● a tablet of paper with the word "stone" written on it—Moses
● a compass with the word "Nineveh" written by the north symbol—Jonah

- a small piece of lamb's wool or fleece—Gideon
- an ear of corn—Joseph's dream
- a stuffed lion—Daniel
- a rock—Goliath
- a cup of water and a cup of wine (or grape juice)—the miracle at Cana
- a can of tuna and a loaf of bread—feeding of the 5,000
- a bag containing thirty pieces of silver—Judas Iscariot
- a gold coin, a bottle of perfume, and an incense stick—the wise men

If you so desire, you can announce the winner as the person (or people) who gets the most correct matches.

Bible Romance Matchup

Overview: Kids will match up biblical husbands and wives. This is a fun Valentine's Day event.

Supplies: You'll need name tags (enough for everyone in the group) and a marker.

Preparation: Write the names of Bible mates on the name tags. For example, one pair of tags would say "Adam" and "Eve," one pair would say "David" and "Michal," one pair would say "Moses" and "Zipporah," one pair would say "Christ and the church," one pair would say "Joseph" and "Mary," and so on. Try to find a few obscure couples to add a challenge to the game. If your group is large and you can't find enough names, repeat some of the pairs.

Time Involved: 10 minutes

Variation

You can also play this game with biblical fathers and sons or other pairs of your choosing.

As kids arrive, give each person a name tag to wear. Have kids wander around the room and find their Bible mates. Allow the game to go on for about ten minutes and then correct any errors.

Use this activity to begin a study on Bible romances or to talk about love relationships in the Bible.

Scripture Relay

Overview: This game will help kids become familiar with any Scripture passage you are about to study.

Supplies: You'll need Bibles, balloons, paper, a marker, and trash bags (optional).

Preparation: Write out a Scripture verse using only one word on each sheet of paper. Place each word inside a balloon and then blow the balloon up and tie it off. Place all of the balloons containing the words of one verse into a pile or a trash bag. Make as many sets as you will have teams.

Time Involved: 10 minutes

Divide the group into teams of five to ten kids, and set one trash bag or pile of balloons on the opposite side of the room from each team. Give each team Bibles, and explain that you'll be giving everyone a particular Scripture reference. Each team must look up the verse, race down to their pile of balloons, and pop the balloons by sitting on them. Instruct kids that once this has been accomplished, they are to place the words contained inside the balloons into the correct order to form the verse. The first team to succeed wins (and actually gets to clean up all of the balloon debris!).

Before you begin your study, have each team explain what the verse means.

Scripture Memory

Overview: Kids will learn to associate Scripture references with specific passages. This game is played like the game

Concentration—one team will reveal a square and the other team must complete the match.

Supplies: You'll need Bibles or concordances (optional), a bulletin board or a larger board divided into one-foot squares, index cards, paper, pencils, tape or thumbtacks.

Preparation: Write several verses on index cards and their corresponding references on separate cards. Tape or thumbtack a reference or a verse to each square face down. Write a number on the back side of each card so that the board looks like a numbered grid.

Time Involved: 10 minutes

Divide kids into two teams. Say: **We are going to review some of the Scripture passages we've been studying. The first team will call out a number and reveal a square. It will either be a reference to a verse or the actual verse written out. The second team will then try to find the corresponding reference or verse. A point will be awarded to the team for every match it finds. If a match is not made, both squares are turned back over. Teams will take turns going first.**

Play until the entire board is matched up. To simplify the game slightly, allow kids to use Bibles or concordances.

Jesus Is the Key

Overview: Kids will use this scavenger hunt as a springboard to discuss John 14:6—"Jesus answered, 'I am the way and the truth and the life. No one comes to the Father except through me.' "

Supplies: You'll need a Bible, lots of old keys (ask members of your congregation to bring keys they no longer use), a lock-and-key set, and paper and a pencil (optional).

Preparation: Hide the keys all over the church or in various places around a campsite. (Remember or write down where you hid them.)

Time Involved: 10 to 20 minutes

Say: **I have hidden lots of keys, and your job is to find them. The object of the game is to find a key, bring it back, and try it in the lock. There is only one key that will open the lock. The person who finds that key wins.**

After all the keys have been returned and the lock has been opened, have a discussion about Jesus being the key to the Father. Have someone read John 14:6 aloud. Afterward, ask:

● **How does the key that opened the lock remind you of Jesus?**

● **What might the other keys represent?**

● **Could you tell as soon as you found a key whether it would fit in the lock?**

● **Do you think it is difficult to tell what way we need to go in life?**

Bible-Warriors Night

Overview: This game, which takes place as a part of a progressive dinner, is modeled after the computer game "Captain Bible." Kids will learn how to fight lies with Scriptural truths.

Supplies: You'll need Bibles, paper, and pencils.

Preparation: Find adults to host each course of your meal (appetizer, soup, salad, main course, and dessert). Write Bible verses on pieces of paper, and give each host or hostess one verse to share with kids.

Time Involved: 2 to 3 hours

Meet at the church. Divide kids into two groups—one group will be the Lies and the other will be the Truths. Say: **Tonight we'll be going on a progressive dinner. At each stop, the host or hostess will share a Scripture. The Truths need to commit it to memory, and the Lies** need to begin creating a lie about the Scripture. For instance, if the verse is "Blessed are the poor in spirit, for theirs is the kingdom of heaven," the lie might be "the poor will never inherit the kingdom of heaven." Later this evening, we will play a game to see if the Truths can win over the Lies.

After the dinner, return to the church or some place that has lots of hiding places. Allow all the kids to hide.

The object of the game is for all of the members of the Truths group to get to the sanctuary. If they run into a member of the Lies group, the member of the Lies group must use one of the lies the group thought up during the evening to try to capture the member of the Truth group. If the member of the Truth group can come up with the correct Scripture verse to fight the member of the Lies group, the member of the Lies group must let the Truths group member continue on his or her way. If the member of the Truths group fails, he or she is captured by the Lies group. The game ends when either all the members of the Truths group are captured or they all make it safely to the sanctuary.

Bring everyone back together for a short discussion. Ask:

● **How important was it to know Scripture well?**
● **What was the most difficult part of this game?**
● **Did you ever feel scared or alone?**
● **How was this activity like real life?**
● **How can we be better prepared to handle the lies that come along?**

Time-Line Trivia

Overview: Kids will put Bible facts into time perspective.

Supplies: You'll need a Bible, paper, marker, tape, orange traffic cones, and a blindfold.

Preparation: Write a historical Bible fact on each piece of paper, and tape each one to a traffic cone. (Some examples of facts are: God makes Eve, Joshua fights the battle at Jericho, Jesus is born, Elijah is in the wilderness, Saul becomes Paul, John is called as a disciple, and so on.) Mix the cones up, and place them in random order.

Time Involved: 10 minutes

Begin by explaining that the object of this game is to place all the Bible events in the order they occurred. The kids will be allowed only five minutes to complete the game. Begin by having the group choose one person to be blindfolded. The idea is for the rest of the group to verbally assist the blindfolded person in placing the cones in the proper order. The game will definitely require teamwork to complete the task in under five minutes. When the time is up, help the kids rearrange the cones in the correct order of events.

Then lead a short discussion by asking:

● **Was it difficult to put these events in order? Why or why not?**

● **Was it hardest for the blindfolded person or for the team? Explain.**

● **Why might it be important to understand the proper order in which events occurred in the Bible?**

● **Who or what might the blindfolded person represent?**

Floor Word-Hunt

Overview: Kids will find key words or phrases to spur discussion. (This fun-filled event resembles the game Twister.)

Supplies: You'll need one four-foot length of one-inch elastic for every two players, a needle and thread or a stapler, and four-inch adhesive letters or large letters typed on individual pieces of paper.

Preparation: Begin by creating a simple word search in a grid pattern by using key words you would like to discuss with your kids such as "grace," "redemption," "salvation," "faith," "justification," "revelation," "joy," "love," "evangelism," and so on. Lay the adhesive letters on the floor in the same grid pattern as your word search. Make sure the letters are approximately four inches from each other.

Time Involved: 1 hour

Sew together (or staple) the ends of each piece of elastic so that it looks like a huge rubber band. Pair kids up, and give each pair a "rubber band." Say: **We are going to explore word meanings. I am going to give each pair a word. Your job is to find the word on the word search and circle it by standing inside your rubber band.**

Add much more twisting fun and confusion by having all the pairs go at the same time.

Once each pair has succeeded, have them take turns sharing the words they found and the meanings of the words.

This game is a great way to discover how much your group knows about particular biblical principles. With this knowledge, you can develop studies based on the ideas kids struggle with most.

Biblical Scavenger Hunt

Overview: Kids will look up particular Scriptures to solve clues.

Supplies: You'll need Bibles, a map of your area, paper and pencils, and a vehicle with an adult driver for each team.

Preparation: Compile a list of local merchants who are willing to help with this game by allowing kids to make contact with them and by signing their clue sheets. Explain to the merchants that your youth group will be doing a scavenger hunt, and give them all the necessary details. Next, prepare a sheet of clues for each team (see the sample list following this game).

Time Involved: 2 hours

Have kids meet at a central location in the scavenger hunt area such as the church or a restaurant. Divide kids into teams, with an adult driver and a vehicle for each team. Give each team a Bible, an area map with the boundaries clearly marked, and a clue sheet. Inform kids they will have one hour to complete their hunt. When the time is up, they need to report back to the central location.

After everyone has come back together, have kids share their experiences. Also, use this time to discuss that it isn't always easy to understand what a particular Bible passage says—we often have to grapple with its meaning!

Sample Scavenger Hunt Clues:

- ❏ Genesis 23:4 (burial site)—a cemetery
- ❏ Deuteronomy 8:3 (bread)—a bakery
- ❏ Judges 16:19 (Delilah cuts Samson's hair)—a barber shop or a beauty shop
- ❏ Psalm 19:8 (enlightening the eyes)—an eyeglass shop
- ❏ Psalm 36:9 (fountain of life)—a fountain
- ❏ Psalm 43:4 (altar)—a church
- ❏ Psalm 74:6 (axes and hatchets)—a hardware store
- ❏ Psalm 103:4, Proverbs 14:18 (crowns)—a card- and gift-store
- ❏ Proverbs 3:15 (jewels)—a jewelry store
- ❏ Hosea 14:5 (lily)—a flower shop
- ❏ Matthew 6:26 (birds of the air)—an aviary
- ❏ Matthew 24:20 (flight)—a local airport
- ❏ Matthew 25:6 (bridegroom)—a bridal shop or a tuxedo shop
- ❏ Mark 1:6 (leather belt)—a leather-goods store
- ❏ Luke 6:40 (student and teacher)—a school
- ❏ John 21:25 (books)—a bookstore
- ❏ Acts 10:12 (animals)—a zoo or a veterinarian's office
- ❏ James 5:9 (the judge at the door)—a courthouse

Babel Mania

Overview: Kids will have a hilarious time studying the Tower of Babel story! This is a great activity to involve the whole congregation by having some volunteers help bake cakes. Everyone in the church will enjoy watching kids build the biggest tower they can from cake "bricks." Afterward, everyone can enjoy eating the masterpiece!

Supplies: You'll need a Bible, lots of cake mixes, petite-loaf pans that make eight loaves each, lots of icing, and a clean plastic tarp.

Preparation: A week in advance, organize a group of people who have petite-loaf pans to bake your bricks. Have the volunteers freeze the cakes and bring them to the event.

Time Involved: 20 minutes

Leader TIP

Each cake mix makes sixteen minicakes and requires approximately one-and-a-half cups of icing.

Read the story of the Tower of Babel in Genesis 11:1-9. Say: **Now we're going to build our own tower to the heavens by using cake bricks!**

Provide the "construction crew" with the bricks and icing and let them go to work building and mortaring the structure. If you have plenty of cakes and kids, you can divide the group into two teams to see which one can build the tallest tower in ten minutes.

Lydia Parachute

Overview: The kids will see how the ministry of Lydia is applicable today.

Supplies: You'll need a Bible; a ball; and one large piece of purple fabric big enough to be a parachute, such as a large purple tablecloth, a king-sized sheet, or a parachute made by someone in your church (which could be used for future youth games).

Preparation: None is needed.

Time Involved: 5 minutes

Begin by reading Acts 16:11-15 to the group, or have one of the students read it aloud. Have kids line up around the parachute and each take hold of the edge. Place a ball in the middle. Next, have the group begin waving the parachute up and down, attempting to knock the ball off the parachute. As this continues, go around the group and have each person share one way in which the fabric parachute could be used to show Christ's love in the home.

Variation

Another option is to have each person share as the ball lands on his or her section of the parachute.

Examples of different uses are:
- a blanket to cover someone who is cold,
- a tablecloth on which to serve a meal to others, and
- a dish towel to help dry dishes.

"We Are Family" Collages

Overview: This game is a good wrap-up of a study of Matthew 12:46-50 as it speaks of spiritual families.

Supplies: You'll need a Bible, newsprint, and markers.

Preparation: Tear off one big sheet of newsprint for each group, and lay some markers near each sheet.

Time Involved: 10 minutes

Separate everyone into groups of five to seven. Say: **Using the big sheets of paper, draw pictures that illustrate how God's family, the church, is like your family at home. Examples would be people eating together,**

people praying together, and people playing together.

Allow five minutes for the drawing, making sure that each person has an opportunity to take part. When this has been completed, bring everyone back together, and have the other groups guess what the different drawings represent. Award points for each correct guess, and name the winner as the team with the most points.

Read Matthew 12:46-50, and begin a discussion by asking:
- **What drawings surprised you?**
- **How is our church family like your own family?**
- **How is the church family different?**
- **What are some of the things that would make the church family more like your family at home?**

Fruit of the Spirit Photo Opportunity

Overview: Kids will begin to see the fruit of the Spirit in action.

Supplies: You'll need a Bible, paper, pencils, an instant-print camera and film or a video camera and a tape for each group, and a vehicle with an adult driver for each group.

Preparation: Make a handout for each team by listing the fruit of the Spirit from Galatians 5:22-23.

Time Involved: 2 to 3 hours

Divide the group into teams. Say: **We're going to try to discover all of the fruit of the Spirit in action.** Read Galatians 5:22-23 aloud, and ask kids to take note of the different fruit of the Spirit listed.

Say: **Your goal will be to go out into the community and capture on film each one of these qualities in action—love, joy, peace, patience, kindness, goodness, faithfulness, gentleness, and self-control. You can either**

find people doing these things or stage short skits for the ones you cannot find.

Have everyone meet back after an allotted time period (this activity will probably take at least an hour and a half). When everyone has returned, view each team's accomplishments and allow kids time to share how each situation depicted one of the fruit of the Spirit.

Scripture Cake Race

Overview: This activity is not only tasty, but it will also help kids begin to understand that checking different versions of the Bible can help them more fully understand the meaning of a passage.

Supplies: You'll need several different versions of the Bible (one must be the King James Version); the "Scripture Cake Recipe" handout (p. 103); the ingredients to make Scripture Cake: 1/2 cup butter, 2 cups sugar, 2 tablespoons honey, 6 eggs, 1 1/2 cups flour, 2 teaspoons baking powder, 2 teaspoons cinnamon, 1/2 teaspoon ginger, 1/2 teaspoon cloves, 1 teaspoon nutmeg, 1/2 cup milk, 2 cups chopped figs, 2 cups chopped raisins, 2 cups chopped almonds, and salt; a greased ten-inch tube pan, mixing bowls, and a mixer or mixing spoons.

Preparation: Make one copy of the "Scripture Cake Recipe" handout (p. 103) for each person.

Time Involved: 20 minutes

Give each person a Bible (randomly scatter the various versions), a copy of the "Scripture Cake Recipe" handout (p. 103), and a pencil.

Say: **Today we are going to bake a Scripture Cake. But first we need to figure out the ingredients using the Bible. Look up each reference, and write down the ingredient most appropriately described by the verse.**

After about fifteen minutes, bring the group back together

and review the ingredients everyone has come up with. Some of the responses you get will be hysterical.

Next, lead a short discussion by asking:

● **We all looked up the same references; why do you think all of us didn't come up with the same ingredients?**

● **Do you think anyone was incorrect in his or her answers? Why or why not?**

● **How was this activity similar to what we discover when we look up Scripture using different versions of the Bible?**

Provide the kids the correct ingredients and have them make the cake.

SCRIPTURE
Cake Recipe

1/2 cup Judges 5:25, last clause
2 cups Jeremiah 6:20
2 tablespoons 1 Samuel 14:25
6 of Jeremiah 17:11
1 1/2 cups 1 Kings 17:12
2 teaspoons Amos 4:5, first clause
a pinch of Leviticus 2:13
2 Chronicles 9:9
1/2 cup Judges 5:25, first clause
2 cups each 1 Samuel 30:12
2 cups Numbers 17:8

*Cream the 1/2 cup Judges 5:25, last clause; the 2 cups
Jeremiah 6:20; and the 2 tablespoons 1 Samuel 14:25.
Add 6 of Jeremiah 17:11 (yolks only). In a separate bowl,
mix all the dry ingredients (1 1/2 cups 1 Kings 17:12; 2
teaspoons Amos 4:5, first clause; a pinch of Leviticus 2:13;
and 2 Chronicles 9:9). Add the dry mixture to the creamed
one, alternating with the 1/2 cup Judges 5:25, first clause.
Stir in the 2 cups each 1 Samuel 30:12. Coat 2 cups
Numbers 17:8 in some extra 1 Kings 17:12 and shake it off.
(This keeps them from sinking to the bottom of the pan.)
Fold in 6 stiffly beaten Jeremiah 17:11 whites. Bake in a
well-greased ten-inch tube pan at 300 degrees for 2 hours.*

(recipe taken from *Cooking From the Heart,* Campus Crusade for Christ, Inc.)

Concordance Challenge

Overview: Kids will use concordances to find and memorize Bible verses.

Supplies: You'll need Bibles, concordances, paper, a pencil, and small prizes (optional).

Preparation: Make a list of Bible verses you would like kids to find and memorize. Choose shorter verses (probably no more than one or two sentences in length).

Time Involved: 15 to 30 minutes

Begin by briefly explaining how to use a concordance. Then tell everyone that this game is a race to see which team can locate and identify the location of a passage by book, chapter, and verse.

Leader TIP

If you don't have enough concordances, have kids share them in groups of three or four.

Read the first verse on your list out loud. Repeat it several times as the kids try to locate its reference in the concordance. This will also help them begin memorizing the verse.

If you like, give a small prize or gag gift to the team that finishes first. Once each team has located the verse, repeat it several times together.

You might want to keep track of the Scriptures the kids looked up in the concordance and study them further the following week.

Bible Facts

Overview: Kids will learn lots of Bible trivia by playing this team-oriented game.

Supplies: You'll need a Bible, index cards, a pencil, and a watch with a second hand or a timer.

Preparation: Prepare Bible trivia cards by writing questions and answers on index cards. You can make your questions as difficult or as easy as you like, based upon your group's knowledge of the Bible. You might also want to consider dividing the questions into difficult, moderate, and easy categories, assigning point values to each category. Here are a few sample questions to get you started in your preparation:

- Name three of the twelve apostles.
- What is the shortest verse in the Bible?
- In what book of the Bible can we find the stories of Abraham?
- What is the last book of the Old Testament?
- Name a book of the Bible named after a woman.

If you'd prefer to get kids involved in the game's preparation, hand out index cards and ask each person to write down a trivia question and its answer. Collect the cards and use them to play the game the following week.

Time Involved: 15 to 30 minutes

Begin by dividing the group into two teams. Assign a Captain or a Spokesperson to each team. Have teams take turns answering Bible trivia questions. If the team which selected the question cannot provide a correct answer in thirty seconds, give the other team an opportunity to answer the question. Keep track of points if you'd like.

A Penny for Your Thoughts

Overview: Kids will have an opportunity to give their interpretations of a verse by playing this discussion-oriented game. This is a great game to play with a group of kids who know each other and who do not feel inhibited in speaking or sharing their ideas with others.

Supplies: You'll need Bibles and pennies.

Time Involved: 15 to 30 minutes

Begin by dividing the group into two teams (either mixed teams or a boys team and a girls team). Next, select a short passage of Scripture to read aloud (the words of Jesus from the Gospels work well).

Say: **In a moment, I will read a Bible passage and then call out the name of someone on a team by saying, "a penny for your thoughts." That person must either respond immediately with a thought about the passage or must pass his or her turn to a person on the other team by calling out one of their names and saying, "a penny for your thoughts." If the person from the first team gives a thought, he or she receives a penny. If that person passes, then the person on the second team must give a thought and receive a penny.**

As the game progresses, continue to read short Bible passages, alternating between teams. Play the game for a prescribed amount of time and, afterward, see which team has the most pennies.

If you like, pause from time to time during the game to talk about some of the insights that kids offer about the Bible passages.

Casting Your Cares

Overview: Kids will write down their personal concerns and struggles and then have a paper fight.

Supplies: You'll need Bibles, $5\frac{1}{2}$ x $8\frac{1}{2}$-inch paper, pencils, tape, and a trash can.

Preparation: Put the pencils and a stack of paper in the middle of the room.

Time Involved: 10 to 25 minutes

Have each student take several sheets of paper. Say: **Write one thing you are concerned about on each sheet of paper. You might write "grades," "family," or "friends." Anything that upsets or discourages you is fair game. Don't put your name on your paper or share it with anyone else. This is strictly between you and God.**

While kids are writing, tape a line down the middle of the floor.

When each person has at least three to five things written, each on a separate page, have kids wad their pages up and form two equal teams. Have the teams face each other standing on opposite sides and approximately three feet from the tape line. If you have more than twenty kids, you might want to consider forming additional teams. Say: **When I say "go," throw all of your concerns onto the other team's side while trying to keep their concerns off your side. The object is to get as many concerns as possible on the other team's side before the time is up. You'll have one minute. Go!**

When the time is up, put a large trash can in the middle of the room and say: **This time, you'll have thirty seconds to work together to get all of the concerns into the trash can. Go!**

After you call time, ask a volunteer to read 1 Peter 5:7 aloud and then ask:

● **Was the way you treated your concerns in this game like or unlike the way kids really treat their concerns?**

● **What happened when you dumped your concerns on each other? What happened when you worked together to dump your concerns?**

● **What thoughts go through your mind when your friends dump problems on you?**

● **What do you think about dumping your concerns on God?**

● **How can you help your friends bring their concerns to God?**

● **What are your thoughts about how God can help you with your concerns?**

● **How does it make you feel to know that God cares for you?**

Gather around the trash can and ask for several people to pray that group members will be able to let go of their concerns. If you have a Dumpster, you may hold a ceremonial trash-dumping after the prayer.

Reaping the Whirlwind

Overview: Kids will experience firsthand the consequences of sowing the wind and reaping the whirlwind.

Supplies: You'll need a Bible, bags of birdseed, box fans, extension cords (if needed), bushel baskets or boxes, and tape.

Preparation: Set up the fans, using extension cords if necessary, approximately three feet behind the baskets or boxes. Then use tape to make a line ten feet in front of the baskets.

Time Involved: 10 to 20 minutes

This game illustrates the futility of sowing "good" seed into the wind.

Establish teams of five to ten students, and have them stand behind the line facing the baskets or boxes. Give each team a bag of birdseed and, one at a time, have kids throw a handful of birdseed toward the team's basket.

The object of the game is to get as much seed as possible into the basket. Players should take turns until they have emptied the entire bag of birdseed.

Leader TIP

If electricity is not available to you, this game works well on a windy day.

After kids have played the game, read your students Hosea 8:7 and then ask:

- **What was it like to play this game?**
- **What could the seed represent in your life?**
- **What could the fan represent in your life?**

Cross the Jordan!

Overview: Kids will work together to cross the gym floor on small squares. This game teaches the story of the Israelites crossing the Jordan River in a way your kids will never forget.

Supplies: You'll need Bibles, two 2x2-foot squares of carpet or cardboard, two brooms, and a long rope that will reach across your playing area.

Preparation: None is needed.

Time Involved: 15 to 30 minutes

If you have more than twenty people in your group, you might want to split into groups of twelve to twenty for this activity. You will need two carpet or cardboard squares, two brooms, and one rope for each group.

Appoint two students to serve as the High Priests who will carry the ark across the river. For the purpose of this game, the Jordan River will be the space between two boundary lines in your gym. The ark of the covenant will be the two brooms which the two High Priests will have to keep on their shoulders at all times. The High Priests will use the two squares of carpet or cardboard to get across the river. Before they begin, have them tie the rope around their waists so they can get the rest of the team across the river.

In order to cross from one side of the gym to the other, the High Priests must stand on one square and throw the next square just far enough ahead to step on it. They are then to reach back and pick up the carpet square behind them and throw it forward. The High Priests must keep the two brooms on their shoulders all the way across.

Once they have reached the other side of the gym, the High Priests are to throw one of the squares as well as one end of the rope back to the next person in line on the other side of the gym. Once this person has a tight hold on the rope, the High Priests are to pull him or her on the square across the gym. This process is repeated until the entire group is across the gym.

After your group has finished the game, have them read Joshua 3:7-17. Then lead a short discussion, using the following questions:

● **What do you think the Israelites were thinking when they saw the priests step into the river carrying the ark of the covenant?**

● **How did you feel about being dragged across the gym by a rope? Explain.**

● **What are the rivers in your life that only God can help you across?**

New Testament Scramble

Overview: Kids will have fun learning the order of the New Testament books.

Supplies: You'll need slips of paper and pencils.

Preparation: Write one of the books of the New Testament on each of the slips of paper.

Time Involved: 10 minutes

Leader TIP

If your group is smaller than twenty-seven people, some people will need to fill more than one position in the line. If it is larger than twenty-seven, more than one person will stand in the same book position.

Mix up the slips of paper, and give one to each person in your group. If you have less than twenty-seven people, give some members more than one book of the New Testament. If you have more than twenty-seven people, give more than one person the same book in the New Testament.

As quickly as they can, have kids try to line up in sequential order of the New Testament. Once they are in order, have them each name their books out loud.

Lukewarm Laodicean Spitballs

Overview: Kids will realize the undesirable aspects of being spiritually lukewarm.

Supplies: You'll need a Bible, newspaper, one bowl for every group of three or four, one straw for each student, colored paper, a sheet of plastic, and tape.

Preparation: Fill the bowls with lukewarm water, and tape the sheet of plastic to a wall of the meeting room.

Time Involved: 10 to 15 minutes

Give each student a straw. Set bowls of lukewarm water on newspaper, and have kids gather in groups of three or four around them. The bowls should be positioned on the floor fifteen to twenty feet away from the wall with the plastic taped on it.

Distribute a different color of paper, if possible, to each group of three or four. The object of this game is to see how many spitballs the members of each team can get to stick to the sheet of plastic by spitting them through their straws. Students should use the lukewarm water to create the spitballs. Have each student tear his or her own spitballs from the sheet of paper. After the game, ask a volunteer to read Revelation 3:14-22 to your group.

For discussion ask the following questions:

● **Why would it be better to be spiritually cold than to be spiritually lukewarm?**

● **What temperature is your spiritual life right now?**

King Ahab's Chariot Races

Overview: Kids will re-enact Elijah's famous sprint down Mount Carmel in front of King Ahab's chariot.

Supplies: You'll need Bibles, tape or chalk, a stopwatch or a watch with a second hand, cups, and ice water.

Preparation: Mark a circle with tape or chalk, approximately thirty feet across.

Time Involved: 10 to 20 minutes

This wheelbarrow race illustrates the historic race between Elijah and King Ahab to reach Jezreel. Have kids form trios. Each trio will have one Elijah, one chariot, and one Ahab. This will be a timed race, one trio at a time. Elijah begins by running around the circle backward. Then the chariot will get down on his or her hands and knees and King Ahab will pick up the chariot's legs (wheelbarrow-race style) and race around the circle just behind Elijah. The fastest trio should be served ice water by the other trios.

After the game, have your trios read 1 Kings 18:41-46. Then have kids discuss the following questions in their trios:

● **How was Elijah able to outrun King Ahab's chariot?**

● **In what areas of your life would you like to experience the power of the Lord?**

Bible Categories

Overview: Kids will learn important facts of the Bible in this *Jeopardy!*-style game.

Supplies: You'll need a copy of the answers (pp. 114-116) and a dry-erase board and a dry-erase marker or a chalkboard and chalk.

Preparation: Write the nine categories on the board from left to right as in the game *Jeopardy!* Under each category, write vertically from top to bottom 10 points, 20 points, and so on up to 50 points. In the "Answers" section, the letter "a" corresponds to 10 points, letter "b" corresponds to 20 points, and so on.

Time Involved: 30 minutes or more

Form teams of no more than five, and have one person on each team volunteer to keep track of each team's points. A team will choose a category and a point amount to select its answer and then try to come up with the correct question as in the game show *Jeopardy!* A round might look like this:

Team 1: "New Testament Figures for 30 points."

Leader: "Jesus' prominent cousin."

Team 1: "Who is John the Baptist?"

After the game, you might want to take a picture of the winning team to put up in the "Bible Categories Hall of Fame."

BIBLE CATEGORIES

1. Old Testament Figures

2. New Testament Figures

3. Places

4. Prophets

5. Books of the Bible

6. Authors of the New Testament

7. Parables

8. Kings

9. Women in the Bible

ANSWERS

1. Old Testament Figures

a. The person who made the axhead float to the top of the water. (Who is Elisha?)

b. One of the two people who held up Moses' arms during a battle. (Who is Aaron or Hur?)

c. The man who was put into slavery by his eleven brothers. (Who is Joseph?)

d. The man who showed up the 450 prophets of Baal on Mount Carmel. (Who is Elijah?)

e. The one who led the army of Israel into the Promised Land. (Who is Joshua?)

2. New Testament Figures

a. Peter's name before Jesus changed it. (What is Simon?)

b. He tried to save Jesus from the guards by cutting off a soldier's ear. (Who is Peter?)

c. Jesus' prominent cousin. (Who is John the Baptist?)

d. He had a life-changing experience marked by a great light. (Who is Paul or Saul?)

e. He was the Caesar at the time of Christ's birth. (Who is Augustus?)

3. Places

a. The place where Mary and Martha were from. (What is Bethany?)

b. The place where Jesus grew up. (What is Nazareth?)

c. The sea at which Jesus spent a lot of his time. (What is Galilee?)

d. The country where Jesus talked to the woman at the well. (What is Samaria?)

e. The place where Jesus told his disciples to stay until the Holy Spirit came. (What is Jerusalem?)

4. Prophets

a. The prophet who told David his sin with Bathsheba was going to be punished. (Who is Nathan?)

b. The prophet who went to heaven in a fiery chariot. (Who is Elijah?)

c. The prophet who saw dead bones get up and dance? (Who is Ezekiel?)

d. The prophet who helped a widow's oil go a long, long way? (Who is Elisha?)

e. The prophet who fled to Tarshish instead of obeying God? (Who is Jonah?)

5. Books of the Bible

a. The book that gives the Ten Commandments. (What is Exodus?)

b. The book that tells about the early church after Christ's ascension. (What is Acts?)

c. One of the books that are collections of King Solomon's wise sayings. (What is Proverbs or Ecclesiastes?)

d. The smallest book of the Bible. (What is Jude?)

e. The book that begins, "In the beginning was the Word, and the Word was with God, and the Word was God." (What is John?)

6. Authors of the New Testament

a. The person who wrote the book of Revelation from the island of Patmos. (Who is John?)

b. The person who wrote the most books in the New Testament. (Who is Paul?)

c. The person who wrote the books First and Second Timothy. (Who is Paul?)

d. The person who wrote the books First and Second Peter. (Who is Peter?)

e. The person who wrote the book listed first in the New Testament. (Who is Matthew?)

116

7. Parables

a. The three parables that spoke of lost items. (What are the parables of the coin, the sheep, and the prodigal son?)

b. The four soils in the parable of the seed and the soils. (What are along the path, rocky, thorny, and fertile?)

c. The man who helped a robbery victim. (Who is the good Samaritan?)

d. The place where the wise man built his house. (What is "on the rock"?)

e. With faith the size of this, you could move a mountain. (What is a mustard seed?)

8. Kings

a. The first king to build the temple in the Old Testament. (Who is Solomon?)

b. The king who also played the harp and wrote songs. (Who is David?)

c. The king who will reign forever and ever. (Who is Jesus?)

d. The king who was evil and married to Jezebel. (Who is Ahab?)

e. The king who had John the Baptist killed. (Who is Herod?)

9. Women in the Bible

a. She was a prophetess, a judge, and a warrior. (Who is Deborah?)

b. She blessed Jesus on the day he came to the temple when he was a baby. (Who is Anna?)

c. She was Abraham's wife. (Who is Sarah?)

d. She brought Samson to his ruin. (Who is Delilah?)

e. This Moabitess took good care of her mother-in-law. (Who is Ruth?)

Your Word Is a Lamp Unto My Feet

Overview: Kids will use teamwork to understand that the Bible is the best source for direction in their lives.

Supplies: You'll need a Bible, paper, a marker, tape, and one newspaper for each team.

Preparation: Prepare four separate sheets of paper as indicated by the following directions: On the first sheet write "Psalm 25:10—Path 1"; on the second sheet write "Psalm 32:9—Path 2"; on the third sheet write "Psalm 78:17—Path 3"; and on the fourth sheet write "Psalm 106:14—Path 4." Before the game begins, determine a starting line and four different finishing points forty feet from the starting line. Tape one of the reference sheets to the floor at each of the finishing points.

Time Involved: 10 minutes

As you begin the game, read Psalm 119:105 to the group. Next, have kids form two teams, and have the members of each team stand in a single file line. Give each team a Bible and a newspaper. Every person on the team should take five pages of the newspaper.

Say: **In this game, we will be learning just how important the Bible is in determining our paths in life. The newspaper will represent God's written word in our lives.**

Explain that the object of the game is to take turns carrying the Bible and laying out the pages of the newspaper like steppingstones toward one of the finishing points. The first person on each team will begin the relay by carrying the Bible and placing his or her pages on the floor in the direction of one of the finishing points. That person should then return and

Leader TIP

If you have a large group, create as many teams and destinations as you like.

118

tag the next person on the team. The second player will walk out on the pages already in place and then lay his or her pages down in the same manner. Continue this same process until all the members of the team have had turns and the path ends at one of the finishing points.

After you've explained the process, say: **There's a catch to winning the game: There are four destinations and only one represents God's will for your life. When the last person on your team reaches the finishing point, he or she needs to look up the passage from the path you chose. If the message in the Bible passage indicates that you chose the right path, you win the game. If, however, the passage indicates that you have taken the wrong or a foolish path, you must pick another one and begin again.**

After the game is complete, have the winning team read the verse and then lead a discussion by asking:

● **Why is it important for us to use the Bible as the source of direction in our lives?**

● **How does this belief differ from what the world tells us?**

● **Is there any situation in which the Bible would not be able to guide us? Why or why not?**

Table Tennis Slalom

Overview: Youth will play a simplified croquet-style game using table tennis balls and straw "mallets."

Supplies: You'll need a Bible; five toilet paper tubes; duct or masking tape; one straw for each person; a stopwatch or a watch with a second hand; at least four table tennis balls; and two sets of gold, silver, and bronze medals (any form).

Preparation: Tape the five toilet paper tubes horizontally to the floor in a staggered croquet course, making sure the holes on each side are exposed. Determine a starting line and a finish line.

Time Involved: 10 to 20 minutes

Form pairs, and have one partner in each pair be the Racer and one person be the Timer. The Racer's job will be to blow his or her table tennis ball through the tubes in the croquet course. As soon as the first Racer blows a ball through the first tube, the next pair may begin. One Racer may pass another Racer if he or she catches up. Two different Racers can be competing for the same tube, but a Racer cannot blow another Racer's ball off-course. (If this happens, the Racer should be disqualified.) After the Racer in each pair finishes the course, the Timer should write down the Racer's time and then the two should switch places and go another round.

After the second Racer in each pair has completed the course, combine the two times for that pair's final score. Award gold, silver, and bronze medals to the pairs with the top three scores. Call kids together, read 2 Timothy 4:7 aloud, and then ask:

● **How was this game like the verse I just read?**

● **How was this game unlike what will really happen at the end of our race in life?**

● **Did you ever want to give up in the race? How was your experience like your daily life?**

Cheaters Lineup

Overview: Kids will do a mock police lineup to discover people in the Bible who were cheaters.

Supplies: You'll need a Bible for each trio, ten pieces of paper, a pen, a ten-foot piece of newsprint, and tape.

Preparation: Tape the newsprint to a wall, and make it look like the backdrop for a lineup in a police station, making a mark at 6 feet, a mark at 5 feet 6 inches, a mark at 5 feet, and so on. Make sure the lines are drawn across the entire piece of newsprint. Also create nameplates by writing the following ten names from the Bible on separate sheets of paper, including a bogus identification number with each, such as Ananias #6783001. The names are: Zacchaeus, Absalom, Ahab, Jezebel, Jacob, Rehoboam, Judas, Achan, Ananias, and Sapphira.

Time Involved: 20 minutes

Gather kids together facing the lineup paper on the wall. Tell them you have found ten individuals cheating in the group, and they will be put through a police lineup. Randomly choose ten people to go and line up against the lineup wall. Next, give each of the ten people a nameplate with a name and an identification number on it.

Form everyone else into groups of no more than three. Tell them their job is to determine what each of these people did to get caught cheating. The first team to accurately identify them all wins. Encourage the groups to use their Bibles.

To conclude the game, lead a discussion by asking:

● **What did the cheaters have in common?**

● **Why do you think these cheaters thought they could get away with their crimes?**

● **What happened to them?**

● **How does this game apply to us today?**

Count the Cost

Overview: Kids will play a type of Capture the Flag game to help them understand there is a cost for true discipleship.

Supplies: You'll need an older, inexpensive Bible; a sock for each of half of the participants; flour; a $1/2$ cup measuring cup; and a piece of black construction paper and tape for each of the remaining participants

Preparation: Fill each of the socks with $1/2$ cup flour, and tie them shut. Also, select a home base for each team and a jail on one side.

Time Involved: 10 to 30 minutes

In this game, one team tries to penetrate the other team's home base and steal the Bible without being caught and sent to jail.

Divide kids into two teams. One team is to be called The Way after the name of the first-century Christian believers. Each member of The Way needs to have a piece of black paper taped to his or her back. Each member of the other team, called the Roman Guards, should be given a flour-filled sock to beat The Way for trying to spread the gospel.

Members of The Way will try to enter the Roman territory, seize the Bible, and bring it back to their own home base before they are beaten. If a member of The Way is hit by a Roman Guard and a flour mark shows up on his or her back, he or she must be taken to the Roman jail. The member of The Way must stay in jail until tagged by another team member. There can be no more than three Roman Guards in the home base territory and no more than three members of The Way in the safety of their own home base.

The game ends when the Bible is brought safely back to The Way's home base. You may want to have kids trade sides and play again so each person gets a feel for what it was like for both the Roman guards and the early believers.

When kids are finished playing, find a quiet place for a discussion and ask:

● **How is this game like what the early believers endured to spread the gospel?**

● **The Apostle Paul was beaten and imprisoned many times for preaching. What do you think motivated him to endure this treatment?**

● **In what ways do you feel that we have to "count the cost" today?**

Sleepyhead

Overview: Kids will use teamwork and cooperation to keep Eutychus awake.

Supplies: You'll need a Bible and a one-minute timer for each group of eight.

Preparation: None is needed.

Time Involved: 5 to 10 minutes

Read Acts 20:7-12 to the group and then say: **Eutychus was the man who fell asleep on a windowsill one night while Paul was preaching. When he fell asleep, he also fell to his death. Paul used this incident to bring glory to God by bringing Eutychus back to life in front of everyone.**

Form teams of eight, and have each team form a circle. Choose one person per team to be Eutychus. He or she will sit in the middle of the circle with a timer set for one minute. The rest of the team will try to form a human structure or pyramid with no more than four feet or legs touching the ground. If the team is successful, Eutychus stays awake. If the first human pyramid on a team is successful, Eutychus should set the timer again and the team should try a different structure.

Leader TIP

For smaller groups, you might consider forming only one team and having kids play against their best time.

If the team is unsuccessful after one minute, Eutychus falls asleep and the team is out. The team that can keep Eutychus awake the longest is the winning team.

Build the Church

Overview: Kids will try to share their faith without using certain Christian "lingo."

Supplies: You'll need the "Taboo List" handout (p. 124) and interlocking plastic blocks.

Preparation: Make a copy of the "Taboo List" handout (p. 124) for each four or five kids.

Time Involved: 10 minutes

Form groups of four or five, and pick one person at a time to begin. Give each group ten interlocking plastic blocks and a "Taboo List" handout, and have each person in a group take a turn at giving his or her personal testimony. If, however, the person uses a word on the "Taboo List," he or she is required to give up one of the team's blocks to the other team. Allow each person a chance to play, but keep the group's total sharing time to about ten minutes. The team with the most blocks in the end will be able to "build a bigger church" with their blocks.

Say: **It's important when we tell others about Jesus that we try to stay away from words they don't understand. So often the words we use can confuse others and even keep them from coming to know Jesus. Let's all be careful to share our faith in words that will help others know how much Jesus wants to have a relationship with them.**

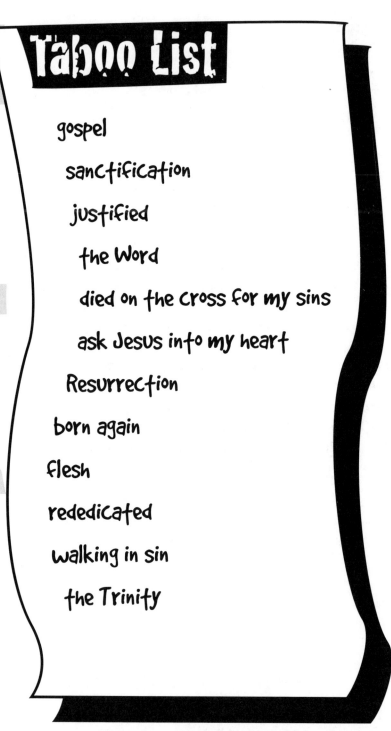

Handout

Taboo List

gospel

sanctification

justified

the Word

died on the cross for my sins

ask Jesus into my heart

Resurrection

born again

flesh

rededicated

walking in sin

the Trinity

Walls of Jericho

Overview: Kids will try to infiltrate the walls of Jericho by finding out who has the password.

Supplies: You'll need a Bible, slips of paper, a pen, and a box or container.

Preparation: Write the word "Jericho" on enough pieces of paper so that there will be enough for half of the kids in your group to each have one. Write the word "Rahab" on one piece of paper. Place all the pieces of paper in the container or box.

Time Involved: 10 minutes

Form two teams. Label one team the Israelites and the other the City of Jericho. Have kids line up and face each other in Red Rover-style, and have the kids on the City of Jericho team each take a slip of paper from the container. All but one of the team members will receive slips of paper that say "Jericho," and one person will receive the paper that says "Rahab."

Next, the City of Jericho team should secretly pick a password such as "popcorn" or "grasshopper" and then line up to create the great walls of Jericho by interlocking their arms together. When they have created the walls, the Israelites team should send a pair of "spies" to the City of Jericho team. The spies will choose three players, one at a time, from whom they'll try to gain the password. When a spy asks, a chosen player on the other team must show the spy his or her slip of paper. If a spy chooses a person who has a paper with "Jericho" written on it, the password is to remain a secret and the Israelites cannot penetrate the wall. If a spy chooses the person with the paper with "Rahab" written on it, the spy will get the password and the Israelites are allowed to penetrate the wall. If the spies find "Rahab," the Israelites win the game. If, however, in their three choices the spies don't find Rahab, they become part of the mighty Jericho walls.

The game ends when either "Rahab" is discovered or the Israelites lose all their members. When the kids have finished one round, have them change teams and play again.

After the game, read Joshua 6:1-23. Then ask:

● **How was the game like this passage in the Bible?**

● **What did you think about being one of the spies? What do you think must have been going through the minds of the real spies?**

● **What would it have been like to be Rahab in the story?**

● **Why do you think God used her as he did?**

Grateful Heart

Overview: Kids will participate in a scavenger hunt to discover the importance of being grateful.

Supplies: You'll need the "Clues" handout (p. 128), scissors, and a watch or timer.

Preparation: Make one copy of the "Clues" handout (p. 128) for each team. Cut the clues apart, and place them in the appropriate places.

Time Involved: 15 to 30 minutes

Form teams of no more than five, and give each team the first clue. Instruct each team not to read the clue until it's the team's turn to go on the Bible scavenger hunt.

Say: **In the Bible, the story is told of ten lepers who were healed by Jesus. Only one returned to Jesus to say, "Thank you." Today we are going to go on a scavenger hunt to find pieces of a sentence telling us about being more grateful. Each clue you find will help you add one word to the sentence. The winning team will**

Leader TIP

The sentence kids are trying to discover is "Give thanks with a grateful heart!"

be most grateful and will be the one with the quickest
time in figuring out the verse.

Send the teams off in five-minute intervals so they won't
just follow each other. Make a record of the time when each
team left and the time when it returns. When teams have found
all the clues, have them return to home base and see which
team has identified the verse and can recite it.

When the kids return, read 1 Thessalonians 5:18 aloud and
ask:

● **Why should we continually be thankful for all of
our circumstances?**

● **What things are you thankful for?**

Clues

Instructions: In each of the locations listed below, place a copy of the next clue so the kids will know where to go.

1. Go to the place where people bring their tithes and offerings. Look in the place where the money is collected.
Key Word: This is where people _____ to the Lord.

2. Go to the place where babies are taken care of.
Key Word: One out of ten lepers in the story gave _____.

3. Go to the place where the handicapped can park with ease.
Key Word: A preposition that starts with a "w" is _____.

4. Go to the place where children swing (or slide).
Key Word: The first letter of the first word in the Greek alphabet is _____.

5. Go to the place where your church sign is.
Key Word: The leader said you would be _____ if you won this game.

6. Go to the place where the "sound" is heard on Sunday mornings.
Key Word: The symbol often used for Valentine's Day is a

_____.

7. Return to home base, and put all your words together to complete the verse.

Picture This!

Overview: Kids will learn more about the Bible by taking pictures with an instant-print camera and taking turns lining the pictures up in their correct order on an indoor clothesline.

Supplies: You'll need Bibles, an instant-print camera (or cameras) with film, clothespins, a clothesline, a laundry basket, a bowl, paper, and a pen.

Preparation: Either set up a temporary clothesline in your meeting room or use an existing one outside. Place clothespins on the line. Select a well-known Bible story, and break the story down into four to six segments. Write each segment on a slip of paper. Some suggested stories are: David and Goliath (1 Samuel 17:21-51); Moses parting the Red Sea and the Egyptians being drowned (Exodus 14); Jesus and the rich young man (Matthew 19:16-26); or Paul on the road to Damascus (Acts 9:4-9). Fold the slips, and place them in the bowl.

Time Involved: 30 to 45 minutes

Divide kids into the same number of groups as there are story segments. Provide each group with a Bible, and instruct each group to select one slip of paper and decide how to pose the group and capture the scene in one picture. Once the group has made its decision, one group member should take the picture. After allowing the picture to develop, have the group place it face down in the laundry basket. Repeat the process until each group has posed its scene and taken its picture.

Once all the pictures have been placed in the basket, select one group to come forward, turn the pictures over, and try to put the story in its correct order. Allow each group sixty seconds to work and then allow another group to try. When a group believes it has the story in the correct order, instruct them to hang the pictures on the clothesline. Check the pictures to verify that they follow the story line. After the pictures are in their correct order, read the Bible story in its entirety to the class.

Bible Billboard

Overview: While traveling, kids will watch for billboards and try to locate forty items that are mentioned in the Bible.

Supplies: You'll need paper and pens.

Preparation: None is needed.

Time Involved: 20 to 60 minutes

There are various journeys recorded in the Bible, many of which revolve around the number forty. For example, the Israelites wandered in the wilderness for forty years; it rained forty days and nights on Noah's journey; and Jesus fasted during a forty-day journey.

Leader TIP

If the region you are traveling in has very few billboards, simply look for real items such as cows, lakes, sheep, and so on.

The object of this activity is to have kids look for forty items on billboards that are mentioned somewhere in the Bible. These would include such things as perfume (used on Jesus' feet), a hotel ("no room in the inn"), and mountains (such as the one Elijah stood on). Tell the kids to be creative and have fun!

Stretcher Bearers

Overview: Kids will have fun helping their paralyzed teammates get through the crowd to see Jesus.

Supplies: You'll need a Bible, one large bedsheet for every five people, and items for an obstacle course, such as traffic cones, old tire tubes, boxes, rope, and furniture.

Preparation: Set up an obstacle course.

Time Involved: 10 minutes

Begin this activity by reading Mark 2:2-5 aloud to the group and then say: **A paralytic wanted to see Jesus, but he was surrounded by too many people. The man's friends devised a plan to get the paralytic to see Jesus. They took him to the top of the roof, made a hole in the roof, and then lowered him down in front of Jesus. Jesus was so impressed with the faith of this man that he healed him.**

Divide the group into teams of five players. Have each team choose one person to be the paralytic and four to be stretcher bearers. The object is for the stretcher bearers to take their paralytic through a series of obstacles and finally arrive at the finish line to see Jesus. The first team to finish is considered healed.

After the game, lead a short discussion by asking:

● **What was so special about the paralyzed man's friends?**

● **Who do you consider the stretcher bearers in your life?**

● **Who are you a "stretcher bearer" for?**

Half-Truths

Overview: Kids will need to circulate throughout the group to find the other halves of their Bible verses.

Supplies: You'll need a Bible, index cards, a pen, scissors, and snack food such as a bag of chips (optional).

Preparation: Compile a list of well-known Bible verses (one for every two students in your class). Print each of these verses on an index card and then cut the index card in half where the natural verse break occurs. For example, print and cut John 3:16 this way: "For God so loved the world that he gave his one and only Son," and "that whoever believes in

Variation

If you want to make this game even more challenging, print only a few complete verses and leave the rest incomplete. The kids will really have to hustle to be the ones to come up with complete verses.

him shall not perish, but have eternal life." The first line of text would appear on half of the index card while the second line would appear on the other half.

Time Involved: 10 minutes

After you have cut and shuffled the cards, give one to each person. Have kids circulate around the room to find the other halves of the verses. You might want to add an additional incentive, such as a bag of chips. Allow the first two students who complete their verse to begin eating the chips; the next two players to complete their verse may join them.

Destined for Doom

Overview: Kids will play an "end times" Tug of War as they represent the four winds from the four corners of the earth.

Supplies: You'll need a Bible, a thick rope, and scissors.

Preparation: Cut the rope in four thirty-foot pieces. Form a large X by tying the pieces together (see diagram below).

Time Involved: 5 minutes

Begin by reading Mark 13:24-27 to the group. Divide kids into four teams, each one named after one of the four winds (north, east, south, and west). Have each team take one end of the rope, and on your command, have teams play Tug of War. The winning team is the first group of "chosen ones." Play several times, mixing up the teams.

After the activity, lead a short discussion using the following questions:

● **When you found your team falling behind, did you want to give up or work harder?**

● **When you feel like bad things are happening in your life, do you give up easily or do you get tougher?**

● **What is the most exciting thing to you about Jesus' promise to come again?**

Overcrowded

Overview: Kids will play a form of Hide-and-Seek and imagine what it must have been like to be Jesus with the crowds pressing in on him.

Supplies: None are needed.

Preparation: None is needed.

Time Involved: 10 minutes

This game is a variation of Hide-and-Seek. When your group has assembled, say: **There are many verses in the Bible about the crowds that pressed in on Jesus! Even when he went to a mountain or out in a boat to be alone, the crowds always seemed to follow him.**

Explain that in this game, one person will play Jesus and will go out and try to hide in an attempt to be alone. On your command, the other kids are to begin searching for Jesus. Once a person has discovered where Jesus is, he or she is to stay there quietly until everyone has found the spot.

Play several rounds by selecting another person to play Jesus each time. When the game is finished, have kids gather and ask:

● **When you played Jesus, how did it feel to have everyone crowding in on you in your hiding spot?**

● **How do you think Jesus felt always being followed by others?**

● **Why do you think it's good to spend time alone or in silence as Jesus modeled?**

Bible Bookathon

Leader TIP

Some Bibles have the list in alphabetical order so you'll have the answers handy without all the work!

Overview: Kids will use teamwork to come up with all the books of the Bible and then alphabetize them as quickly as possible.

Supplies: You'll need a Bible, paper and a pen for every two people, and boxes of Cracker Jack (optional).

Preparation: None is needed.

Time Involved: up to 10 minutes

Leader TIP

You might consider handing out boxes of Cracker Jack to those who remember and alphabetize the most books.

Form pairs, and give each pair paper and a pen. Have partners write down as many books of the Bible as they can remember (both Old Testament and New Testament). Next, have the pairs put the books in alphabetical order. See if anyone can get all sixty-six books!

The Greedy Shall Inherit...Nothing!

Overview: While building towers, kids will have to choose whether to be greedy and risk it all or play it safe.

Supplies: You'll need a Bible, enough three-ounce paper cups for each team to have about twenty, a timer, and candy (optional).

Preparation: None is needed.

Time Involved: 5 to 10 minutes

Divide your group into teams of three or four. Before the game begins, read Luke 12:13-21 to kids and then say: **We're going to play a game in which your destiny is uncertain. You'll be given cups to build a tower. To build a tower, your team will place one cup on the table with the opening up and then another cup on top of it with the opening down. Continue the process, reversing each cup, as you build your tower taller and taller. The object is to see which team can build the biggest tower in the allotted time. However, your time limit is uncertain, so you're allowed to stop at any time. If the tower falls because you have decided to be too greedy, you may not have time to rebuild, so playing it safe may be a wise strategy. The choice is yours.**

Determine an allotment of time, and set the timer. A good place to start is twenty-five seconds. For the second round, give teams one minute, and for the third round, give teams fifteen seconds.

When the timer goes off, the team with the most cups stacked up is the winner. You might want to consider giving candy to the team that wins each round.

When the game is finished, ask:

● **How was building the tower like the man building the barns in the Bible?**

● **What made you keep building?**

● **What made you want to stop building?**

● **How did it feel when your tower crashed and you had nothing?**

● **How is this game like greed in our lives?**

Tossed by the Waves

Overview: Kids will create a storm of waves in a swimming pool and try to get the beach ball across to the opponent's side. The object is to demonstrate how easy it is to influence an object that is not anchored or grounded.

Supplies: You'll need a Bible, a beach ball, a piece of string or rope the width of the swimming pool, and a small magnet or another weighted object.

Preparation: Rope off two lines in the middle of the swimming pool with about three feet between the lines.

Time Involved: 5 to 10 minutes

Form two teams. Have one team stand in the water on one side of the pool, while the other team stands in the water on the other side. Throw a beach ball into the center of the pool. Instruct each team to begin making waves to keep the ball from coming across their team's line. When the ball crosses a line, start again. Play in this fashion for several rounds.

Next, tie a magnet or other small weighted object to the nozzle of the ball and play the game again. The players will discover that with the weight on it, the ball won't move as easily. Play for a few minutes and then have the kids gather around the edge of the pool. Read Ephesians 4:11-16 aloud, especially emphasizing verse 14. Ask:

● **What influenced the movement of the ball?**

● **What prevented the ball from being tossed back and forth?**

● **What prevents us as Christians from being tossed around by every bad thing in the world?**

Carrying Someone's Burdens

Overview: Kids will use teamwork to carry each other's burdens.

Supplies: You'll need a Bible, one 2-inch x 6-inch x 12-foot. wood plank, two sturdy chairs, six backpacks, and twelve bricks or heavy books.

Preparation: Lift the plank off the ground and place it on the seats of the chairs. Give each person a backpack full of books or bricks.

Time Involved: 5 to10 minutes

The object of the game is to have all six people with loaded backpacks change both packs and positions with each other without falling off the plank. This activity is not as much a game of competition as it is one of teamwork.

Begin by reading Galatians 6:2 aloud. Next instruct six kids to each put on a loaded backpack and stand up on the plank. When they are all situated, have kids each pass his or her pack to the person standing behind him or her. The last person in line should pass his or her pack forward. Eventually the packs will get congested and the team will have to start working together.

After all the packs have been passed and everyone has one on again, have all six players change positions on the plank without falling off. To do this, have the line reverse its order on the plank. If you have more than one team, you can add a competitive element by seeing which team can do it the fastest.

Squirt-Ball Battles

Overview: Kids will use water guns to squirt table tennis balls off of two-liter bottles while learning about the Israelites confronting their enemies before crossing the Jordan River.

Supplies: You'll need a Bible, tape or chalk, eight two-liter bottles, a marker, eight self-stick labels, eight table tennis balls, a water gun, a bucket of water, and a watch with a second hand.

Preparation: Mark a shooting line on the ground with tape or chalk. Write the names of the following nations on labels and secure them to the bottles: Hittites, Hivites, Jebusites, Moabites, Canaanites, Perizzites, Girgashites, and Amorites. Place a table tennis ball on top of each bottle. Place the bottles approximately ten to twelve feet from the shooting line. Position the bucket of water next to the shooting line for refilling.

Time Involved: 10 minutes

In this game, kids become the Israelites from the book of Joshua trying to rid the land of evil inhabitants. Each bottle is labeled with one of these groups. Before the game begins, read Joshua 3:1-10, and spend a few minutes discussing what the people must have been feeling before crossing the Jordan to confront their enemies.

Next, explain that each person will get a chance to try his or her expertise at shooting the water gun. The object is to defeat as many nations as possible in thirty seconds by shooting the table tennis balls off the bottles. The Israelite that defeats the most evil inhabitants gets to be hero for the day!

Game Selection

Overview: Kids will discover both how difficult it can be to make group decisions and what compromise is all about.

Supplies: You'll need a Bible, a large selection of board games, and a selection of sports equipment.

Preparation: Lay the sports equipment and the board games out in the middle of the room.

Time Involved: 15 to 30 minutes

As kids arrive, invite them each to select one game or sport they would like to play. After everyone has assembled, say: **We'll play whatever game the group decides on. The only catch is that everyone must agree on the same activity!**

Allow kids two or three minutes to come to a consensus. The larger the group is, the more difficult this will be. After ten minutes, ask:

● **Did you decide what game we'll play?**

● **How did you decide?**

● **Did anyone feel pressured to change his or her mind?**

● **How did you feel as you tried to agree on an activity?**

● **What hindered you from coming to an agreement?**

Have someone read 2 Corinthians 13:11 aloud. Lead your group in a discussion on being "of one mind."

Say: **As Christians, we don't always agree. But we are instructed to "be of one mind" and "live in peace" with each other.** Ask:

● **Why do you think it's often difficult for members of a group to agree on something?**

● **What things can we do as a group to be of one mind?**

● **What are some things that hinder us from living in peace with one another?**

Finish by playing the game the group agreed upon or allowing them to form smaller groups and play the games of their choice.

Team-Building Games

The Gigantic

Book of Games
for Youth Ministry,

Volume 1

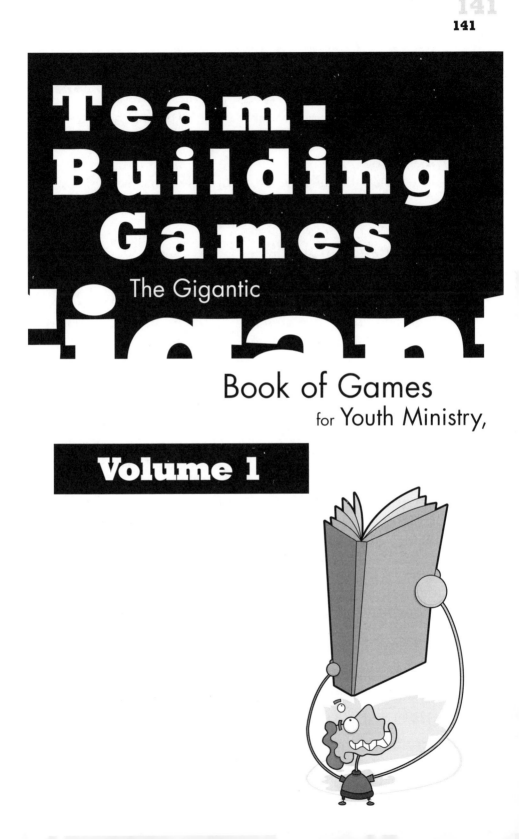

Puffed Up

Overview: Kids will race to blow up and stick balloons to teammates and then complete an obstacle course.

Supplies: You'll need a roll of two-inch masking tape and thirty one-inch balloons for each team and chairs.

Preparation: Arrange an obstacle course for each team using four or five chairs.

Time Involved: 10-20 minutes

Divide the group into two or more teams with three or four people on each team. Give each team a roll of masking tape and thirty balloons. On your command, have members of each team roll the masking tape (sticky side out) around one of their teammates below the neckline. Next, have kids blow up their balloons as quickly as they can and stick as many as possible to the taped-up team member.

When the balloons have been attached, have the player go through the obstacle course and back to the team. Balloons that fall off during the race can't be reattached.

The team that has the most balloons still attached when the balloon person finishes the obstacle course wins the game.

If the teams want to play again, have them each select a new team member to be the balloon person.

Tie It Up

Overview: Kids will search for hidden pieces of yarn and tie them together in relay fashion.

Supplies: You'll need yarn and scissors.

Preparation: Cut the yarn into small sections of four, six, eight, ten, and twelve inches. Hide the longest sections around the meeting area, and put the shorter sections out where kids can see them.

Time Involved: 10 to 20 minutes

Divide kids into teams of two or more. Have each team designate a home base where they will return after finding a piece of yarn. Explain to kids that the object is to see which team can tie the longest strand of yarn together. On your command, have team members locate pieces of yarn, bring them back to their home base, and begin tying them together. Each person, however, can only pick up one piece of yarn before returning to home base, and home base is the only place where yarn can be tied together.

Variation

If you have a large group, get various colors of yarn and cut the same size and number of pieces from each. Assign each team a specific color to find.

Start the game and play until you think most of the yarn has been found. Ask teams to stretch out their pieces to determine the winner.

When the game is over, ask:

● **In what ways was it easy to cheat in this game?**

● **Why do you think the team that won was able to do so?**

● **Why is it important to play by the rules?**

● **What would happen to our group if some of us chose to ignore the rules?**

● **What are some rules or guidelines which help our group function better?**

Blanket Slide

Overview: Kids will complete a relay race by sliding team members around an obstacle course on a blanket.

Supplies: You'll need one old (but sturdy) blanket for each team, chairs, and tape or chalk.

Preparation: Arrange an obstacle course for each team using

---

five or six chairs. Make sure you leave enough room for the blanket to get by without hitting the chairs.

Time Involved: 5 to 10 minutes

Divide kids into two or more teams, and give each team a blanket. Mark a starting line with tape or chalk, and then demonstrate how each team is to complete the obstacle course.

Begin by having one person from each team sit on the team's blanket. Have the other team members grab hold of the blanket's edges. The object is for the team to pull the person on the blanket around the obstacle course and back. If team members throw the person off, they must begin again with that person. Each time a team gets back to the starting line, a new person should jump on the blanket and the team should run the course again. Continue this process, and declare the winner as the first team to get all its members through.

> **Variation**
>
> Blindfold all the players on the team except the person riding on the blanket, who will direct the others through the course.

At the end of the game, discuss the following questions:

● **In what ways did you have to work as a team to complete the race?**

● **What were some things that happened during the game that you didn't expect?**

● **In what ways did this game help build a team spirit in our group?**

Video Scavenger Hunt

Overview: Kids will play video scavenger hunt and watch for various listed items.

Supplies: You'll need a TV, a VCR, a videocassette of a popular movie, paper, pencils, popcorn and bowls, and soft drinks.

Preparation: Preview the video the students will be watching.

Look for obscure and barely noticeable objects, names, places, and things for the kids to look for. Write a list of questions pertaining to these items and make enough copies for each participant to have one.

Time Involved: 60 to 90 minutes (depending on the length of the movie)

Divide your group up into smaller groups of five or six people. Tell them that they are going to play Video Scavenger Hunt. Give each group a pencil and a handout with the list of items they'll be looking for. For example, if you are showing the movie the *Wizard of Oz*, your list may look like this:

1. What color are Dorothy's magical shoes?
2. How many times did the lion act afraid?
3. In which room did the Wicked Witch melt?
4. Where was the Munchkin with the purple pants hiding?

Your questions should be ones without obvious answers, so kids will have to pay attention to the details of the movie. At the end of the movie, go over the answers and award bowls of popcorn and soft drinks to everyone for their efforts.

Water Relay

Overview: Kids will pass water from one end of the team to the other.

Supplies: You'll need four two-liter bottles, water, and small paper cups.

Preparation: Fill two of the bottles with water, and mark the empty bottles with a permanent marker around the middle (so each bottle is divided in half by a line).

Time Involved: 10 minutes

Divide your group into two even teams. If you have an uneven number of kids, have one of the leaders play. Have the two teams line up facing each other and sit on the floor with their legs crossed. Give cups to all the members of each team. Place an empty bottle at one end of each team. Place the bottles filled with water at the other ends of the teams.

On the word "go," the first team member is to use the bottle to fill the next person's cup with water. The second team member will then pour his or her water into the third person's cup. When the second person's cup is empty it can be refilled by the first person's water bottle. When the water reaches the last person in line, he or she will pour it into the empty bottle.

The first team to fill its empty bottle past the halfway point wins.

Toilet Paper People

Overview: Kids will wrap their teammates in toilet paper.

Supplies: You'll need several rolls of toilet paper.

Preparation: None is needed.

Time Involved: 10 minutes

Divide the group up into smaller teams of six. Give each team a few rolls of toilet paper. Tell kids that when you say "go," one member of each team is to wrap the other team members in toilet paper. Explain that the first group to have all its team members wrapped in toilet paper wins.

The object is for all the team members to be wrapped together and not individually.

Water Hula Balloons

Overview: Kids will race to get water balloons from one place to another.

Supplies: You'll need balloons, water, Hula Hoops, four buckets, two chairs, and tape.

Preparation: Fill the balloons with water, and put them in two of the buckets. Identify and mark a starting line with tape.

Time Involved: 15 minutes

Divide the group into two teams. Give each team a Hula Hoop, a bucket of water balloons, and an empty bucket. Have each team line up single file and stand at one end of the activity area. At the other end (at least thirty feet away), place a chair in front of each team.

Say: **When I say "go," you are to get as many people on your team as possible in the Hula Hoop. The people inside the Hula Hoop will need to have their stomachs against the Hula Hoop. Next, place one water balloon between all of your backs, in the center of the hoop. The object is to run down around the chair and back without allowing the water balloon to break or fall. When you return to the starting line, place the water balloon in the empty bucket. Get out of the Hula Hoop and pass it to the next few people in line. The first team to get ten water balloons in its empty bucket wins.**

Be sure to tell kids that if the water balloon breaks before they have made it back to their starting point, they must go back and start again.

Flashlight Freeze-Tag

Overview: Kids will play Tag with their flashlights. This game works best in a dark area at night so that the flashlights will shine brightly.

Supplies: You'll need flashlights, green and red transparent plastic cups, masking tape, and a whistle.

Preparation: Tape the red and green cups to the ends of all the flashlights except for four.

Time Involved: 30 minutes

Divide kids into two teams. Give two students on each team plain white flashlights. Give the other members of one team red flashlights and the members of the other team green flashlights.

Explain that you are going to have teams stand at opposite ends of your playing area. The four kids with the white flash-lights are to stand in the middle. With the exception of the kids with the white flashlights, the object of the game is for a team to get all of its members to the other end of the field. Say: **When I give the command to begin, the members of each team are to try to get to the other end of the field without being tagged. If you see someone with the other color of flashlight, tag him or her with your light. When someone is tagged, he or she has to freeze in place. When a person is frozen, the only thing that person is allowed to do is turn his or her flashlight on and off so that everyone knows he or she is frozen. The only per-son that can unfreeze a frozen person is a teammate with a white flashlight. When a white light unfreezes a frozen person, that person can resume play.**

The first team that gets all its players to the other end of the field wins the game.

Creepy Crawlers

Overview: Kids will perform tasks while connected to one another.

Supplies: You'll need a chalkboard and chalk or newsprint and a marker (optional).

Preparation: None is needed.

Time Involved: 10 to 15 minutes

Divide the group into teams of four players each. Have team members stand so their left shoulders touch. Using their left hands, kids are to grab the **left wrists** of the people in front of them (see diagram).

Creepy Crawlers

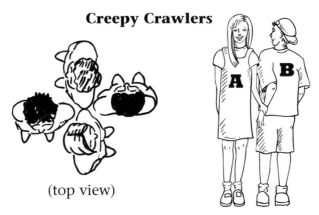

(top view)

All teammates should now be connected by their left hands while their right hands hang free. Explain that teams have become giant spiders and team members' right hands represent insect antennae. These creepy crawlers must perform a series of tasks, each more difficult than the previous one. In order to succeed, the "spiders" must work together.

At no time are the parts of a spider allowed to become disconnected. If a team becomes disconnected, it must perform some silly task chosen by other teams. (A sample task might be hopping on one foot while singing "Mary Had a Little Lamb.")

The following is a sample list of spider activities, each one progressively more difficult than the one before. You may want to display these on a chalkboard or a piece of newsprint. (Be sure to add others to the list.)

● Sit on the floor. Count aloud to ten. Stand up.

● Move to any wall in the room. One person is to touch the wall with his or her right hand. Repeat the task with the remaining three walls, with each one touched by a different teammate.

● One person must remove his or her right shoe and scoot it on the floor to the person on the opposite side of the spider. Each person on the team should continue to pass the shoe around until it comes back to the owner.

● All teammates are to remove their right shoes. Simultaneously scoot the shoes around the outside of the spider.

● One person is to remove an object from his or her pocket. The object is to be passed to the person on his or her right and on around the spider until it reaches its owner.

Once the spiders have completed all the assigned tasks, have everyone sit on the floor. With the teams still connected, lead a brief discussion on patience, teamwork, and cooperation.

Fetch-a-Sketch

Overview: Two blindfolded kids draw an object as described by a third teammate.

Supplies: You'll need blindfolds (two per team) and a chalkboard and chalk; or a dry-erase board and dry-erase markers; or newsprint, markers, and tape.

Preparation: If you choose to use newsprint rather than a chalkboard or a dry-erase board, hang the paper in an appropriate place so players can draw on it.

Time Involved: 5 to 10 minutes

Divide the group into teams of three, and select a leader for each team. Secretly inform the leaders of an object that you want each team to draw. The object should be different for each team. Objects might include such things as a cat, a tree, a house, the church, and so on. Begin the game by asking each team to stand at one end of the room. Point out the chalkboard, the dry-erase board, or the newsprint on the opposite side.

Instruct teammates to stand side by side with the leader in the middle and their arms locked. Provide blindfolds to the two outside players on each team. Explain that the leader is to guide his or her team to the board and the blindfolded players are to each pick up a piece of chalk or a marker. Next, the team leader is to instruct his or her teammates to draw the object assigned to that team.

With only the leader giving instructions, both blindfolded kids are to proceed to draw the picture together. One person should draw with his or her left hand while the other must use his or her right hand.

Call time after three minutes. Have kids remove their blindfolds, and see how long it takes the kids to guess what has been drawn by other teams. Repeat the game, allowing a different member to serve as leader of each team.

When the game is finished, ask:

● **Was there anything frustrating about this game? If so, what was it?**

● **How important was it to trust the team leader while you were drawing?**

● **In what ways did patience and teamwork play a role in this game?**

Greeting Card Sorter

Overview: Kids will race to be first in assembling greeting card puzzles.

Supplies: You'll need greeting cards (one per team), scissors, and blindfolds (one per team).

Preparation: Cut cards into puzzles of eight to ten pieces.

Time Involved: 10 to 15 minutes

Have kids form pairs. Give a blindfold to one person in each pair and a greeting card puzzle to other. Explain that the blindfolded person on each team must assemble the card puzzle as guided by the other partner. There is no time limit, but greeting cards must be assembled completely. Once the game begins, only the blindfolded kids may touch the puzzle pieces.

Begin the game, and see how long it takes each pair to finish. Then have kids switch roles and play the game again. Be sure to shuffle the puzzle pieces before beginning each new round.

After the second round, lead the group in a brief discussion by asking:

● **Which was easier, giving directions or assembling puzzles? Why?**

● **Did you trust the person giving directions? Why or why not?**

● **What role did patience play in this game?**

● **What does this activity tell us about teamwork?**

Land of the Least

Overview: Kids connected back-to-back try to hug human statues scattered around the room.

Supplies: None are needed.

Preparation: None is needed.

Time Involved: 10 minutes

Start by selecting eight people to serve as "statues." Scatter these kids around the room. Ask them each to stand in any position they wish and freeze as soon as they "take shape."

Have the rest of the group form pairs. Ask partners to stand back-to-back and hold hands. Explain that each pair is to run and hug as many statues as many times as they can in two minutes. Hugs are made by trapping a statue between two back-to-back players. Note that no statue may be hugged twice in succession by the same pair. Also, no statue can move in any way during the game.

Play for two minutes, and call time. Repeat the game with partners holding hands while facing one another. This variation should be much easier.

When the game is finished, ask:

● **Which was easier, hugging while standing back-to-back with your partner or hugging while facing your partner? Explain.**

● **Which is easier, relating to someone who has turned his or her back on you or meeting him or her face-to-face?**

● **Did having a partner help in sharing hugs? Explain.**

● **Does having someone with you help when you're confronted with a problem? Why or why not?**

● **How do you handle it when you have to make decisions on your own?**

Pipe Bridge

Overview: Blindfolded players stack as many cotton balls as possible between two pipe cleaners.

Supplies: You'll need pipe cleaners (two per team), cotton balls, one blindfold for each team member on one team, and a watch with a second hand.

Preparation: None is needed.

Time Involved: 5 to 10 minutes

Divide the group into teams of three or more players each. Distribute blindfolds to the members of one team. Ask the team with blindfolds to scatter themselves out in the center of the room. Instruct everyone else to gather in a large circle around them, and sit down. Explain that when all the blindfolds are in place, you're going to scatter the pipe cleaners and the cotton balls on the floor around the blindfolded team.

The first thing the blindfolded team should do is locate cotton balls and construct a bridge by laying both pipe cleaners on top of their cotton balls as illustrated in the following diagram.

Pipe Bridge

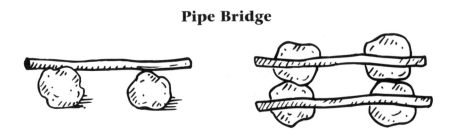

While two team members build the bridge and hold it together, the other team member (or members) is to crawl around and locate the scattered cotton balls. To help in this process, group members seated in the circle may yell directions such as "Move to the right" or "There's one next to your foot!"

Call time after three minutes, and see how many cotton balls stayed on the bridge. Repeat the game with a different team trying to beat the previous record.

When all the teams have built at least one bridge, ask:

● **What did you find challenging about this activity?**

● **In what ways was it important to trust your teammates?**

● **Did your teamwork factor into your success or failure? If so, how?**

Push Me...Pull Me

Overview: Kids standing in a circle pull against one another to tag items scattered around the room.

Supplies: None are needed.

Preparation: None is needed.

Time Involved: 5 to 10 minutes

Arrange kids so they are standing in a circle facing out in the center of the room. As far as you can, alternate boys and girls. Ask kids to lock arms with their neighbors. There will be people facing all four walls in the room.

Select any four objects in the room, one near each wall. Objects may include such things as a doorknob, a window, a picture, or a chair. If you wish, use only the walls themselves. Next, select four people to serve as Taggers. Make sure these players are facing the four different objects.

Explain that on your command, each Tagger is to try to be first to tag his or her assigned object. Be sure to tell kids that at no time can the circle be broken. The process is that while one person may be trying to reach a doorknob, someone else might be struggling to tag a window on the opposite side of the room.

Play and watch as each player pulls against the others to win. Repeat with different Taggers and objects.

When the game is finished, have kids sit in a circle and ask:

● **What was challenging about this game?**

● **What was rewarding?**

● **Were there any frustrations? If so, what were they?**

● **To those who were not Taggers, how did it feel to be pulled in different directions?**

Lead a brief discussion about teamwork, endurance, and decisions which seem to pull you in opposite directions.

Shifty Sheets

Overview: Kids move back and forth across a newspaper-covered floor while carrying a bedsheet between them.

Supplies: You'll need one bedsheet per team (they all need to be the same size) and several old newspapers.

Preparation: None is needed.

Time Involved: 5 to 10 minutes

Divide the group into even-numbered teams of four to six players. Give each team a bedsheet and assemble all the teams at one end of the room. Have the team members position themselves around the sheet, each grabbing hold of a corner or edge. The sheet should then be pulled tight until it is flat.

Explain that teams are to carry their sheets back and forth across the room. The sheets are to remain pulled tight the whole time. Tell them that when they start moving across the floor, you are going to place a few newspapers on the floor behind them.

The object is for the teams to avoid stepping on the newspapers as they walk back and forth across the room. This will be more difficult than it sounds since the teams are to keep the sheets pulled tight. If any team member steps on a paper along the way, the team is out and must sit on the side of the room.

Continue placing more and more newspapers on the floor with each successive trip the teams make. Soon the floor will be nearly covered with newspapers. Play until only one team is left.

With teams seated on their individual bedsheets, ask:

● **Was there a strategy to winning this game? If so, what was it?**

● **What, if any, frustrations were experienced along the way?**

● **How important was teamwork in playing the game? Explain.**

Squigglers

Overview: Kids will use their feet to pass a ball in and out of a circle.

Supplies: You'll need balls of various sizes such as table tennis balls, soccer balls, beach balls, foam balls, and footballs, a whistle (optional), and a stopwatch or a watch with a second hand.

Preparation: None is needed.

Time Involved: 5 minutes

Have kids form a standing circle (or several circles with larger groups), alternating boys and girls as much as possible. Ask kids to lock arms with those on either side. Next, place a soccer ball on the floor between the feet of one player. Designate this person as the Starter. The Starter will choose which direction the ball will go around the circle.

Explain that the ball is to be passed around the circle, through and between each person's feet as illustrated in the following diagram.

The object is for players to work together to move the ball around the circle as quickly as possible. When the ball reaches the Starter, the game is over. Time each round, and see if the group can beat its previous record.

For added fun, blow a whistle to signify that the kids are to change directions with the ball. If you want to keep the group on its toes, sound the whistle several times during the game. Repeat the game several times using balls of different sizes, shapes, and weights. Playing with a football will be especially interesting!

When the game is finished, ask kids to be seated and ask:

● **Did you find anything frustrating about this activity? If so, what?**

● **How important was cooperation during the game?**

● **In what ways was the game a test of patience?**

● **What does this activity teach us about the importance of teamwork?**

Stick and Stack 'Em!

Overview: Teams try to build the tallest toothpick-and-marshmallow structures while blindfolded.

Supplies: You'll need a box of toothpicks, one bag of miniature marshmallows, one blindfold for each person, and a tape measure or a yardstick.

Preparation: None is needed.

Time Involved: 10 to 20 minutes or more, depending on the number of teams

Divide the group into teams of two or three players, and ask them to be seated. Choose one team to start, and give a blindfold to each of its members. Place a box of toothpicks and a bag of marshmallows near the team.

The object is for each blindfolded team to take three minutes to build the tallest marshmallow-and-toothpick structure it can. Explain that everyone is to remain silent during the activity while each team takes its turn.

Team members will need to work together and visualize what the structure should look like along the way. After a team has been given three minutes to build its tower, have kids remove their blindfolds. Continue the process until each team has had an opportunity to play. Measure the height of each structure as it is finished. Challenge each successive team to build a taller and stronger tower.

When the game is finished, lead a brief discussion by asking:
- **What did you find challenging about this activity?**
- **What did you find frustrating?**
- **In what ways was trust a part of this activity?**
- **What does this game teach us about teamwork?**

Yards of Yarn

Overview: Kids will weave a piece of yarn in and out of their shoes and then maneuver through an obstacle course.

Supplies: You'll need yarn, scissors, and obstacles such as chairs or other furniture.

Preparation: Cut the yarn into twelve- to fifteen-foot pieces (enough so every team has one piece). Arrange the furniture into an obstacle course. Before your meeting, instruct kids to wear sneakers or other shoes that have eyes.

Time Involved: 10 minutes

Divide the group into teams of four, and provide each team with a piece of yarn. Explain that this activity involves two parts. The first part is a race to see which team can be the first to thread a piece of yarn through the shoes of each person. This involves everyone on the team taking turns threading the yarn through one eye on each of his or her shoes, wrapping it around his or her ankles, and then passing the end onto the next teammate. The process should continue until the loose end returns to the first player. He or she then ties the end to his or her own shoe. Be sure to have kids leave approximately one foot of yarn between each other.

The second part of the activity is a race in which teams maneuver around the obstacle course while they're connected. Have everyone start simultaneously and at the same place in the room. After a winning team has been determined, have all the teams remain connected and sit down together. Lead a short discussion by asking:

Variation

You can make this activity more challenging by having all the kids put on blindfolds.

● **What did you find challenging about this activity?**

● **How important was it to remain patient? Explain.**

● **What happened when one player**

moved too fast across the room?

● **What does this activity teach us about teamwork?**

Table Talent

Overview: Kids will give affirmations to one another while waiting for food. This creative activity keeps kids at a restaurant from finding out how many open sugar packets it takes to aggravate their group leader.

Supplies: None are needed.

Preparation: None is needed.

Time Involved: 5 to 15 minutes

The object of this game is to challenge each of the kids in the group to positively affirm others around the table while waiting for their food to arrive. Choose a category from the "Compliment List" below. Explain the activity to kids, and start them off with the category you've chosen. For example, if the category is Eyes, the first person might begin by saying, "I like Anna's eyes because they're blue," "I like Jan's eyes because they're curious," or "I like Frank's eyes because they're full of laughter." Continue in this manner around the table.

COMPLIMENT LIST	
● Eyes	● Ideas
● Menu choice	● Laugh
● Hair	● It's important you're part of our group because...

Be sure to monitor the activity to ensure that negative comments don't make their way into the game. Challenge the kids to make up their own categories, too. After a few rounds, ask:

● **Why do you like hearing people say positive things about you?**

● **What other times and places could you give some-one a compliment?**

● **How does affirmation build our group?**

This Napkin Names Our Group

Overview: Kids will fold paper napkins to illustrate some-thing they like about the group.

Supplies: None are needed.

Preparation: None is needed.

Time Involved: 5 minutes

While waiting for food at a restaurant, challenge kids to fold their napkins into shapes that symbolize something they like about the group.

As each person tells about the shape he or she folded, suggest that he or she com-pletes this sentence: "Our group looks like this napkin because...but it is different from this napkin because..."

After everyone has had an opportu-nity to share, discuss the following questions:

● **What actions on our part will make certain our group keeps these good qualities?**

● **What other qualities might God want us to add?**

● **What actions would help us to grow closer as a group?**

● **What actions or things might God**

Variation

Simply have kids fold napkins in cool ways and teach each other to do the same. Then thank God for cre-ativity as the food arrives.

Leader TIP

To keep the restau-rant from having to supply extra napkins and won-der why Christians would be wasteful, explain to kids that the one rule is that they have to be able to use their napkins again dur-ing the meal.

want us to remove from our group? Why?

● **How does deliberately building positive things and relationships in our group keep us from excluding or hurting group members?**

Quarter Qualities

Variation

● If you're traveling on a bus, print the list and challenge seatmates to race to complete it before pairs in other seats.

● Have kids come up with their own riddles about things to find on the quarter, similar to the bow riddle. Gather the riddles and present them for Quarter Qualities, Round 2.

Overview: Kids will complete a scavenger hunt on the surface of a quarter.

Supplies: You'll need a quarter for each person.

Preparation: None is needed.

Time Involved: 15 minutes

To begin the activity, give each person a quarter. The object is for kids to find the things on the quarters that you call out. When kids find an item, they are to hold their quarters in the air. Guessing from memory is not allowed. Wait until all the kids have found the item before you call on the first one to hold his or her quarter in the air to provide the answer.

Quarter Scavenger Hunt List

● The animal (an eagle)
● The president (George Washington)
● The direction the president is facing on the quarter (left)
● The direction the animal is facing (left)
● A two-word phrase that means twenty-five cents (quarter dollar)
● A word that means freedom (liberty)
● An item that answers this riddle: I can play a violin and tie a package large or thin (a bow, found in George Washington's ponytail)

- The phrase that names the trustworthy one (In God We Trust)
- The phrase in a language other than English (E Pluribus Unum)
- The country in which the quarter is made (United States of America)

Wide Ages Mean Wisdom

Overview: Kids will work in multi-age teams to complete a task.

Supplies: You'll need Bibles, index cards, and pencils.

Preparation: None is needed.

Time Involved: 5 to 10 minutes

Begin by dividing the group into teams of five to six players. Each team must include at least one person from each age group represented by those present at your activity. Hand out cards and pencils, and instruct kids to each write a school challenge they are currently facing. Then have them share the challenges with their teammates. As each person shares his or her challenge, the others on the team should share a Bible verse that might provide some help for the challenge. When everyone has finished sharing, have each team member write the other team members' names on his or her hand. This will help remind kids to pray for each other's challenges.

Follow this activity by asking:

- **How else might we help each other from week to week?**
- **In what other challenges can we give each other encouragement?**

Variation

On subsequent weeks, vary the challenge to address problems kids have at home, with friendships, at church, with chores, and so on.

Igloo Insights

Overview: Kids will build an igloo that holds all of them.

Supplies: You'll need lots of snow suitable for packing and refreshments such as hot chocolate in insulated containers.

Preparation: Arrange for a home or field to meet in. Make sure you have a warm spot for kids to gather after the activity.

Time Involved: 2 or 3 hours

When there's lots of snow on the ground, gather your group in an area with lots of room. Keep the parents happy and the toes warm by insisting that everyone bundle warmly and bring extra gloves. Tell the group that the object is for them to build an igloo big enough to hold all of them.

To build an igloo, follow these steps: (1) Pack snow into bricks about approximately 1x2 feet in size; (2) Assemble the bricks in a circle or an oblong shape. Each level needs to move a bit closer to the center until you've constructed a dome; and (3) Make sure you include a door opening as you begin your construction.

Your igloo will be surprisingly warm inside. Serve refreshments inside and ask:

● **Our igloo took a long time and many people to build. Was it worth it? Why or why not?**

● **This igloo will melt more slowly than the surrounding snow. Why?**

● **How do we want our group to be like an igloo—a haven from the wind, something we work at steadily, and something we pack with shared times so we can withstand the weather together?**

Shred-Free Environment

Overview: Kids will race to put shredded paper back together.

Supplies: You'll need two paper shredders, leftover Sunday bulletins or other paper with print, and transparent tape.

Preparation: None is needed.

Time Involved: about 30 minutes

Divide the group into two equal teams. Give each team six Sunday bulletins (or other paper with print), and have the kids shred them, sending one bulletin through at a time. Then challenge the teams to get the pieces out of the shredder and race to see who can put them back together the quickest, using tape. After several minutes, ask:

Leader TIP

It will be a more powerful and meaningful discussion if kids lead it themselves with minimal participation from adult leaders.

● **What strategies did you use to get the bulletins back together?**

● **What made your task challenging?**

● **How is shredded paper like the results of slams and criticisms we aim at each other, even if we're just kidding?**

● **How do the words we say either hurt or glorify God?**

● **How can we overcome our assumption that "people-shredding" is no big deal?**

● **What personal actions can we all take to make sure we don't shred people with our comments?**

Olympic Gold

Overview: Kids will participate in several activities to determine who gets a gold medal in each event.

Supplies: You'll need three different-colored ribbons (such as blue, red, and green) for the winners in each event, a broom, a table tennis paddle, a table tennis ball, an old necktie, paper and pencils, and one watch with a second hand for each timed event.

Preparation: Arrange the various events described in the following box around the room. Assign a leader at each station to record the scores of players.

Time Involved: 30 minutes

Divide kids into teams equal to the number of events you have.

Before beginning the activity, describe each event and tell kids what they are to do at each one. Have each team send one person to each event to compete with kids from the other teams. Make sure each person has an activity in which to participate. If not, you can allow a team to send more than one person to an event. After the events are over, award medals to the three winners in each event.

Olympic Gold Events

● **Foot Standing:** Ask each person to stand on one foot, and see who can do it the longest.

● **Arm Raising:** Ask each person to raise his or her right arm up in the air. See who can hold it up the longest without help from the other hand.

● **Toe Standing:** Ask kids to stand on their toes. See who can stand on them the longest without touching the ground with the rest of his or her feet.

● **Tie Tying:** Give each person the necktie, and time him or her to see how long it takes to get it properly tied around his or her neck. Award the medal to the fastest time.

● **Stare Down:** Divide kids into pairs. Tell partners to look directly into each other's eyes until one person blinks. Form new pairs using the winners in each round until only one person is left.

● **Broom Balancing:** One at a time, ask each person to balance a broom in the palm of his or her hand. See who can balance it the longest.

● **Paddle Ball:** One at a time, give each person a table tennis ball and a table tennis paddle and see who can bounce the ball against the floor the most times without missing.

(Make up other games if you want the event to run longer.)

At the end of the games, discuss these questions.

● **What would happen to our group if some people started thinking they were better than other members?**

● **In what ways is everyone in our group a winner even though he or she may not have won a medal?**

● **What can the group do to make sure we make everyone feel like they are winners?**

● **In what ways do you think being a child of God and being a winner are the same?**

Pass the Picture

Overview: Kids will commit to pray for each other's needs during the meeting.

Supplies: You'll need a large bowl and a photograph from each participant.

Preparation: The week before the meeting, ask each person to bring a photograph representing a person, place, event, or situation he or she would like prayer for. Tell kids to write any significant information on the backs of the photographs, such as names, dates, locations, or other issues of concern.

Time Involved: 15 to 60 minutes

[]

Leader TIP
At the next meeting, you might consider letting kids share how God interceded during the week.

Place the photographs in a bowl, and have each participant select one. Then have each person go to the person whose name is on the photograph he or she selected and discuss how he or she can pray for the person. Depending on the size of the group, either have kids sit in a circle and take turns praying, photograph by photograph or divide them into smaller, more intimate groups to pray.

Once the praying part of the activity is finished, ask for volunteers to share how they felt when someone else prayed for them. Encourage group members to continue praying for one another throughout the coming week.

Making a Global Impact

Overview: Kids will learn how to impact their world through prayer and experience a "global impact" by using a globe beach ball. This prayer session will help expand the vision of those in the group.

Supplies: You'll need a plastic blowup globe beach ball, paper, and pencils.

Preparation: None is needed.

Time Involved: 15 to 45 minutes

Begin tossing the beach ball around the room to the kids while discussing the importance of praying for people around the world. To challenge your kid's world-praying experience, have each person who catches the globe share a quick prayer for the foreign country his or her thumb landed on as he or she caught the ball.

When you've finished playing the global-impact game, select one of the countries already discussed and pray for it in more depth.

Have kids break into small groups of three or four. Assign each group a different cause to pray for during your meeting. Examples would be issues such as economic problems, religious freedom, and missionary involvement.

Before the meeting ends, challenge each group to keep a written account of specific world-prayer needs to share at the following meeting. Suggest that kids be attentive to newspaper articles or news programs.

Variation

Assign each group a "homework" assignment, asking them to dig into encyclopedias, the Internet, periodicals, and so on to learn more about a country and its background. Have kids share the information at the next meeting.

Say What?

Overview: Kids will learn to think on their feet as they respond to phrases and sayings using the first words that come to mind.

Supplies: You'll need a bowl; paper; a pencil; and a selection of funny jokes, quotes, phrases, or verses.

Preparation: Write down the phrases, jokes, quotes, or verses on slips of paper. Try to select some that are funny, some that are thought-provoking, and others that challenge kids' thinking. Good resources include the Bible, a trivia game, and *Scholastic Dictionary of Idioms: More Than 600 Phrases, Sayings and Expressions,* by Marvin Terban.

Time Involved: 30 to 60 minutes

Variation

Other topics might include character qualities; fruit of the Spirit; or interpersonal relationship elements such as honesty, diligence, love, loyalty, anger, or purity. Comical statements or sayings which lighten the mood and bring laughter are important too, because they help provide balance to the game.

Have kids sit in a circle. Pull one slip of paper out of the bowl, and read it aloud. Have the person on your right say the first word that comes to his or her mind after hearing it. Quickly go around the circle, and have each person do the same. Have a few kids share their thoughts as to why they chose those particular words.

Next, ask the person on your right to select the next slip and read it aloud. Go around the circle in the same manner. Have the person who selected the paper choose one person and ask why that individual chose the word he or she chose. Continue the game until each person has had a chance to lead a round.

Pass the Parcel

Overview: Kids will be divided into small groups and take turns answering fun questions.

Supplies: You'll need colored tissue paper for wrapping; scissors; tape; checkbook-sized boxes filled with assorted goodies such as candy bars, gum, mints, bookmarks, pens or pencils, and notepads; a pen; and slips of paper.

Preparation: Depending on the size of your group, calculate an approximate number of goodie boxes you'll need (one per team, and teams should be no larger than five people). Fill the boxes with treats. Using the colored tissue paper, wrap each box.

Write enough questions on separate slips of paper for each wrapped box to have six. Suggested questions include "What is your favorite thing to do?" "What do you like most about your family?" "What do you think is the hardest part of growing up?" "How would you like to see our country change?"

Tape a question to the top of each wrapped box and then wrap each box with another layer of tissue paper and attach a second question. Repeat the process until each box has six layers of paper and questions.

Time Involved: 15 to 30 minutes

Divide the group into teams of four to five players. Have each team sit in a circle, and give a box to each one. Explain that the teams will need to answer each question attached to their boxes. The object is for each team to tear off one layer of paper at a time and then take turns answering each question. This process should continue until each team has answered its final question. When all teams have finished, they can open their prize boxes and distribute the treats.

Scramble Scrabble!

Overview: Kids will enjoy a time of working together to search for the letters to complete words, phrases, and sentences using a Scrabble game.

Supplies: You'll need Bibles, a concordance, paper, pencils, sets of letters from Scrabble games (one for every six kids), dictionaries (optional), and assorted king-size and miniature candy bars (at least one for every player).

Preparation: Using a concordance, write down about twenty well-known Bible passages. Circle one of the words in each passage. This word will be the one kids will have to find and spell out using their Scrabble letters. (You can also select twenty words of various length from the dictionary.)

Time Involved: 30 to 60 minutes

Divide the group into smaller teams of no more than six per team. Have kids scatter out on the floor so there is enough elbowroom for each team to work. Provide a set of Scrabble letters to each team, instructing kids to open the game boards and turn all the letters right-side-up.

Explain that you will read a well-known Bible passage aloud, leaving one key word out. The teams are to decide what word is missing and then spell the word using their Scrabble letters. If teams can't figure out what the missing word is, have them look it up in the Bible. Once a team thinks it has correctly spelled out the word, have team members raise their hands so you can walk over and check it. Tell kids not to shout it aloud, because if the first team misspelled the word, the other teams will continue to play. The first team to find the word and spell it correctly wins that round.

Continue the process until your verses are used up or until time runs out. Keep track of each team's score and invite the members of winning team to each select a king-size candy bar. Hand out miniature candy bars to the remainder of the kids.

Umbrella Catch

Overview: Kids will prompt a blindfolded team member to identify items missionaries might use.

Supplies: You'll need two umbrellas; two blindfolds; two boxes; wrapping paper; tape; scissors; pens; paper; envelopes; and items missionaries might use such as toiletries, paper products, personal-care items, office supplies, children's toys and clothing, and so on.

Preparation: Select a missionary (or a missionary family) to send some needed items to. Ask each member of the group to bring an appropriate item to the next meeting. Also place a note in the church bulletin and request gifts for the missionaries to be donated prior to the meeting. Equally divide all the missionary items into two boxes.

Time Involved: 20 to 30 minutes

Divide the group into two teams. Have one member from each team put on a blindfold. Provide an umbrella to each blindfolded person. Instruct both blindfolded kids to open their umbrellas and stand ready to "catch" items as soon as they correctly guess what each item is.

Team members should begin describing how each item is used without describing what it looks like. As soon as the blindfolded member guesses what the item is, another member should throw the item into the open umbrella. The first team to catch all the items contained in its box wins.

After you have completed this portion of the activity, provide wrapping paper and have kids wrap each item. Have them each write an individual letter introducing himself or herself to the missionary. Ask kids to include their promises to pray at least one time weekly for the missionary.

At the close of the meeting, ask each team to take time to pray for the missionary and his or her special needs.

You might want to challenge kids to take turns writing to the missionary for the remainder of the school year. If you decide to do this, have each team set up a schedule for writing during the upcoming months. Be sure to have kids share with the entire group any letters received from the missionary.

Grab a Book

Overview: Kids will go into a library and search for books that describe them best.

Supplies: None are needed.

Preparation: None is needed.

Time Involved: 45 to 60 minutes

Have kids meet you at the local library. When they arrive, instruct them to look for books that best characterize each of them personally. Tell kids to examine the front covers, back covers, endorsements, thickness of the books, the books' subjects, and so on. As kids find their books, have them sit quietly for about ten minutes and gather their thoughts about how the books characterize them. When kids have had a chance to put their thoughts together, have everyone sit in a circle. One at a time, have kids hold their books up and share thoughts about how the books characterize them.

Grab Bag Fun

Overview: Kids will select grab bags and answer the questions written on the paper inside.

Supplies: You'll need brown-paper lunch bags; slips of paper; a pen; powdered sugar; flour; rice; gummy worms; tape, glue, or a stapler; and assorted treats as prizes.

Preparation: Write a "get to know you" question on each slip of paper and place one inside each bag. Some suggested questions are: "What is the most important person in your life like?" "How do you see yourself when you're in your twenties?" "Who do you admire most?" "What is something you absolutely hate?" "What kind of friend would you describe yourself as?" and "What do you remember about the best or worst day of your life?" To prepare the bags, pour into each a small portion of one of the following ingredients: powdered sugar, flour, rice, or gummy worms. Tape, staple, or glue the edge of the bags shut securely. Write instructions on each bag explaining how to open it. Examples might include: "open with your teeth only," "open with your pinkie fingers only," or "open with your nose and your knees."

Time Involved: 30 to 60 minutes

Divide the group into two or more teams. Instruct the kids on each team to take turns selecting and opening a bag following the instructions written on the bag. The person who opens the bag is responsible for retrieving the question from inside it, using the same method as he or she used to open the bag. This person should then read the question aloud and give everyone on the team an opportunity to respond to it. Have kids continue selecting and opening bags and answering questions until all of the questions have been answered. Then let kids enjoy the treats!

Fishbowl Fun

Overview: Kids will direct their blindfolded team members toward "catching" magnetic items inside a fishbowl.

Supplies: You'll need two clear plastic (or glass) fishbowls; two magnetic strips; two pens; string; paper; a pencil; two blindfolds; and assorted magnetic items such as paper clips, pins, metal buttons, tacks, and nails.

Preparation: Place the magnetic items inside the two fishbowls (make sure the same items are included in each bowl). Make two lists of all the items. Next, make a simple fishing pole for each team by tying one end of the string to a pen and the other end to a magnetic strip.

Time Involved: 20 to 30 minutes

Divide the group into two teams. Blindfold one member of each team, and provide both blindfolded kids with magnetic fishing poles. Give each team a list of the items its members must "fish" for in the goldfish bowl. The fisherman must retrieve items in the order specified on the list or they must be thrown back. Other team members are to call out instructions to help their blind fisherman get all the items he or she needs. The first team to catch all its items wins.

Variation

To make this game more challenging, have the blindfolded team members hold the poles in their mouths while fishing. Or you might consider rotating fishermen after each item has been caught.

Newspaper Newsies

Overview: Kids will work together reading newspapers and cutting out words and sentences to create a funny story.

Supplies: You'll need a stack of newspapers, scissors, glue, and paper.

Variation

To make the teams work faster, you can give them a specific time limit. Particular themes can also be predetermined prior to handing out the newspapers. Some suggested themes include: stories of courage and rescue, stories that tickle the funny bone, stories of true love, and stories of unusual or unique action.

Preparation: None is needed.

Time Involved: 20 to 30 minutes

Divide the group into teams of four or less, and give each team newspaper, scissors, glue, and paper. Instruct each team to quickly look through the newspapers and begin cutting out words, phrases, and sentences to create their own funny news stories. They can also find and cut out pictures to add to their stories. Once all the teams have compiled their stories and glued them to the paper, have kids read them to the rest of the group.

Building a Firm Foundation

Overview: Kids will follow instructions to create Lincoln Log houses as quickly as possible.

Supplies: You'll need Lincoln Log building sets (enough for each group to have a set), paper, and pencils.

Preparation: Write down several different floor plans for building Lincoln Log houses, each getting progressively more difficult. For example, a simple plan would include walls, a roof, and a door. A medium plan might include walls, a roof, two windows, and a door. A difficult plan would be two stories, a balcony, two windows, and a door. Copy the floor plans for each group to refer to during the game.

Time Involved: 30 to 60 minutes

Divide the group into teams of six players or less. Provide

each team with a Lincoln Log set and a copy of the simple floor plan. Tell them that this game is a relay, so they will need to work together and quickly build their houses. After a team has completed its simple plan, check to make sure the team included all the necessary elements and then give it the next plan. Continue this process until the teams have all finished their projects. The winning team is the one who is the first to correctly build all three models.

After the game, you can discuss the importance of building firm foundations in Christ using the Lincoln Log houses as the lesson object.

You Oughta Be in Hollywood

Overview: Kids will cooperate to create short videos that will be shown to the larger group.

Supplies: You'll need a video camera and a videotape for each group of four kids, the "Video Segment List" handout (p. 179), adult volunteers/drivers, popcorn and soft drinks, a VCR, and a TV.

Preparation: Make one copy of the "Video Segment List" handout (p. 179) for each group.

Time Involved: 60 to 90 minutes

Have kids form groups of four. Assign an adult volunteer/driver to each group, and give him or her a videocamera and a videotape.

Announce that in sixty minutes (or thirty—it's up to you), you'll meet back at your starting point for the "New Faces Video Festival."

Say: **I've got popcorn, soft drinks, and everything we need except for the videos. This will be your part of the**

Leader TIP

Assign kids to groups in order to intentionally develop relationships, and keep visitors together with the kids who invited them.

activity. **Your job is to travel as a group and shoot up to four minutes of compelling video to showcase your talents and persuasive powers. Here are the rules of the game:**

1. The adult will drive and obey all traffic laws.

2. Adults will be the designated videographers.

3. Plan shots carefully—only the first four minutes of your tape will be shown.

4. Video segments must come from the "Video Segment List."

5. Only tapes turned in by the deadline will be entered in the festival.

Distribute the "Video Segment List." Give groups five minutes to plan what they want to shoot, and send them out.

When they return, serve snacks and show the videos. Ask each group to answer the following questions:

● **What was the strangest thing that happened on your video shoot?**

● **What was the funniest thing that happened?**

● **Who would you nominate for New Actor of the Year?**

Sum up by saying: **You did a great job! Those of you who asked people to do something bizarre on tape discovered it can be uncomfortable to take a risk. As Christians, Jesus asks us to do some uncomfortable things, too—such as turning the other cheek, forgiving others, and living as servants.**

Have kids pair up in their groups and discuss the following question:

● **What's the thing Jesus asks you to do that you find the hardest?**

After partners have shared, ask them to pray for each other.

VIDEO
SEGMENT LIST

- Convince a total stranger to impersonate Elvis.

- Go to a copy shop and photocopy your faces.

- Pretend you're in a car, walk through a fast-food restaurant's drive-through window, and order one small soft drink.

- Crowd around a pay phone, call someone's mother, and serenade her.

- Get a woman who's over forty to go on camera and tell her age and weight.

- Visit the police station and convince the desk sergeant to say "Let's be careful out there."

- Act out your favorite scene from a classic movie.

- Buy a stalk of celery at a grocery store and trade it to another shopper for another vegetable.

- Convince a clerk at a gas station to let you have the key to the employee restroom.

Fast on Your Feet

Overview: Kids will work together to brainstorm ways to use nylon hose.

Supplies: You'll need a bag of clean, used nylon hose (one piece of hose for each person).

Preparation: None is needed.

Time Involved: 5 to 10 minutes

Ask kids to form trios.

Give each person a piece of nylon hose and say: **It's true that you can't do a job without the right tools. That's why I've given each of you a tool that fits any situation.**

> ## Leader TIP
> If you want to encourage relationships, form the trios so kids who don't know each other or who need to work out a relationship are in the same trio.

I'll give you a series of situations. I'd like you to quickly discuss in your trios how these pieces of nylon hose can help you solve the dilemmas. And when I say "quickly," that's exactly what I mean. You'll have forty-five seconds and then it will be time to show the rest of us what you came up with.

Give each group a situation from the "Situations" box, and give kids forty-five seconds to create. Be sure to applaud all efforts. Collect the nylon-hose pieces for use another time.

Situations

1. You're hiking, and you see a bear following you. What will you do?

2. It's time for your Valentine's Day date, and you forgot to get a present. There's no time to buy one—what do you do?

3. You have a toothache. The dentist can't see you for two days. Now what?

4. Aliens are attempting to contact you via radio signals. You need to respond. What do you do?

5. You're standing in line at the bank, and robbers rush in. What do you do?

Team Matchups

Overview: Kids will work at creating a machine and learn that all the parts are necessary to make it work effectively.

Supplies: You'll need paper, a marker, and tape.

Preparation: Write down parts of various machines on individual pieces of paper. Each machine should have the same number of parts. For instance, you could use a **washing machine:** (1) the dial, (2) the agitator, (3) the water hose, (4) the motor, and (5) the tub; or a **computer:** (1) a keyboard, (2) a monitor, (3) a power supply, (4) a disk drive, and (5) computer chips. List each separate part on a sheet of paper. Develop as many machines as necessary to have enough parts for your entire group. (Some machines may have the same parts—that's OK).

Time Involved: 10 minutes

As kids arrive, tape a piece of paper with a machine part written on it to each of their backs. Explain that they are to create several working machines by finding the other people who have the rest of the parts for their machines. Let kids know how many parts are in the machines they are trying to build, but don't tell them what machines they are part of. Give kids five minutes to figure out what machine they belong to.

After five minutes, have kids tell which machine they think they are and identify all the parts of the machine. Some kids will not be in the correct group or in any group at all. Reveal the correct combinations, and have them get into their machine groups. Ask:

● **Why was it difficult to figure out what group you**

182

should be in?

● **How did you feel when you couldn't find all your parts?**

● **If you did not find your group at all how did you feel?**

Use this activity as a springboard into a conversation about 1 Corinthians 12:12-27 (the body of Christ has many parts).

Find "Freddy"

Overview: Kids will be awarded points for finding particular things on some very peculiar people!

Supplies: You'll need five adults in disguise, including one who will play the part of Freddy and dress in a specific outfit such as a red-and-white striped shirt and a hat; four things that belong to Freddy, such as a teddy bear, a Walkman, a water bottle, and eyeglasses; photographs of the five adults dressed normally; and the "Freddy's Point Sheet" handout (p. 184).

Preparation: Find a group of crazy adults who will disguise themselves and wander through a chosen populated place, such as a mall.

Give each adult one of Freddy's belongings, and tell him or her that the item must be visible on his or her person at all times during the game. Make one copy of the "Freddy's Point Sheet" handout (p. 184) for each person.

Time Involved: 1 hour and 15 minutes

Leader TIP

Make sure you gain permission for your event, since mall security guards might get nervous around suspicious-looking people in disguise.

Meet the adult actors at one mall location while your kids gather with another sponsor at a different point at the mall. Instruct the adults to disperse into the mall and not stick together. Suggest they always appear to be busy, doing things such as if they were shopping, standing at a counter, or sitting on a bench talking with someone. When the kids approach one of the adults, they should ask, "Are you Freddy?" or "Is that Freddy's _____ you have?" If the kids are correct, the adult will sign the line corresponding to that item on their point sheets.

If the management has limited the places your group may go or there are large department stores in the mall that would make it impossible for the kids to find the adults, inform everyone of areas they should avoid. Finally, explain where everyone will meet after one hour.

Divide the kids into groups of three or four. Have the other sponsor give kids a copy of "Freddy's Point Sheet." When the game is over, award Freddy's belongings to the team with the most points. Take a few minutes to lead a short discussion by asking:

● **How did you feel about walking up to strangers and asking for specific things?**

● **Did you ask a question of someone who wasn't part of the game?**

● **If so, how did you feel when you made this mistake?**

● **Have you ever had to talk to a complete stranger about anything? If so, about what?**

This conversation is an effective introduction to a unit on evangelism or ministering to strangers or new families in church. You could also use it to begin a study about the disguises we often hide behind by asking:

● **What kind of disguises do you hide behind?**

● **How do you feel when you are trying to be something you are not?**

● **Why is it better to be the person God created you to be rather than to be fake?**

Freddy's
Point Sheet

YOU are on a mission to find Freddy and his belongings. Five of our adult church members are wandering around in disguise. Attached are pictures of these people without their disguises so you'll know who you're looking for. When you discover Freddy or one of his belongings, ask the person, "Are you Freddy?" or "Is that Freddy's _____ ?" (item from your list). If it is, have the person sign the line by that item.

Freddy and his belongings can be found anywhere except the following locations, which are off-limits:

Freddy's Items:

_____ Freddy (10,000 points)

_____ Freddy's teddy bear (5,000 points)

_____ Freddy's Walkman (8,000 points)

_____ Freddy's eyeglasses (6,000 points)

_____ Freddy's water bottle (3,000 points)

Faith in a Cup

Overview: Kids will learn that trusting a teammate requires action.

Supplies: You'll need one pitcher of water, one foam cup for every two people, and towels.

Preparation: None is needed.

Time Involved: 5 minutes

Divide your group into pairs. Give each pair a pitcher of water and a foam cup. Ask:
  ● **Do you believe that I can pour a cup of water without spilling a drop?**
  The kids will more than likely answer "yes." Pour the cup of water and then ask:
  ● **Do you believe that your partner can pour a cup of water without spilling a drop?**
  Everyone will again probably answer "yes." Instruct kids each to perform this action and then dump the water back into the pitcher. Ask:
  ● **Do you believe your partner can pour a cup of water from his or her waist and into a cup on the floor without spilling a drop?**
  Let kids respond. Some may say "yes," some may say "no." Instruct each pair to have one of the partners lay on the floor with a cup next to his or her right ear.
  Say: **If you believe it's possible, we're going to put your faith into action.** Have the partner who remains standing attempt to pour water into the cup. Next, ask:
  ● **Why did you believe your partner either could or couldn't do this?**
  ● **Did you change your mind after you realized your partner was going to attempt this with the cup next to your head? Why or why not?**
  Continue your discussion by asking kids about other times

in their lives when they said they trusted someone but their actions didn't show it.

Shoe-Shucking Race

Overview: Kids will have to remove their shoes while balancing a pan of water on their feet.

Supplies: You'll need a dishpan filled with water for each team and towels.

Preparation: None is needed.

Time Involved: 10 minutes

Divide kids into teams with a minimum of four players per team. Have the members of each team get into a circle, lie on their backs, and put their feet into the air together so their legs are touching. Place a dishpan of water on the combined feet of each group. The object of the game is to have the members of each group remove their shoes without the use of their hands and without spilling the water. Give kids a three-minute time limit. After the time is up, ask:

- **Was it difficult to succeed at this game? Why?**
- **What did you have to do to succeed?**
- **How did you determine who would go first, second, and so on?**
- **If you were the one who made the water spill, how did you feel?**

Use this activity to begin a brief talk about the importance of working together and encouraging one another.

Live Detective Night

Overview: This game is modeled after the board game Clue. The kids will play the game as various fictitious characters.

Supplies: You'll need a game of Clue, slips of paper, pencils, the "Team Detective Sheet" handout (p. 188), masking tape, and a die or a spinner.

Preparation: Use tape to form a large grid that looks just like the board game. Create 2x2-foot squares and 6x6-foot rooms. Write each suspect, weapon, and room from the "Team Detective Sheet" (p. 188) on a separate slip of paper, just as in Clue. Make one copy of the "Team Detective Sheet" (p. 188) for each team.

Time Involved: 20 minutes to 1 hour

Divide kids into six teams, and name each team after a particular character (such as Yolanda Yellow, Carrie Crimson, Pamela Purple, Larry Lime, Brian Blue, and Wanda White). Provide each team with a copy of the "Team Detective Sheet," and ask each team to appoint one person to serve as its "playing piece." Follow the instructions included with the board game, except that each guess must be the decision of the entire team. Play until one team solves the case.

Variation

For added fun, provide the live playing pieces with color-coded costumes and use different rooms in the church for the locations in the game.

Team DETECTIVE *Sheet*

Suspects	Weapons	Rooms
Yolanda Yellow	*Switchblade*	*Hallway*
Pamela Purple	*Soda Bottle*	*Bathroom*
Larry Lime	*Gun*	*Dining Room*
Brian Blue	*Overdose*	*Kitchen*
Carrie Crimson	*Rake*	*Game Room*
Wanda White	*Hammer*	*Den*
		Music Room
		Garage
		Deck

Cellophaning

Overview: Kids who don't know each other well will learn to have fun together.

Supplies: You'll need a roll of cellophane for each team.

Preparation: None is needed.

Time Involved: 5 minutes

Start by forming trios. Have each trio wrap one of its members in cellophane from the shoulders down. The object is to use the entire roll and wrap the person so that nothing but his or her neck and head are exposed. The trio that finishes first wins the game.

You can continue the activity by seeing which trio is the quickest at unwrapping the person and rolling the cellophane back onto the cardboard tube! (By concluding the game in this manner, the cellophane is not wasted and can be used to play the game again.)

Five Kernels of Corn

Overview: This activity works especially well near Thanksgiving and is a great way to remind kids of the history of Thanksgiving while motivating them to think of those who are less fortunate.

Supplies: You'll need five kernels of unpopped popcorn for each team and an adult volunteer/driver for each team.

Preparation: None is needed.

Time Involved: 90 minutes

Divide your group into teams of no more than five players. Give each team five kernels of popcorn, and say: **There is a legend that is told about the Pilgrims each bringing five**

**kernels of corn to the first Thanksgiving dinner to re-
mind them of both the rough winter they had survived
and the wonderful new friends God had given them.**

Explain that the object of the activity is for the teams to go
door-to-door asking residents for canned-food donations that will
be given to a local food pantry. Instruct kids to trade their kernels
of corn for as many canned goods as they can get people to donate.
Each team has the option of either giving all five kernels away at
the first house or giving one kernel at the first house, another at
the second house, and so on. Give kids an hour time limit. The
winning team is the one that returns with the most canned food.

After kids arrive back at the church, lead a discussion by asking:

● **What was your greatest success in getting donations?**

● **Did you find it hard to ask people for food?**

● **How do you think the poor in our community feel
about having to always ask for food?**

● **What are some other ways we can help those who
have less than we do this Thanksgiving?**

Go together as a group to deliver the food and end the activity with a popcorn party!

Balloon Hugs

Overview: Since we live in a "no-touch" society, this activity
will provide a way for kids to give appropriate hugs because all of
us need to feel loved.

Supplies: You'll need lots of balloons.

Preparation: Blow up all the balloons.

Time Involved: 5 minutes

Divide kids into pairs. Give each pair several balloons. Tell
them that they need to pop the balloons as quickly as possible
by squeezing them between their bodies.

Name Acrostics

Overview: Kids will begin to build confidence in themselves and learn how others in the group feel about them.

Supplies: You'll need paper and pencils.

Preparation: None is needed.

Time Involved: 5 to 10 minutes

Have kids sit in a circle, and give each person a piece of paper and a pencil. Have each one write his or her first name, one letter at a time, vertically down the left side of a piece of paper. Then tell kids they'll be writing a compliment about each person on that person's paper. Each compliment must begin with one of the letters in that person's name. Have kids pass the sheets of paper to the left around the circle to complete the acrostics. After this process is complete, have each person introduce the person whose paper he or she is holding. This can be done by having each person state the person's name and read the compliments aloud. Return the papers to their proper owners.

Variation

This activity can be used to compliment your pastor or others in positions of leadership within your church. You might also consider taking compliment acrostics to shut-ins. Everyone can use a boost at one time or another!

Here's a sample name acrostic:

S (secret keeper)
A (attentive)
R (really listens)
A (attractive)
H (happy)

Once everyone has been introduced, ask:

● **How did you feel as someone read compliments about you?**

● **Did you feel uncomfortable hearing about the special ways we are important to other people?**

● **How could you use this lesson at school to help a person with a low self-image feel better about himself or herself?**

Say: **Think of one person you know who could use a compliment. Write his or her name down the back of your paper, and do a compliment acrostic.**

Working Together Balloon-Volley

Overview: Kids will work in teams helping others keep their balloons afloat. This game will remind kids of their need to help one another.

Supplies: You'll need lots of balloons in two different colors (at least one balloon for each person), clothes hangers, twist ties, and knee-high nylon stockings.

Preparation: Blow up the balloons and make a racquet for each person in your group. Use the following instructions to make a racket: (a) pull the bottom of the hanger down to form a diamond shape; (b) slide the knee-high nylon stocking over the body of the hanger; (c) pull the open end of the stocking up to the top of the hanger, and secure it with the twist tie; (d) bend the curved end of the hanger into a handle (see diagram).

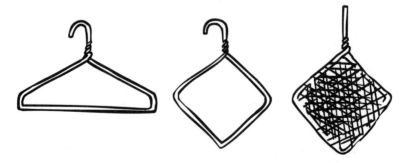

Time Involved: 15 minutes

Have kids get into two teams. Distribute the balloons of one color to the first team and the balloons of the other color to the other team, and give each person a racquet. Demonstrate how to gently tap a balloon with a racquet to keep it afloat. Let each student practice for a minute.

Say: **The object of this game is to keep your balloon afloat. Remember, though—you are a team. If you see one of your teammates' balloons starting to fall, try to help that person out. The team that has a balloon on the floor first loses the round.**

Allow kids to play this several times and then come back together for a short discussion. Ask:

● **How were the balloons like people in a church family?**

● **How should the people in our church work together like the teams did in this game?**

Road Mapping

Overview: Kids will be reminded that there are often several choices in certain matters, all of which can be right. This activity can be a great icebreaker when your group is getting ready to discuss a subject that has no definitive right or wrong answers.

Supplies: You'll need one road map for each team, paper, and pencils.

Preparation: Make a list of four destinations that can be found on the road maps, and give each team a copy.

Time Involved: 15 minutes

Divide the group into teams of four. Give each team a road map and a list of destinations.

Say: **I will give each team ten minutes to find the locations written on the list and decide how to get to each one and in which order to go to the locations. The**

194

rule is that everyone must participate in the decision.

After ten minutes, ask:

● **Did everyone agree about the best way to go and the order in which you should visit the four locations?**

● **How did you decide which way was best?**

● **How is this activity like deciding the direction our group will go?**

● **How is it like the disagreements we might have?**

Stretcher Race

Overview: Kids will learn more about the concept of helping a weaker brother or sister.

Supplies: You'll need queen-size sheets, obstacles such as old tires, plastic traffic-cones, chairs and so forth.

Preparation: Set up two identical outdoor obstacle courses.

Time Involved: 15 minutes

Divide the group into two teams. Explain that the object is to get each team through the obstacle course. The tricky part, however, is that only two team members can walk, the rest must be carried on the sheets, either one-by-one or in groups. Begin by having each team select two stretcher bearers and then devising a plan to get through the obstacle course. Give each team five minutes to deliberate and then give them a command to begin. The fastest team wins.

When the race is completed, ask:

● **What was it like to be one of the people carrying the rest of your team?**

● **What was it like for those of you who were carried?**

● **In what ways do we often have to be stretcher bearers for others in our group? In our homes? In our schools?**

Togetherness Olympics

Overview: Kids will be reminded that sometimes it is easier to work independently but that we are called to work together.

Supplies: You'll need several lengths of rope that are long enough to tie four or five kids together at the waist, paper, and a marker.

Preparation: Write down specific "Olympic" instructions, and place them at various outdoor locations. Examples might include:

- The entire team must do ten jumping jacks before going to the next stop.
- The entire team must walk backwards to the next event.
- The entire team must go to the next event with all of their backs touching.
- Each teammate must carry a full glass of water to the next location without spilling it, or the team must start over!

Time Involved: 20 minutes

Have kids divide into teams of four or five. Have each team form a standing circle and then tie a rope around all of their waists with about a foot in between each person. Tell kids that they need to complete all of the events in the Olympic relay as a team. If any team fails to complete an event, they must start over at the beginning of the entire course. Give teams ten minutes to get through all the events.

When the teams have finished, bring them together for a short discussion. Ask:

- **What were your concerns about waiting for other teammates to do something before you could go on?**
- **Would these activities have been easier if you had not been tied together? Why?**
- **In what ways did you encourage each other to succeed?**

Snow Mountain

Overview: This event is a great ski-trip game. Kids will learn to work together to be human snow-movers!

Supplies: You'll need a twenty-five-gallon trash bag for each team, scissors, and a watch with a second hand.

Preparation: Cut two holes in the bottom of each trash bag so a person can put his or her legs through it like a pair of pants.

Time Involved: 15 minutes

Divide the group into teams of three. Mark a starting and finish line in the snow. Have one member of each team put on a pair of trash-bag pants. Say: **The object of this game is to move the greatest amount of snow from the starting line to the finish line within five minutes. The two people without trash-bag pants on each team must fill the third person's plastic pants with snow and then help him or her waddle to the finish line and dump the snow. The pants cannot be removed to dump the snow. Be sure to stack the snow as high as possible. After each round, the team should run back to get another load. Continue this process for five minutes. The team with the tallest pile wins!**

This is a great game to close out a day of skiing before returning to the lodge for hot chocolate and a fire.

Leader TIP

It's best for the person with the plastic pants on to have ski pants on underneath so he or she doesn't get too soaked and cold.

Shoe Matchup

Overview: Kids will participate in a fun time trying to match teammates with their shoes.

Supplies: You'll need blindfolds.

Preparation: None is needed.

Time Involved: 10 minutes

Divide kids into two equal teams. Tell them to throw their shoes into one big pile in the center of the group and mix them up. Each team needs to choose one member who will be blindfolded. The object is for the blindfolded person to return the correct shoes to their owners by listening to the directions provided by their team members. Of course, both teams will be shouting directions at the same time, so chaos will rule!

Corporate Construction

Overview: Kids will learn to work together successfully as a team while building with children's construction sets.

Supplies: You'll need plastic sandwich bags, as many children's construction sets as possible, and a copy of a construction pattern for each person (patterns can be found in the boxes with most construction sets).

Preparation: Place ten construction pieces in each plastic bag. You'll need one filled bag for each person.

Time Involved: 15 to 25 minutes

As kids arrive, give them each a bag containing construction pieces and a construction pattern. Explain that the object is for kids to construct the patterns illustrated on their sheets by finding other people in the room who have parts they need. Once a pair joins together, the partners must remain as a team. However, they can locate others to join them as well. Kids will probably need to find several others to help complete the task. The first team to complete a pattern wins.

Life's Little Puzzle

Overview: Kids will work together to see who can build a puzzle the quickest. This activity is a great way to arbitrarily split kids into teams for other events.

Supplies: You'll need several preschool jigsaw puzzles.

Preparation: None is needed.

Time Involved: 10 minutes

As kids arrive, give them each the piece to a jigsaw puzzle. If you have extras left over, place them back into the correct puzzle frames. Put all the frames in the center of the room. Have kids locate the correct puzzles to which their pieces belong. The first group to completely put a puzzle together wins.

Team Accountability

Overview: Kids will work together to see which team can gather the most points over the course of two weeks.

Supplies: You'll need the "Teamwork Point Sheet" handout (p. 199).

Preparation: Make one copy of the "Teamwork Point Sheet" handout (p. 199) for each team.

Time Involved: 2 weeks

One week prior to using this activity, divide kids into two teams. Give each team a copy of the "Teamwork Point Sheet" handout. The object of the game is for each team to use the handout and accumulate as many points as possible over the course of two weeks.

TEAMWORK
[POINT SHEET]

- 25 points for each team member who attends both sessions
- 15 points for each new person brought by a team member
- 20 points for each person on the team who brings a Bible to the meeting
- 10 points for each guest who brought a Bible
- 15 points for wearing red
- 20 points for each guest who is wearing red
- 10 points for each team member who is not wearing white socks
- 30 points for each team member who can recite a verse from the Old Testament (no two teammates are allowed to recite the same verse)
- 30 points for each team member who can recite a verse from the New Testament (no two team-mates are allowed to recite the same verse)

Kindling Cabins

Overview: Kids will work together in a race to build the best mini-cabin possible.

Supplies: You'll need campfire wood and kindling.

Preparation: None is needed.

Time Involved: 30 minutes

This game would be great at a camp or a retreat center.

Divide kids into teams of equal size. The object is for each team to collect enough wood and kindling to create a one-foot-square log cabin with a roof. Select some players or adult leaders to act as judges and vote on the best cabin. Save the kindling for your campfire.

Communication Creation

Overview: Kids will work together to complete a puzzle— without talking.

Supplies: You'll need construction paper in the following colors: red, green, blue, black, and yellow; scissors; and envelopes.

Preparation: Cut construction paper into shapes according to the diagram following this activity. You'll need one complete set of shapes for each group. Place all of the red shapes in one envelope, all of the blue shapes in another envelope, and so on. When you finish, you should have five envelopes for each group.

Time Involved: 20 to 30 minutes

Divide the group into five teams of five players each. Provide each person with an envelope containing puzzle pieces. (Make sure that each group has all five colors represented and thus a complete set of pieces. If you have a group of four, assign two envelopes to one person. If you have a group of six, assign two people to share one envelope.)

Tell kids that the object of the game is for each group to form five rectangles, all of equal length and width, using all of the envelopes and pieces in the group's possession. There are three stages to this activity:

● **Stage One (5 to 10 minutes)**— Group members may not speak to each other. The only thing a person can do is offer one of his or her pieces to another member of the group. A person cannot indicate a need for a particular piece and may only take a piece if it is offered. (If a piece is offered to a person, he or she must take it.)

● **Stage Two (5 to 10 minutes)**— Group members still may not speak; however, a person can indicate his or her need for a particular piece.

● **Stage Three (up to 5 minutes)**— Group members may speak.

● **Stage Four (optional)**— Groups may help each other. After all of the groups have completed their puzzles, ask:

● **Was communication with your group easy or difficult? Explain.**

● **Do you feel that the other members of your group were helpful or not helpful? What made you feel that way?**

● **How important was it for the members of your group to work together? Explain.**

● **How does good communication help us to work together better?**

The following combinations of shapes and colors are what a group's finished product should look like. Cut the construction paper so that the pieces fit together as illustrated.

Communication Creation

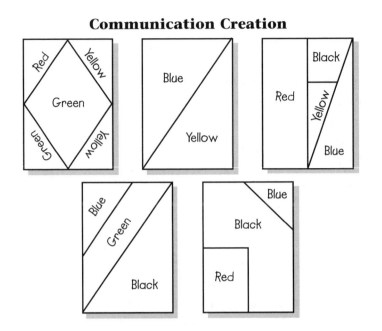

Beware the Alligators!

Overview: Kids will help each other across a "river" full of vicious "alligators."

Supplies: You'll need 2x2-foot cardboard squares (one less cardboard square than the number of kids in your group) and masking tape.

Preparation: Use masking tape to mark the sides of the river, approximately thirty feet in width.

Time Involved: 20 to 30 minutes

Tell kids that the space between the masking tape lines is a large river. Their job is to work together to get the entire group across. They are to travel across by walking in a single file line on the cardboard "steppingstones." If a player accidentally steps into the "water," he or she will be devoured by a vicious alligator (and thus will be out of the game).

Begin by having kids move forward across the river by stepping forward on the pieces of cardboard. As they move forward, they are to pass each vacated steppingstone behind them up to the first person in line. If, at any time, a steppingstone is left vacated and no one is touching it, an alligator may push it out of the way (and thus keep kids from using it).

As many kids as necessary (or possible!) may stand on a steppingstone at one time as long as each person has both of his or her feet on the steppingstone. As kids progress across the river, you (and other adult helpers, as well as any unfortunate alligator "victims") can act as the alligators, catching people who fall off the steppingstones and removing the steppingstones when they are vacated.

Pyramid Basketball

Overview: Kids will work together in pyramids to score points for their teams.

Supplies: You'll need a basketball and a basketball hoop or a box.

Preparation: None is needed.

Time Involved: 10 to 30 minutes

Have kids remove their shoes and socks. Form trios of kids who are about the same size and then form two teams so that each team includes the same number of trios. Have each team select a trio to play center and develop a strategy for placing the rest of their trios around the playing area. Tell trios that they will be forming pyramids with two players on their hands and knees on the floor and the other player kneeling on their backs.

Basic basketball rules will apply except for the following exceptions: (1) each basket scored is worth six points, (2) the top person in a trio may dismount to chase the ball but must switch places with one of the bottom players to reform the pyramid, (3) points will count only if the ball is shot from an intact pyramid, (4) fouls will be declared if any person comes into physical contact with a member of another pyramid or if any person causes another pyramid to collapse.

Call the centers to "jump" for the ball. Play for one-fourth of your designated time (or one quarter) and then let teams reconvene to adjust their strategies. Trios may re-form at this time.

After four quarters, you may want to gather and discuss the challenges of working together by asking:

● **What was the hardest thing about working within your pyramid?**

● **What was hard about working with other pyramids?**

● **What strategies did you develop to overcome the obstacles you faced?**

● **How were your strategies like or unlike those that you use to communicate when you face other challenges in teamwork?**

Hose Hockey

Overview: Kids will shoot a stream of water at a lightweight ball to score goals. This is a great game for a super-hot summer day, since everyone will wind up soaking wet!

Supplies: You'll need masking tape, two garden hoses (at least one hundred feet in length) with sprayer attachments, a water faucet, a faucet coupler, a lightweight children's ball, and two blindfolds.

Preparation: Mark a goal with masking tape on each side of the playing field, and one hundred feet apart. Make sure each goal is an equal distance from the water source.

Time Involved: 10 to 30 minutes

Form two teams, and show them where the goals are. Explain that team members must hold and direct their hose so that the front player can shoot water to move the ball into the team's goal. The complication is that the water shooter will be blindfolded. The rest of the team must direct the shooter so that the team will be successful.

To begin, place the ball in the center of the playing field and turn on the water. Each time a goal is scored, place the ball back in the center of the field and have the next person in line become the new water shooter.

Gummy Pass

Overview: Kids will work together in a race to bag a team of sticky characters.

Supplies: You'll need gummy bears, gummy worms, or other gummy candies, small plastic bags, toothpicks, tape, and a rectangular table for every two teams.

Preparation: Fill one plastic bag with five gummy candies for each team. Tape two filled plastic bags to the short end of each table, and tape two empty plastic bags to the other end of each table (see diagram).

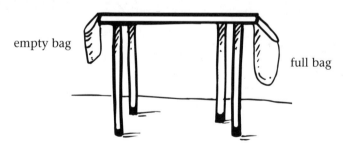

empty bag

full bag

Time Involved: 5 minutes

Divide kids into teams of five, and give each person a toothpick. Have members of each team line up evenly spaced down the long side of one of the tables. The person at the end next to the filled bag is the only person on each team who can use his or her hands. The rest of the kids must place their toothpicks in their mouths and kneel with their hands behind their backs.

On your command to begin, the person on each team who can use his or her hands must spear a gummy character with the toothpick and pass it along the table to the next person on the team. Because they can't use their hands, team members will need to use the table to pass the gummy characters. The second person will spear the gummy character, and the first person will remove his or her toothpick. The second person will pass to the third person in the same way. The first person may spear the second gummy character as soon as the second person has taken possession of the first gummy character.

The last person in line must remove his or her toothpick using the edge of the table and make sure the candy lands in the empty plastic bag. If the candy misses the bag, the first person must retrieve it after all the rest of the candy has been passed and pass it down the line a second time. The winning team is this first to have all five candies in the second plastic bag. Continue the game until all the teams have completed the task!

Share and Snap

Overview: Kids will share a stick of bubble gum and "pop" their way to victory.

Supplies: You'll need one stick of sugarless bubble gum for each team.

Preparation: None is needed.

Time Involved: 5 minutes

Form equal-sized teams of no more than six people. Have members of each team stand in a circle. Give one person on each team a stick of bubble gum. On your cue, the team member will unwrap the gum, pull off a piece, and pass the stick on. The first person must chew the piece of gum and snap it loudly enough that the next person can hear it. The second person may not snap his or her gum until he or she hears the first person's snap. When play has gone around the circle and the first person hears the last person snap, he or she must yell "Snap!" and quickly sit down, followed by each of the other team members in order. The first team to be seated wins.

Conclude the game with a short discussion by asking:

● **What was this experience like for the first person in line? The last person? Those in the middle?**

● **What problems did you encounter in the process of playing the game?**

● **How is this experience like your life when you feel short of time? What problems do you encounter?**

● **How does this experience remind you to handle time pressures more effectively?**

Bubble Sculptures

Overview: Kids will use bubble gum to form artistic sculptures.

Supplies: You'll need a pack of bubble gum and a wax paper square for each team, and small prizes (optional).

Preparation: None is needed.

Time Involved: 10 to 15 minutes

Have kids form equal-sized teams. Give each team a pack of bubble gum and a wax paper square. Provide a predetermined amount of time for teams to secretly plan a sculpture to be constructed using bubble gum. Allow teams five minutes to carry out their plans.

When time is up, have teams guess what each sculpture depicts. Award prizes to each

Variation

Assign each group a Bible character or an animal to sculpt.

team in categories such as: "Most Easily Recognized," "Most Creative," "Looks Least Like Bubble Gum," or "Best-Blown."

Beach-Towel Volleyball

Overview: Kids will play in pairs to score points in a volley-ball game played with water balloons and beach towels.

Supplies: You'll need balloons and a beach towel for every two players and a volleyball net.

Preparation: Fill balloons with water.

Time Involved: 20 minutes

Divide the group into two teams, and have members of each team form pairs. Give each pair a beach towel. Place one team on each side of the net. Have teams choose a number between one and ten to determine which side will go first.

Begin by having the first pair launch a water balloon with its beach towel. Award a point each time the team can successfully volley a water balloon between pairs (up to three times). If the water balloon hits the ground during an attempted volley, resume play by having the other team launch a new water balloon. On or before the third volley, the team must pass the water balloon to the other side of the net. If the team receives the water balloon, they may begin volleying for points. Award one point to the op-posing team whenever the water balloon hits the ground.

Have teams continue the round until one team accumulates fifteen points.

Viper

Overview: Kids will work as a single team to maneuver together over a challenging obstacle course.

Supplies: You'll need objects to create an obstacle course such as tires, chairs, Hula Hoops, boxes, masking tape, or natural obstacles.

Preparation: Set up a series of obstacles that will prove challenging to your group and determine the order in which your "viper" will proceed.

Time Involved: 10 to 15 minutes

Have kids form a viper by sitting on the ground, one behind the other, with their legs extended out beside the people in front of them. Instruct kids to put their hands on the shoulders of the people in front of them.

> # Variation
> This game can also be played as a relay by setting up two or more identical courses.

The viper will move by scooting along the ground and swaying back and forth. You may wish to have your group coordinate their efforts by singing this tongue-twisting song to the tune of "Row, Row, Row Your Boat":

Ssss, Ssss, Ssss, we hiss
Through the jungle mist—
Slithering, sliding, slimy snake
Slinks slowly south of thisss...

The members of the group must stay connected as they negotiate the obstacle course. The course will be most fun if you set your obstacles close enough so the "tail" is still maneuvering around one obstacle while the "head" has moved onto the next.

210

Stuff It

Overview: Kids will affirm each other as they race to stuff balloons in each other's shirts.

Supplies: You'll need two XXXL sweatshirts, two plastic trash bags, and about sixty balloons.

Preparation: None is needed.

Time Involved: 10 minutes

Hand out the balloons. Ask kids to blow them up and tie them off. As they do, have them think about things that are good, honorable, and praiseworthy in themselves. After kids blow up all the balloons, have them stuff an equal number into each trash bag.

Form two groups, one of all males and the other of all females. Have members of each group stand in a circle, and say: **When we are in the habit of looking for things that are good, honorable, and praiseworthy in ourselves, we tend to be able to see those things in others as well. In this game, you will need to come up with good things about others quickly, so I hope you primed your minds as you blew up the balloons!**

Variation

This game can also be played as a whole-group race against the clock instead of as a relay. The key is just to make sure the game moves quickly.

Place a bag of balloons in the center of each circle, and have one person in each circle put on one of the sweatshirts. The other members of each team will each race to the bag, grab a balloon, and stuff it inside the sweatshirt as they shout out an affirmation that applies to the team member who is wearing the sweatshirt. They must continue until all the balloons have been stuffed into the shirt. When they're done, the person wearing the sweatshirt is to remove it and dump the balloons. The next person in the circle should put the sweatshirt on, and the team repeats the process. (Forget the bag at this point...the balloons will be everywhere!)

When all members of a team have been affirmed, have them shout in unison:

Two, four, six, eight—
In Christ, we can appreciate!
Go team!

Love Loop

Overview: Team members will pass around a ring as a reminder of the need to share God's love in spite of obstacles.

Supplies: You'll need one key ring loop.

Preparation: None is needed.

Time Involved: 5 to 10 minutes

Have members of the group stand in a circle and hold hands.

Say: **Dearly beloved, we are gathered together here with our hands clasped to remind us of the high calling God has given us to pass on his love. As a symbol of that love, we have a shared ring. Our goal is to pass that love without letting go of the fellowship that binds us together (in other words, each others' hands!)**

Place the ring on your ring finger with great fanfare, and continue: **Since it is such a high calling, we must pass this ring from ring finger to ring finger without letting go of anyone's hands.**

After the ring has been successfully passed around the circle, discuss how it really feels to try to pass God's love to someone.

212

Human Conveyor Belt

Overview: Kids will work together to form a human conveyor belt that "goes the distance."

Supplies: None are needed.

Preparation: Designate and mark a starting line and a finish line. The distance between the two should be about three times the length of the single file line your group will form.

Time Involved: 10 minutes

Have kids get into a line on their hands and knees, shoulder to shoulder. Have the first person in line lay on his or her stomach across the backs of the other kids. The object is for the person to slither along the kids' backs, keeping his or her body as flat as possible. As each person moves in turn along kids' backs, he or she may not use elbows, hands, or knees. The only method allowed to move oneself along is stretching and pulling with the arms. The rest of the kids may help the person along by arching their backs and pushing the person forward. This activity takes a lot of coordinated effort and teamwork!

When the first person gets to the end of the line, he or she is to join the line. As soon as the first person's feet have cleared the second person's back, the second person should also begin slithering along kids' backs. Kids must continue to move in this way until the whole group reaches the finish line.

When individual people begin crossing the finish line, they are to stand and cheer the rest on. By the time the second to the last person gets to the finish line, there should be only one remaining person to climb over.

Cover Me!

Overview: Kids will protect each other from attack in this summer game.

Supplies: You'll need a high-powered water gun, a 9x12-inch sheet of black construction paper for each person, masking tape, and markers.

Preparation: Fill the water gun with water.

Time Involved: 10 to 15 minutes

Give each person a sheet of construction paper and a few pieces of masking tape. Have each one draw a round target on the paper and attach it to his or her chest. Then have kids form a circle, and choose one player to be "It." Give "It" the loaded water gun, and have that person stand in the middle of the circle.

Instruct "It" to close his or her eyes, and have the circle begin moving clockwise in a sidestep fashion. On the count of twenty, the circle should freeze while "It" immediately opens his or her eyes and begins shooting at someone's target.

Variation

You may wish to introduce multiple water guns and more players in the middle of the circle to make this game very fast-paced! In this case, the first person tagged by the water comes into the circle with a shout and the counting begins again.

No matter who the water is aimed at, any person is allowed to intercept it with any part of his or her body. If any person's target is tagged by a stream of water, he or she becomes "It." However, if the water hits any area other than a person's target, "It" remains "It" and must try again. When a new person becomes "It," have the circle repeat the earlier process. Have kids continue the game until the tape no longer holds their targets on.

Mix 'n' Match

Overview: Kids will get to know each other better as they try to find a girl or boy who matches the leader's commands. This is a wonderful game for mixing a large group of kids or for organizing guy-girl pairs for other games.

Supplies: None are needed.

Preparation: None is needed.

Time Involved: 20 minutes

Begin by dividing those present into two groups—guys and girls. Then give the following instructions: **In a moment, I will call out a command. I will instruct the guys to each find a girl partner who matches the command. Likewise, girls might be asked to find guy partners who match the command. For example, if I say, "Guys, find a girl who has red socks," the guys must look for girl partners with red socks. Once a guy has found a girl partner who matches the command, they are to remain together for the duration of this game. I will continue calling out commands until everyone has a partner.**

Begin calling out commands such as: "Girls, find a guy with chin whiskers"; "Guys, find a girl whose middle name is Mary"; "Girls, find a guy who has been to Hawaii"; and "Guys, find a girl who has a pet cat." Make up other commands that will get the kids talking as well as mixing.

Continue until each person has a partner and then give the couples a choice of completing one of two team-building exercises:

● Partners must create a brief youth group song; or

● Partners must work to create an original youth group slogan.

Chapel of Cards

Overview: Kids will work together in teams to construct a chapel of playing cards.

Supplies: You'll need a deck of cards for each team, toothpicks, and tape.

Preparation: None is needed.

Time Involved: 20 to 30 minutes

Divide kids into teams of four or five players. Give each team a deck of playing cards, two toothpicks, and a piece of tape. Then say: **Some of you have probably tried to make a house out of cards before. But today we'll be making a chapel out of cards. Each team has fifteen minutes to construct its own chapel, using only the playing cards. The completed chapel must also have a cross on top—which can be fashioned out of the two toothpicks and tape.**

After your command to begin, allow fifteen minutes for each team to finish its project. If you choose, provide prizes for the tallest chapel, the fanciest chapel, the neatest chapel, the most creative chapel, and so on. You might consider using this game to lead into a discussion about the church, spiritual gifts, or working together within the Christian community.

Feet Ball

Overview: Kids will have to work together to pass a ball around the circle.

Supplies: You'll need a lightweight ball.

Preparation: None is needed.

Time Involved: 10 to 15 minutes

Invite kids to take off their shoes and sit in a circle on the floor with their feet touching in the middle. Place the ball inside the circle, and ask kids to pass the ball around the circle using only their feet (this is more difficult than it sounds).

Once kids have mastered sending the ball around the circle, ask them to reverse the ball's direction, skip the ball back and forth, or work it around the circle in other creative ways.

Once they have mastered the skill, have kids play other games such as Hot Potato.

Remember This?

Overview: Kids will create specific actions and words based on the memory of a specific group event. This game will help your kids remember positive and funny events in their shared past.

Supplies: You'll need a chair for each person.

Preparation: Arrange the chairs in a circle.

Time Involved: 15 to 30 minutes

Variation

After the first person has shared an action, have the next person repeat it prior to presenting his or hers. The third person is then to repeat both actions before presenting one. Continue this process until the last person in the circle has to remember all the actions before presenting one.

Ask kids to sit in the circle of chairs and each silently think of a significant group memory such as a camp or a mission trip (it's OK if several kids choose the same event). Next, ask each person to come up with both a word and a physical movement or motion that recalls a specific memory from the event. For example, if Kristie chose the memory of a winter-camping experience, she might throw her arms up over her head in a dive movement, as if she were going down a toboggan run on her stomach, and say "Swoosh!"

After everyone has chosen a particular word and movement, go around the circle and have each person provide a demonstration. Have the other kids try to guess what each action represents. Ask each person to explain his or her memory. (This will give kids a chance to share memories and laugh together.)

Blanket Ball

Overview: Kids will experience teamwork with every play in this game.

Supplies: You'll need a volleyball net, beach balls, and one blanket for each team.

Preparation: Set up the volleyball net.

Time Involved: 20 to 45 minutes

Form teams of six to ten students, and give each team a blanket. The object is for one team to use its blanket like a bat and hit the beach ball over the net while the other team tries to return the hit using its blanket.

Scoring can be done either by counting how many consecutive times the ball goes over the net without falling to the floor (cooperative) or teams may score points in the standard volleyball point system (competitive).

Basket-Disc-Ball

Overview: Kids will work together in this hybrid of basketball and flying discs.

Supplies: You'll need a flying disc and basketball hoops.

Preparation: None is needed.

Time Involved: 20 to 60 minutes

This variation of basketball encourages a complete team effort. Form teams of four to eight, and explain that the goal is to throw the flying disc through a hoop as in basketball. The difference is that the disc must be thrown to each team member before a shot is attempted. A person may not move after he or she has caught the disc. If a team recovers a rebound after a missed shot, members must again pass the disc through the entire team before another shot is attempted. **This is to be played as a non-contact sport.**

Nose-Nudging Fruit Relay

Overview: Kids will nudge fruit across a swimming pool with their noses.

Supplies: You'll need apples or oranges (one piece of fruit for every four kids) and a stopwatch (optional).

Preparation: None is needed.

Time Involved: 10 minutes

Form groups of four, and give each group a piece of fruit. Have members of each group stand in a single file line at one end of the shallow end of a swimming pool. The object of this game is for the members of each group to nudge their piece of fruit with their noses from one side of the pool to the other. The piece of fruit must be pushed only with a person's nose and may not be pushed with a person's mouth or hand. Each group member must give the piece of fruit one nudge and then move to the back of the line while the next team member gives the fruit a nudge, and so on. If the shallow end of the pool or lake area is not large enough to accommodate the whole group at once, consider using a stopwatch to time each team.

Shh!

Overview: Kids will work in a growing team and try to make the others laugh.

Supplies: None are needed.

Preparation: None is needed.

Time Involved: 10 to 20 minutes

This game is sure to bring laughter to your group. Have kids sit in a circle, and ask one volunteer to stand in the middle. This person will point to another person in the circle. The person he or she points to must say "Shh!" and then stay straight-faced and quiet. The person in the middle should use funny gestures and expressions in an attempt to break the other person's silence. When the quiet person giggles or laughs, he or she must also move into the middle and choose another person. Kids in the middle can work together to get the next person to laugh. Play continues until everyone has had a chance to be in the middle.

Twisted Soccer

Overview: Kids will throw competition "out the window" with this soccer variation.

Supplies: You'll need a soccer ball and soccer goals.

Preparation: None is needed.

Time Involved: 15 to 30 minutes

Split your group into two even teams of five to ten people each. Explain to kids that you'll be playing a game of soccer with several significant changes. First, there will be no designated goalies; second, whenever a goal is scored the team it was scored against gets the point; and finally, whoever scores a goal switches to the team with the most points. At the end of your allotted time for this twisted soccer game, ask if your group can tell who really won.

I Can't Hear You!

Overview: Kids will sing their answers to questions.

Supplies: None are needed.

Preparation: None is needed.

Time Involved: 30 to 60 minutes

Divide the group into two teams. Ask the first team to come up with a silly interview question to ask someone on the second team–the sillier the question, the better!

The second team will have one minute to come up with an answer based on lyrics from a familiar song or commercial jingle. Once the second team decides on its answer, members must choose one person to sing the lyrics to the first team. For example, the first team might ask, "What is your favorite thing to eat for breakfast" A member of the second team might respond, "Great green gobs of greasy grimy gopher guts!" or "Break me off a piece of that Kit Kat bar!"

If no one on the first team has heard the lyrics or if the first team doesn't think the second team put enough "feeling" into the response, the first team can reject the response and ask for another one by yelling, "I can't hear you!" The second team will then be allowed another minute to come up with a new song lyric to answer the same question. If the team can't respond within one minute, they will lose a turn.

After the first round, have teams switch roles so the second team must come up with a question for the first team. Have the teams continue taking turns until everyone on each team has had a chance to sing. Here are some other silly interview questions teams might try:

221

- If you could choose anything in the world to do and get paid for it, what would it be?
- If (a famous person) asked you out on a date, what would you say?
- How would you describe your worst enemy?
- What will you wear on your wedding day?

Add-a-Word

Overview: Kids will work together to make silly sentences.

Supplies: You'll need a watch with a second hand, and index cards and a marker (or the letter tiles from a Scrabble game).

Preparation: If you don't have Scrabble pieces, make your own letters of the alphabet by writing one letter on each index card. Make at least two copies of each letter and at least five copies of more common letters such as A, E, R, S, T, and N.

Time Involved: 20 to 30 minutes

Form groups of four to six players. Turn the letters over so the group selecting them won't know what they are.

Have one group begin. Allow each of its members to select a letter but not show it to the rest of the group. Next, have group members line up. Call out any subject—music, television, books, places, animals, famous people, and so on. Allow the group one minute to come up with a complete sentence pertaining to that subject. (The sentence must be somewhat grammatically correct.) Each group member is to contribute to the sentence by coming up with a word that begins with the letter he or she is holding. Also, the words have to be in the same order as the group members are standing in.

If the group cannot come up with a sentence within a minute or if the sentence doesn't make sense, that group loses its turn. Make sure you allow enough time for each group to come up with a sentence. After several rounds, remix the pile of letters and continue play. Encourage creativity, and be sure kids don't use foul language.

Common Denominators

Overview: Kids will form teams by discovering interests or traits they have in common.

Supplies: You'll need paper, pens, and pencils.

Preparation: None is needed.

Time Involved: 10 to 60 minutes

Give each person a piece of paper, a pen, and three minutes to write down as many facts about himself or herself as possible, such as "I have one sister," "I play on a hockey team," "I like mystery novels," or "I went to the beach last summer." These facts can be well-known or not so well-known and can include interests, hobbies, family information, and so on. Kids should list only one fact at a time, such as, "I have red hair" instead of "I have short, red hair."

Exchange pencils for pens, and have kids mingle to compare their lists with others' lists. The object is to search for traits kids have in common. If two kids have a characteristic in common, they should both circle the characteristic on their lists and then team up together. Since the team that has the most interests in common is the winner, encourage kids to keep circulating to try to find other people or teams with whom they have more than one trait in common.

If some kids can't find teams, ask the group questions such as, "Whose parents own a blue car?" If an unmatched person raises his or her hand, have that person join the team of another person who raised a hand.

Getting to Know You

Overview: Kids will form pairs and interview each other to find out as much about their habits and preferences as possible.

Supplies: You'll need the "Getting to Know You 1" handout (p. 224); the "Getting to Know You 2" handout (p. 225); pencils; and tokens such as marbles, pennies, nails, or other similar items.

Preparation: Make a photocopy of "Getting to Know You 1" handout and the "Getting to Know You 2" handout for every person in your group.

Time Involved: 15 to 30 minutes

Have kids form pairs. Explain that partners are to take five minutes each to interview one another about food preferences. (To develop kids' listening skills, tell them that taking notes is not allowed.)

After ten minutes, ask the partners to stand or sit some distance away from each other. Give everyone a copy of the "Getting to Know You 1" handout and a pencil, and provide five minutes to fill in the blanks.

Next have kids take turns guessing how their partners answered the first question. Give a token to each person that provides a correct answer. The winning team is the one with the most tokens.

If there's a tie, tell partners to take five minutes each and interview one another about sports preferences. After ten minutes, distribute a copy of the "Getting to Know You 2" handout and give each student a few minutes to fill in his or her answers. As before, ask partners to guess how their teammates responded. Continue until time is up.

Getting to Know You ①

1. My favorite kind of **cheese** is_____.

2. The **fast-food** chain I like most is _____.

3. The last thing I want to hear that we're having for **dinner** is _____.

4. If I had a vegetable garden and could **grow** only one thing, it would be _____.

5. Given a choice between a salty snack or a sweet **dessert,** I prefer _____.

6. Almost every time I go to the **movies,** I order _____.

7. I like my **marshmallows** toasted _____.

8. For my birthday, I usually want this kind of **cake–** _____.

9. The one item I always pass up at a **salad bar** is _____.

10. Given a **choice** between plain or peanut candy, I usually pick _____.

Getting to know You ②

1. My favorite **athlete** is _____.

2. The **Olympic** event I like most is _____.

3. The worst sports **injury** I ever received was

_____.

4. If I could be a **professional** athlete, I would be a _____.

5. Given a choice between playing **individual** or team sports, I prefer _____.

6. If I had to play on a **softball** team, I'd like to play this position _____.

7. I think this **sport** requires the most intelligence–

_____.

8. If I had to take up **dancing** or table tennis, I would prefer _____.

9. The one form of **exercise** I can't stand is

_____.

10. Given a **choice** between baseball or football, I prefer to watch _____.

Whodunit?

Overview: Kids will pantomime historical events while team-mates try to identify the central characters.

Supplies: You'll need paper, a pen, and a container to hold pieces of paper.

Preparation: Tear a piece of paper into twelve small pieces and then write the name of a famous person such as Abraham Lincoln, Neil Armstrong, or Elvis Presley on each piece. Underneath the name, write one thing the person did or for which he or she is known. Fold up the pieces of paper, and put them into a container.

Time Involved: 10 to 60 minutes

Divide the group into two teams of roughly equal size, and have teams go to opposite ends of the activity area. Divide each team into two halves: Actors and Guessers. Allow someone from each group of Actors to draw a piece of paper and share it with the rest of the Actors on his or her team. Then tell the acting groups to pantomime the events or actions that made their people famous. None of the Actors are allowed to speak or use props. Meanwhile, the Guessers on their respective teams are to try to identify the characters the Actors are trying to depict. The team that guesses correctly and in the shortest amount of time is the winner. Continue the game as time allows, letting the groups take turns being Actors and Guessers.

Eureka!

Overview: Kids will "search" for their partners using only their senses of hearing and touch.

Supplies: You'll need several containers such as cans, jars, boxes, or baskets; noise-making objects such as buttons, utensils, nails, pebbles, or sand; blindfolds, index cards, and pens.

Preparation: Make noisemakers by filling cans, jars, boxes, or baskets with buttons, utensils, nails, pebbles, or sand. No two noisemakers should be alike; that is, each container should consist of and contain different material. Make half as many noisemakers as there are kids. Write a description of each noise-maker on an index card. Gather half as many blindfolds as there are kids.

Time Involved: 10 to 60 minutes

Divide kids into two equal groups, and tell them that speaking during this game is not allowed. Give each person in one group an index card that describes a noise-maker to be retrieved and a blindfold. Ask him or her to memorize that description and then put on a blindfold. Give each person in the other group a noisemaker, and ask him or her to select a spot in the playing area where he or she will stand for the rest of the game. On your command to begin, kids should start shaking their noisemakers while the members of the blindfolded group try to "find" the noisemakers described on their index cards.

Variation

You can modify this game to form groups or teams instead of pairs by having several people find one noisemaker.

Blindfolded participants are to yell "Eureka!" whenever they think they have found the right noisemakers. When a player calls out "Eureka!" everyone must freeze until you determine whether the noisemaker matches the description on the card. If so, remove the person's blindfold and have that person stand with his or her partner. Signal for the game to resume, and continue to play until everyone has found his or her noise-making partner.

Leader TIP

Allow each person either one guess based on his or her sense of hearing or two guesses based on hearing and on touch.

Shanghai Shuffle

Overview: Kids will participate in a relay race using an object and a technique that will slow them down considerably.

Supplies: You'll need construction paper, scissors, masking tape, two identical objects such as balls, pillows, or rolls of toilet paper, and two boxes or baskets (optional, if you're playing outside).

Preparation: Cut at least one strip of construction paper for each student in your class, and tape these "tokens" to the wall at one end of the room or hallway. (If you play this game outside, place the tokens in two boxes or baskets at one end of the playing area.) Use tape to mark a starting line opposite of the tokens.

Time Involved: 10 to 30 minutes

Divide kids into two teams of equal size, and have members of each team line up single file for a relay race. Give the first person on each team one of the objects. Explain that each person is to place the object between his or her knees, shuffle to the end of the playing field, grab a token, and then shuffle back to the starting line with the object still between his or her knees. If the person accidentally drops the object, he or she must stop and remain at that location until the end of the relay. The next person in line is to run out, pick up the object, place it between his or her knees, and continue the race. Each person who reaches the wall will receive a token. When a person gets back to the starting line, he or she is to drop the object on the ground in front of the next person.

After a predetermined time limit, call for an end to the relay. Using masking tape, have each team build a chain with its paper tokens. The team with the longest chain wins.

Truth Matchup

Overview: Kids will learn new and interesting truths about each other.

Supplies: You'll need markers and paper.

Preparation: None is needed.

Time Involved: 20 minutes

Choose seven kids out of the group, and give each one a piece of paper and a marker. Have each of the seven secretly write an interesting fact about himself or herself. An example might be, "I ate cat food when I was little." Encourage the kids to make their truths interesting and unique to them. You should have seven papers with one truth on each paper when kids have completed this part. Mix the papers up, and redistribute each one to one of the seven kids.

Have the seven kids stand in front of the group and read the truths on their sheets one at a time. After each truth has been read, instruct the rest of the group to try to guess which truth belongs with which person. It might be helpful to reread the truths before the groups vote.

Play another round by choosing seven different kids, until everyone has had a turn.

"Far Side" Counterpart

Overview: Kids will meet and interact with new people in a fun way.

Supplies: You'll need "Far Side" cartoons with captions underneath and scissors.

Preparation: Cut apart the cartoons and their captions.

Time Involved: 15 minutes

Give each person in your group either a cartoon or a caption. The object is for each person to find the other half of his or her cartoon. This is a great way to get people into pairs for another activity or to introduce new people to one another.

Mr. Potato Head

Overview: Kids will creatively make their own potato people. This is a fun, non-threatening way to introduce kids to the idea of working together.

Supplies: You'll need potatoes, toothpicks, vegetables, a knife, and prizes (optional).

Preparation: Cut the vegetables into small pieces.

Time Involved: 30 minutes

Break the group into teams of four kids, and give each team a potato, toothpicks, and vegetable pieces. The object is for each team to make the funniest, most creative potato person possible. If you desire, you can turn this into a competition between the teams and give out prizes.

Movements

Overview: Kids will learn more about each other by moving to various locations throughout the activity area. This team builder is great because you can play it anywhere, and it's a great filler if you have extra time between activities.

Supplies: None are needed.

Preparation: Choose a category such as birthplaces, and designate a location in your activity area for Californians to stand in, one for New Yorkers to stand in, one for Texans to stand in, and so on.

Time Involved: 15 minutes

Begin by telling people to stand in the designated locations of the state in which they were born. Then have them see if they can put all the states in proper geographical order. For example, a person born in Oregon should stand right above a person born in Northern California, and so on.

> # Leader TIP
>
> If you have kids who were born in other countries, have the kids stand in the geographical order of the world.

After this portion of the activity, have kids stand in locations representing places they would like to live someday or places they would like to travel to.

There are many variations to this team builder. Once you get the hang of it, try to make up some of your own.

Change Three

Overview: Kids will become more aware of characteristics of other members of the group.

Supplies: None are needed.

Preparation: None is needed.

Time Involved: 15 minutes

Divide the group into pairs. Have partners face one another and pay close attention to the details of each other's hair, clothing, accessories, and so on. Then have partners turn their backs on each other and change two things about their appearances. (This might include such things as taking an earring out, taking a belt off, and so on.)

When partners have made their changes, have them turn around and guess which two things are different. As an additional challenge, you might consider trying this activity again with the same pairs.

Windshield-Wash Relay

Overview: Kids will work together to compete in a relay while doing a service project.

Supplies: You'll need one roll of paper towels and one bottle of window cleaner for each team, slips of paper, and a pen.

Preparation: On each slip of paper, write a note that says "Your windshield has been cleaned courtesy of your church youth group." You'll need to prepare enough of these to put one on the windshield of each vehicle parked in the church parking lot during the time you choose for this activity.

Time Involved: 30 to 45 minutes.

Divide the group into teams of two to three. Provide each team with a bottle of window cleaner, a roll of paper towels, and several slips of paper with the note written on them. Explain that on your command to begin, each team is to go out into the church parking lot and clean as many car windshields as it can. (None of the teams are to return until all the windshields have been cleaned.) When a team is finished cleaning a windshield, have one of the kids place a note under one of the vehicle's windshield wipers.

> **Leader TIP**
>
> For safety purposes, be sure to station an adult at all parking lot entrances to watch for entering traffic.

The team that cleans the most windshields wins the relay.

Random Choices

Overview: Kids will make humorous choices and then defend them.

Supplies: None are needed.

Preparation: None is needed.

Time Involved: 15 minutes

Ask all the kids to come to the center of the room. Tell them that you're going to provide two choices. If a person chooses the first choice, he or she is to move to the left side of the room. If a person chooses the second one, he or she is to move to the right side of the room. Here are some examples of choices:

● Would you rather wear a sweater in the pool or a bathing suit to school?

● Would you rather smash your finger in a car door or have your best friend see you pick your nose?

● Would you rather have an ugly dog or a beautiful, bad-tempered cat?

● Would you rather drive across the country with a chronic liar or a panophobe (one who is fearful of everything)?

● Would you rather have bad breath or red bumps all over your body?

● Would you rather be on a tiny ledge on the highest building carrying a bowling ball or have your car break down in the desert?

After everyone has made a choice, have kids gather with the others who made the same choice and discuss why they made the choice they did. Continue this activity for several rounds.

Likenesses

Overview: Kids will enjoy learning about one another.

Supplies: You'll need paper and pens.

Preparation: None is needed.

Time Involved: 30 minutes

Break the kids into groups of five. Have the members of each group try to discover how many things they have in common and then record them on a piece of paper. An example might be, "We all use Crest toothpaste."

In order for a characteristic to be recorded, it must be true of every person in that group. After ten minutes, the group with the most common characteristics wins. Have someone from each group read their list aloud.

Newspaper Fashion-Show

Overview: Kids will work together to create a fashionable outfit.

Supplies: You'll need newspapers, tape, pens, and paper.

Preparation: None is needed.

Time Involved: 1 hour

Break kids into groups of eight. Give each group a stack of newspaper, tape, pens, and paper, and have the group design an outfit for one of their teammates using the supplies provided. Instruct each group to write a commentary describing the outfit after they've designed it. Explain that the more adjectives they use in their commentaries, the funnier they will be. For example a group might say, "Today our suave maiden follows the waxing and waning of style with a draped and elegantly placed scarf."

Instruct each group to choose one person to be the model and one to be the commentator. When groups have finished their designs and commentaries, have the models line up. Instruct the models to walk, one at a time, in front of the group while their commentators describe their outfits. Encourage the "audience" to cheer and shout for each model.

Spoons With Questions

Overview: Kids will learn more about each other as they play the popular game Spoons.

Supplies: You'll need several decks of cards, spoons, tables, and chairs.

Preparation: None is needed.

Time Involved: 10 minutes

Create groups of eight people each. Have each group sit at a different table and play the game of Spoons. Have one person in each group act as the dealer. Have the dealer give every person four cards. In the middle of each table, place one fewer spoons than the number of kids in a group.

Variation

Put the spoons under the table within equal reach of all players. This adds a lot of excitement to the game.

The object of the game is to form a "four of a kind." To start the game, the dealer is to pick up one card from the stack of remaining cards and discard one by handing it to the person on his or her left. Each person discards a card by passing the discard to the next player on the left. The dealer continues to pick up and discard cards until someone gets four of a kind.

When a person has a four of a kind, he or she must quickly pick up a spoon while all the other players scramble to do the same. The player who is left without a spoon loses the round.

Leader TIP

No player is allowed to have more than five cards in his or her hand at a time.

The person who wins each round may ask the person who loses a question of his or her choice. (Remind kids to make sure the questions are clean!) Encourage kids to come up with creative questions.

Red and Black

Overview: Kids will play a game and learn about their natural inclinations to either compete or cooperate.

Supplies: You'll need two dry-erase boards and red and black dry-erase markers or two easels with paper and red and black markers and the following chart.

Red and Black		
Voting	Team A	Team B
Both Black	+1	+1
Team A Black Team B Red	-3	+1
Team A Red Team B Black	+1	-3
Both Red	-1	-1

Preparation: Make one copy of the chart for each team.

Time Involved: 45 minutes

This game is played with two teams, each in a separate room with its own writing surface, markers, and chart. Each team must work by itself and try to anticipate what the other team will do. The entire game centers around voting, and points are based on how well a team anticipates what the other team will do.

Label one group Team A and the other group Team B. Once each team is in its own room, have members decide if they want to vote red or black, both by referring to the chart and by trying to anticipate what the other team will do. Once both teams have come up with their decisions, have them write their decisions on their board, and

Leader TIP

This game will reveal kids' instinct for survival and competition as well as how important it is to cooperate. There's also a lot of strategy involved in this game. It's a great time to see where leaders emerge and to talk about different styles of leadership.

bring kids back together to reveal the results for everyone to see.

After the results have been revealed, continue the game by having both teams return to their rooms and vote again. Continue this process for seven rounds.

After you have completed this activity, take advantage of the opportunity to discuss the following questions:

- **Who emerged as the leader of your team?**
- **How did this person's leadership help or hinder the team process?**
- **How did you make decisions as a team?**
- **How did you communicate as a team?**
- **What did you learn about cooperation and competition?**

Count to Ten

Overview: Kids will need to cooperate in order to count to ten.

Supplies: None are needed.

Preparation: None is needed.

Time Involved: 15 minutes

The goal is for the group to count to ten aloud together while following certain rules. On your command, have the group count to ten. Explain that if two or more people speak at the same time or say the same number, the group must start over. The object is to have someone begin by saying "one," another person continue by saying "two," and so on. (Don't let kids make any plans among themselves before they begin.) In order to succeed, kids must concentrate and work together.

Square Off

Overview: Blindfolded kids will make a square and then overlap it with another group's square.

Supplies: You'll need rope, scissors, and blindfolds.

Preparation: Cut the rope into forty-foot sections, and tie the ends of each rope piece together.

Time Involved: 45 minutes

Give each group of four a rope and four blindfolds. Instruct kids in each group to stand shoulder to shoulder in a tight circle and place the rope at their feet. Then instruct kids to put their blindfolds on. Once the blindfolds are secure, have each group pick up its rope and back up to make a square. Once kids are in position, have them move as they try to overlap their square with the square of the group next to them.

After the activity, gather everyone together and lead a short discussion by asking:

● **What did you do as a group that helped you succeed?**

● **Did one person stand out as a leader? Explain.**

● **What's one thing you learned about yourself either in the context of leadership or in the context of working as a team member?**

Ant March

Overview: Kids will need to work together in order to solve a human puzzle.

Supplies: You'll need nine pieces of paper or wood squares.

Preparation: Place four pieces of paper (or wood) in a row on the ground, and place the other four in a row across from them. The distance between the two rows should be equal to the width of the paper. Place one additional piece between the two rows (see diagram).

Ant March

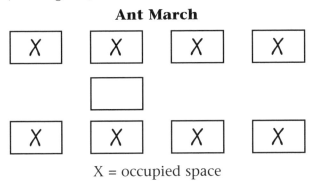

X = occupied space

Time Involved: 45 minutes

Begin by having eight kids stand on each of the pieces of paper. The two rows of kids should be facing each other. The object is for the eight kids to strategically move themselves so they each end up on the opposite side occupying one space. Basically the two groups of kids (four on each side) must trade places.

The rules of the game are as follows: A person can only move forward into an open space. Once a person moves forward, he or she can't move backward. A person may only move around another person when he or she is facing that person and there's an open space for the first person to move into. The game starts with someone stepping into the open space and continues until kids either can't move any more or they have successfully solved the challenge.

This game is very mentally challenging, and kids will get frustrated and want to give up. Continue to encourage them to keep trying.

Once the brain teaser has been solved, you may wish to discuss teamwork with kids by asking:

● **What things helped you to work together as a team?**

● **What hindered you from working together as a team?**

● **If you got frustrated, how did you act?**

- Did your frustration help or hinder you?
- Who emerged as a leader?
- How did his or her leadership help the group?
- Did you feel like giving up? What helped you to hang in there?
- How is this game like life?
- What did this game teach you about your role on a team and how to react to difficult situations?

Energy-Burning Games

The Gigantic

Book of Games
for Youth Ministry,

Volume 1

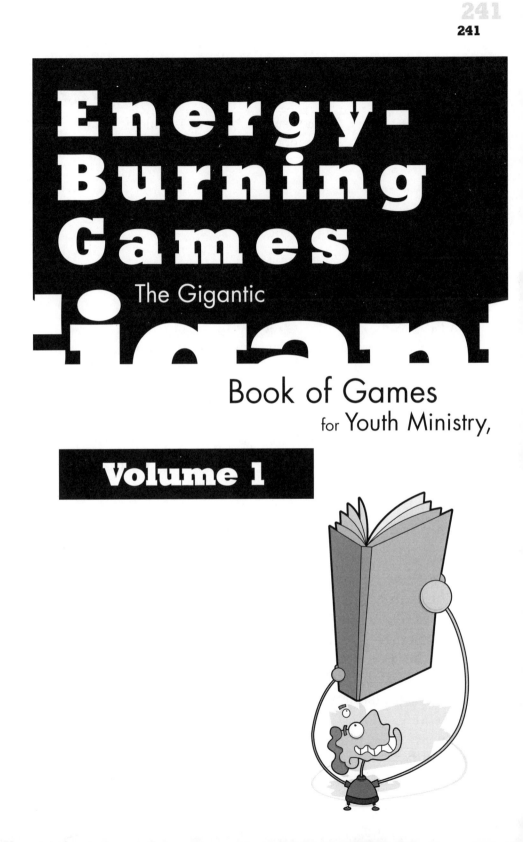

Back-to-Back Taggies

Overview: While locked back-to-back, kids will try to tag teammates positioned on opposite sides of a swimming pool. This activity is a fast-paced game combining strategy and strength.

Supplies: None are needed.

Preparation: None is needed.

Time Involved: 20 minutes

Divide the group into Team A and Team B. Select one Tagger from each team. Position the remaining kids in an alternating fashion at the shallow end of pool as illustrated in the following diagram.

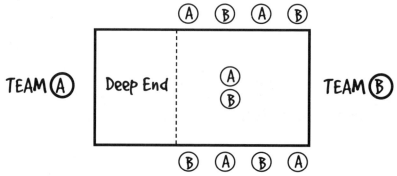

Instruct both Taggers to stand back-to-back, lock arms, and position themselves in the middle of the pool.

On the signal, the Taggers will push or pull against each other as they try to reach the hands of teammates seated on the sides of the pool. To tag someone, the Tagger can make use of his or her head, hands, knees, or feet.

Once tagged, a seated person jumps into the water and locks arms with his or her Tagger. Both now move to tag a teammate on the other side of the pool. Only the Tagger is allowed to make contact with seated teammates.

Tagging must be done while the two teams are still locked

back-to-back. Additional team members must each lock an arm with the last person tagged. This back and forth tagging continues until an entire team is connected in the pool.

As more members join the Tagger, the team's muscle-power increases. This makes it easier to push or pull the opposing team across the pool. The challenge is increased by the fact that kids have to move in the water.

Fluff and Fold

Overview: Kids will fold clothes, pack them into a suitcase, and unpack the suitcase in the fastest time possible.

Supplies: You'll need one suitcase and five different articles of clothing (a shirt, slacks, a sweater, socks, and so on) for each team.

Preparation: None is needed.

Time Involved: 5 to 10 minutes

Divide the group into teams of five. At one end of the room, have teams form single file lines, with teams standing an arm's length apart.

Across from each team at the opposite end of the room, place an empty, closed suitcase and five pieces of clothing. Scatter the clothes on the floor around the suitcase.

On the signal, the first person in each line is to rush to the opposite end of room, quickly fold each item, and place it into the suitcase. When the clothes are all in the suitcase, the suitcase is to be closed and secured. Then the person will race back to tag the next person in line. The starting person should then take his or her place at the end of the line.

The second person will then race to open the suitcase and unfold and scatter the clothes. Once this is done, he or she will run back and tag the next person in line. The relay continues by alternating the folding and packing with the unpacking, unfolding, and scattering.

Run the relay through twice so each person will have the opportunity both to pack and to unpack. Play should continue until everyone has rotated through twice and the first person is back at the front of the line. When this happens, the entire team should rush to the suitcase, each fold one item and place it into the suitcase, and return to the starting line.

The last person to place an item into the suitcase should close it and carry it back to the starting line. The first team to finish is the winner!

Greasy Slide

Overview: Kids will use water guns to shoot objects of different sizes across an oily dropcloth.

Supplies: You'll need a small bucket; paper towels; a large plastic dropcloth; vegetable oil; water guns; water; lightweight objects such as paper clips, pencils, foam plates, foam cups, foam bowls, plastic toys, and so on (avoid using soakable objects such as cardboard and paper products); and towels (optional).

Preparation: Spread a dropcloth over an open area and cover it with vegetable oil. Fill the water guns and the bucket with water.

Time Involved: 15 to 20 minutes

Begin by setting one of the small objects at one end of the dropcloth. Have kids use the water guns to shoot the object over the slick area as fast as possible. This game can be played individually or all together as a competition.

Next repeat the game using the larger objects, such as the foam plates, cups, and bowls. (See if the kids are skilled enough to keep these objects from turning upside down during play.)

Play the game once again using heavier objects such as plastic toys or blocks. As needed, allow the kids to refill their guns from the water bucket. To add speed and promote teamwork, allow several kids to target the same object.

For a really messy end to the game, let the kids take turns sliding themselves across the oily dropcloth. Be sure to have plenty of towels on hand for the cleanup!

Growing Pains

Overview: The next time you want to form teams to play an activity or a game, try this creative way. This activity helps avoid the situation in which some kids are always picked last.

Supplies: None are needed.

Preparation: None is needed.

Time Involved: 5 minutes

Begin by enlisting the tallest participants to serve as team captains. The object is for each captain to move quickly around the area gathering members for his or her team. Inform captains of the total number of players they are to pick for their teams. Have captains form teams based on height. Each captain should begin by tagging a person shorter than he or she is. The person who is tagged should grab the captain's waist from behind. Both team members are then to move together and select another teammate.

The next person tagged, however, must be taller than the first person tagged. Have each captain continue selection by alternating between tagging shorter and taller players until reaching the desired number. Each new team member should in turn grab the waist of the last player in line. The first team finished gets prime position on the playing field.

To make team selection even more fair, suggest that teams must have an equal number of males and females.

Lockup!

Overview: Kids lock arms with teammates running back and forth across the floor.

Supplies: None are needed.

Preparation: None is needed.

Time Involved: 10 to 15 minutes

Divide the group into four teams with at least four members each. You can use an uneven number of teams; however, there should be the same number of kids on each team.

Split each team in half, placing team halves on opposite sides of room (see diagram). Both halves of each team should stand in single file lines facing their teammates on the other side of the room.

Lockup!

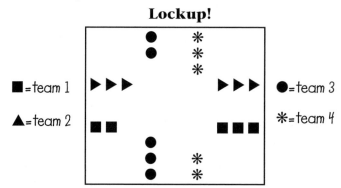

■=team 1 ▲=team 2 ●=team 3 *=team 4

Designate a starter from each half of the team. Explain that this person is to run and lock arms with the first teammate in line across the room.

> **Leader TIP**
>
> Don't overlook the safety factor in playing this game. Remind participants to watch out for each other along the way.

Both kids are to return together and lock arms with the next team member across from them. Have kids continue this back and forth action until the whole team is connected. When members of an entire team are "locked" together, have them make one more trip across the room and quickly sit on the floor.

Measles

Overview: Kids try to lick and stick the most red-hot candies onto partners' faces in the time allowed. This activity is especially suited for festive times such as Valentine's Day or Christmas.

Supplies: You'll need red-hot candies, wet wipes, and bubble gum bandages (optional).

Preparation: None is needed.

Time Involved: 5 minutes

Begin by pairing off in guy-girl pairs (if possible). Ask the guys to lay on their backs on the floor while their partners kneel beside them.

Hand each kneeling player some red-hot candies. Say: **An outbreak of measles has hit the area and I expect many of you to start showing symptoms soon.**

Give kneeling partners two minutes to lick candy pieces and stick them on their partners' faces and necks. Let kids know that the pair with the most "measles" at the end of two minutes is the winner. Since being the winner means the pair has the worst case of measles, reward the winning pairs with boxes of bubble gum bandages...to help ease the pain they surely must be feeling!

Roll-a-Rama

Overview: Teams roll inner tubes around a set course in the fastest time possible.

Supplies: You'll need four inner tubes for each team, a watch with a second hand, and course markers such as traffic cones.

Preparation: Arrange a course with the course markers as in the following example:

248

Roll-a-Rama #1

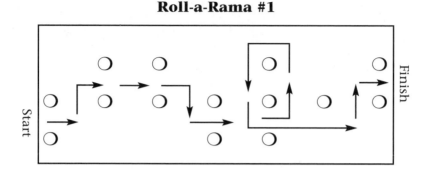

Time Involved: 10 to 20 minutes

Divide your group into teams of four. Depending on the number of teams and available inner tubes, you may choose either to have one team at a time run the course or to have all teams race together.

Instruct members of each team to line up, forming a "monster truck" with really large wheels. To stay connected, members in the rear must each use one hand to hold on to the person in the front. The other hand must be used to balance and roll the inner tube as in the following diagram:

Variation

● If all the teams are racing simultaneously, add the rule that once they cross the finish line, they must run the course again...backward.
● Blow a whistle during play, signaling the teams to turn around and run in the opposite direction. Be sure to have them change direction once more so the teams can cross the finish line.
● Yell "Switch!" during play, signaling each team to change its members' positions and continue to race.

top view

Roll-a-Rama #2

side view

On your signal, have teams race around the course by holding onto and rolling the tires. This is harder than it looks!

If an inner tube drops during play, the team must stop and "change the tire." A tire change is accomplished by having team members exchange inner tubes and then continue the game.

As a team finishes the course, be sure to record its time. The fastest time wins!

Roll 'Em...Run 'Em!

Overview: Kids will roll dice to determine how many times they are to run around a chair before returning to the team. This is a game in which the winner is determined purely by chance, not by skill.

Supplies: You'll need one die and one chair for each team, masking tape, and a whistle (optional).

Preparation: Place a masking tape starting line on the floor at one end of the room. Set a chair approximately ten to twelve feet away from each team.

Time Involved: 5 to 10 minutes

Start by dividing the group into teams of four or more. Next, ask the teams to form standing single file lines behind the designated starting line. Teams should be facing the chairs at the opposite end of the room.

Hand the first person in each team one die. Explain that each person will roll his or her die and then run around the designated chair the number of times indicated.

Variation

For an added twist, blow a whistle during play to signal kids to run backward around the chairs. This will really keep kids on their toes!

Once he or she has completed the correct number of trips around the chair, the person must return and tag the next person in line. Continue in this manner until each person has had a turn. The first team to finish is the winner.

Rubber Band

Overview: Kids will roll a ball back and forth among rotating teammates.

Supplies: You'll need one rubber ball for each team and a whistle (optional).

Preparation: None is needed.

Time Involved: 5 to 10 minutes

Variation

For a wild variation, blow a whistle and yell, "Switch!" during play, signaling all the team halves to switch sides before continuing. This adds difficulty to the game, but it also adds lots of excitement.

Divide the group into four even-numbered teams consisting of six or more kids each. Smaller groups may be used, but the game may not prove quite as challenging. For larger groups, you can add more teams and players.

Divide each team in half and place the team halves on opposite sides of room. Then place a rubber ball on the floor in front of one half of each team as in the following diagram.

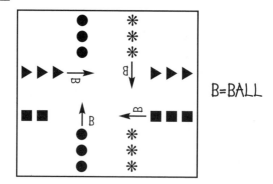

B=BALL

Explain that the teams are to use their hands and roll their rubber balls back and forth across the floor as fast as possible. When one person rolls the ball to his or her teammate on the opposite side of the room the player then moves to the back of the line. Continue the rotation until everyone has had a turn.

The challenge is for a team to move its ball quickly without hitting another ball along the way. The more teams that are on the court, the more challenging the game will be.

Sandwich Maker

Overview: Kids will try to make sandwiches behind their backs.

Supplies: You'll need sandwich fixings such as bread, mayonnaise, mustard, cheese, lettuce, ham, salt, pepper, and so on; knives; paper towels; a tablecloth; and a table.

Preparation: Cover the table with the tablecloth, and set out the sandwich fixings, knives, and paper towels.

Time Involved: 5 to 10 minutes

Variation

Another way to play the game is to allow the volunteer to prepare the sandwich however he or she wishes. The only rule is that every fixing must be used and no peeking!

Ask a volunteer from your group to stand facing away from the table. Explain to this person that the group is really hungry, and they would like a sandwich.

Have the volunteer begin making a sandwich behind his or her back while the rest of the group shouts out things they would like on it. The volunteer is to carefully prepare the sandwich without looking. When it's finished, he or she is to bring it to the front for presentation. Allow other members of the group to try their hands at making sandwiches.

Snow Bombing

Overview: Kids will build miniature snowmen and then try to knock them down with snowballs.

Supplies: You'll need lots of snow.

Preparation: None is needed.

Time Involved: 20 to 30 minutes

Start by having each person build a miniature snowman about one foot tall. Tell kids not to spend too much time making their snowmen because the object of the game is to bomb them with snowballs.

When everyone has finished, mark a twenty- to thirty-foot circle in the snow around the snowmen.

Next, position kids around the perimeter of the circle. Give the group two minutes to make as many snowballs as possible. If kids run out of snowballs, they'll be allowed to make more.

Start the "bombing" portion of the game by having kids take turns trying to knock down snowmen by throwing snowballs at them. Continue until everyone has had an opportunity to play and then repeat until all the snowmen have been demolished. You can keep score by giving one point for knocking down part of a snowman and three points for knocking down an entire snowman. Declare a winner and reward him or her with a snow cone!

Although this game may be played whenever there's snow on the ground, playing at night will really test everyone's aim and accuracy.

Sponge Relay

Overview: Teams will race by passing waterlogged sponges over and under their teammates. This game can really cool off a hot summer afternoon!

Supplies: You'll need sponges, a five-gallon bucket for each team, and water.

Preparation: Fill the buckets with water, and set them aside.

Time Involved: 10 minutes

Start by dividing the group into equal teams of five or six players. (An uneven-numbered team may run one person twice.) Arrange members of each team in a single file line, and have teams stand about five feet away from each other.

Place a water-filled bucket ten to twelve feet away from the first person in each line. Hand a sponge to the first person in each line.

On your signal, the person with the sponge should rush to the bucket, soak the sponge with water, and run back to the end of the line. Next, he or she should pass the sponge to the front of the line in an over and under fashion until it reaches the person in the front. The first person in line should then take the sponge, rush to the bucket, and repeat the process. Continue the game until each person has had a chance to run to the bucket. The game is over when the last person in a line has finished passing the sponge.

Stuff 'Em!

Overview: Kids will try to stuff as many objects as possible into a pair of pantyhose.

Supplies: You'll need one pair of oversized pantyhose for each team; blindfolds (optional); and lots of accessories such as combs, socks, belts, hairbrushes, baseball caps, and so on.

Preparation: None is needed.

Time Involved: 5 minutes

Divide the group into teams of four kids each. Give each team a pair of pantyhose, and explain that the team will have two minutes

Variation

For added fun, blindfold a member of each team. This person becomes the only one allowed to place items inside the pantyhose. Teammates provide assistance by handing him or her objects and offering words of encouragement.

to place as many personal items as possible into the pantyhose. (You may want to have extra items on hand just in case some teams come up short.)

Each item is to be inserted through the waist end of the pair of pantyhose without tearing them. Declare the team with the most items inside the pantyhose the winner.

Water Bowling

Overview: Kids will use water guns to try to knock down foam cups.

Supplies: You'll need ten foam cups, a water gun, water, paper towels, and prizes.

Preparation: Arrange the cups as you would arrange ten bowling pins.

Time Involved: 20 minutes

The object of this game is to see how many cups the kids can knock down with a water gun.

There are two ways to knock down cups: (1) Allow each person to take only three shots at a time, or (2) Allow each person to shoot until the gun is empty.

Begin by having each person stand five feet away from the cups and then move further back with each round. Award token prizes to both the person who shoots the most cups from the furthest distance and the person who knocks over the most cups with a single shot.

Water Weight

Overview: Kids will see who can stuff the most water balloons under a T-shirt.

Supplies: You'll need balloons, water, oversized T-shirts, and trash cans.

Preparation: Fill balloons with water and set them in trash cans.

Time Involved: 10 to 15 minutes

Divide the group into teams of five members each with at least one guy on each team. Place an oversized T-shirt on one of the guys from each team. Next, have members of each team scatter in around one of the cans filled with water balloons.

Explain to the group that team members will have three minutes to stuff as many water balloons as possible beneath the oversized T-shirts. Remind players to pack the balloons carefully so they won't pop them in the process.

The winning team is the one with the most unpopped balloons when the time is up. Any balloon which has popped does not count. After this portion of the game, hold a contest to see which boy might claim the title "World's Greatest Muscle Ballooner!" You might even have the contestants strike crazy poses along the way.

Finish the activity by having balloon-bearing contestants pop their balloons by running into one another. The unused balloons remaining in the cans are then hurled at the leader.

Toe Race

Overview: Kids will use their toes to accomplish a common task.

Supplies: You'll need marbles, two wading pools (for more than twenty kids, use additional pools), and a stopwatch or a watch with a second hand.

Preparation: Place all the marbles into one wading pool. Put the empty pool a few feet away.

Time Involved: 10 minutes

Ask for estimates on how long kids think it will take for the whole group to move the marbles from one pool to the other using nothing but their toes. Take every estimate, no matter how crazy. Then challenge kids to meet or beat the time they predicted. Explain that you will transfer back five marbles for every finger that touches a marble. Begin the game on your command, and keep time to determine how long the transfer actually takes.

After one round, invite ideas for faster strategies such as lining up, moving around the pool after dropping marbles to keep from colliding with another person, letting the strongest toes go first, and so on.

After kids pick a new strategy, challenge them to try again. Repeat the game as often as time allows, urging kids to improve their strategies and times. Consider adding extra challenges such as moving the pools further apart.

Conclude by discussing the following:

● **What's cool about toes?**

● **Not many people pay much attention to toes, but we can't walk or balance without them. Like toes, what other good resources are we currently neglecting in our group?**

● **What cool things would happen if we give these neglected resources the opportunity they deserve?**

Team Tag

Overview: Kids will play a fun game of group tag. Nobody likes to be "It" during a game of Tag, but being "It" with a partner makes the game more fun.

Supplies: None are needed.

Preparation: Set boundaries for the game.

Time Involved: 15 minutes

Enlist two kids with birthdays closest to today's date, and

have them hold hands to serve as the first "It" team.

Say: **Your job is to tag the rest of the group while holding hands. If you let go of each other, your tag doesn't count. When you tag someone together, that person becomes part of your tag team. All the other players must stay within the established boundaries while trying to elude the tag team.**

Narrow the boundaries as the tag team grows larger to make it easier to nab the remaining kids.

After the game, have a discussion by asking:

● **What did you like about being part of a tag team?**

● **What got complicated about tagging with a team?**

● **What strategies made the team approach work?**

● **How might we use the same strategies to work as a team in our church rather than as isolated players?**

Variation

If you have handicapped kids in your group, challenge the group to discover ways that everyone can be involved. For example, team members might carry one another piggyback. Your kids will undoubtedly come up with even better ideas.

Dunk It

Overview: A team of kids will score points by getting a ball into the other team's goal.

Supplies: You'll need two large trash cans, masking tape, a small inflated or foam ball (four to six inches in diameter), and a whistle.

Preparation: Place a trash can at each end of the playing area, and mark a five- to seven-foot circle around each can with masking tape.

Time Involved: 10 minutes or more

Divide the group into two teams. Explain that the object of the game is to get the ball into the other team's trash can located at the opposite end of the playing area.

Give the following instructions:

Each team will be assigned one end to protect. One person on the team will be assigned as goalie (up to three can serve as goalie together if the teams are very large). The goalie's job is to block any shots made against his or her team's goal. Each time your team gets a ball in the trash can, your team will be awarded ten points. Only the goalie is allowed inside the tape circle.

Additional rules are as follows:

● The person who has the ball is not allowed to move. He or she must pass it to another teammate in an attempt to move the ball toward the goal.

● When the other team intercepts or knocks down a pass, that team gets to keep the ball.

● Any ball that is dropped goes to the other team.

● A team member can't touch another person at any time by trying to hold him or her or take the ball away. A team member can only intercept the ball or knock it down.

● When the goalie catches a ball, he or she should throw it to a teammate to start the play moving the other direction.

● You are allowed to change your team goalie at any time during the game.

● When a team scores a goal, the ball is to be given to the other team.

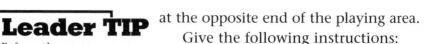

Air Hockey

Overview: Kids will try to blow a table tennis ball off the other team's side of the table.

Supplies: You'll need three six- to eight-foot tables that are the same height, a table tennis ball, and chairs.

Preparation: Place the three tables side by side to make one large square table (see diagram). Put one chair for each person around the enlarged table.

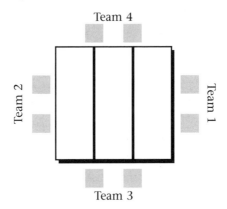

Time Involved: 10 minutes

Divide the group into four teams with at least two people on a team. Have members of each team sit in chairs on one of the four sides of the table.

Give kids the following instructions: **Each team is to try to blow the table tennis ball off the opposing team's side of the table. At no time are you allowed to put your chin on the table or use your body to stop the table tennis ball. Team members are only allowed to use air. Whenever the ball goes off the table in one team's area, the other three teams are awarded ten points each. If you touch the ball or stop it with any part of your body, the other three teams will be awarded five points each.**

Variation

As the game progresses, add additional balls so kids are playing with several at once. Each time a ball falls off the table, stop the game and start over again.

Play the game in rounds of fifty points. Take a break every now and then to let everyone take care of their "lightheadedness."

Hula Hoop Ringtoss

Overview: Kids will toss Hula Hoops onto coffee cans.

Supplies: You'll need Hula Hoops, coffee cans, white paper, tape, markers, and sand (optional).

Preparation: Mark a starting line with masking tape. Cover the cans with white paper. Label each can with a different point value: 10, 20, 30, 40, and 50. To add additional stability to the cans, fill them with sand. Set the cans in numerical order with 10 being closest to the starting line and 50 being farthest away. Put the first can eight feet from the starting line. Then put the second can four feet past the first can, and continue placing cans at four-foot intervals.

Time Involved: 20 to 30 minutes

Have kids line up behind a starting line and toss the Hula Hoops around the cans to earn points. Whoever has the highest point accumulation after three tosses is the winner.

Human Tick-Tack-Toe on the Beach

Overview: Kids will play Tick-Tack-Toe using their bodies as playing pieces.

Supplies: You'll need sticks to draw lines in the sand (or masking tape if you're playing someplace other than a beach).

Variation

This activity is also fun in snowy areas. Have the winning team serve hot chocolate to the losing team.

Preparation: Prepare the Tick-Tack-Toe grid.

Time Involved: 20 to 30 minutes

Divide your group into two teams.

Designate one team as "X" and the other team as "O." Teams should decide together where to put their marks. After the decision is made, have a member of the team lie down in the grid forming either an "X" or an "O" with his or her body. The first team to make three in a row wins. Play several games.

Weave a Web!

Overview: Kids will crawl and duck under a "woven web" inside a meeting room as they try to unravel pieces of string and get to a small treasure box.

Supplies: You'll need yarn; scissors; small gift boxes filled with memory verses, candy, nuts, or other edibles to munch on during the study, coupons for fast food, or inexpensive gifts; and flashlights (optional).

Preparation: Cut a fifty- to one hundred-foot piece of yarn for each person. About an hour before the group's arrival, begin weaving a web inside your meeting room. Take one piece of yarn and tie it to a common stationary object near the entrance to your meeting area such as a stair banister or a heavy piece of furniture. One piece at a time, weave the yarn around, over, under, and between as many objects as possible. Repeat until you have a web of yarn around the room. At the end of each string, attach a small gift box filled with goodies.

Time Involved: 30 to 45 minutes

When kids arrive, instruct them to each grab a piece of yarn and begin untangling his or her portion of the web.

While kids are busy unraveling the yarn, you can offer parallels about potentially "sticky" situations and how much trouble it takes to remove ourselves once we're "tangled up" in the effects of wrong choices. As kids begin to move around, bumping and

Variation

Give everyone a flashlight, turn out the lights, and have kids unravel the web in the dark.

jostling each other, the mood will lighten up and a fresh sense of camaraderie will surface!

Kitchen Jingles

Overview: Kids will quickly work their way through a kitchen looking for items that match with famous advertising slogans.

Supplies: You'll need paper; a pencil; tape; a timer; and kitchen items with famous advertising slogans such as soup, soap, cereal, juice, or coffee.

Preparation: Take inventory of your kitchen's wares, and choose items that are in your pantry. Look at the labels to help recall particular well-known jingles. (One example is "Good to the last drop.") Lay out all the items you are going to use and write each item's slogan on a slip of paper. Tape the slips to the bottom of kitchen items other than the ones to which the slogan pertains. Reserve one slip to begin the game. Replace all the items in various places in your kitchen.

Time Involved: 60 minutes

Divide the kids into teams of four or less. Explain that they must locate food items found in the kitchen area by using the clues you will give them. Members of each team must work together to locate all the slogan items as quickly as possible. Only one team is to play at a time, and there should be no peeking by other teams.

Provide each team with the first clue. They should begin searching the kitchen looking for the item that corresponds to the jingle or slogan written on the piece of paper. Once the correct item is found, tell the kids to turn the item over and read the next jingle. Have the team repeat this process until all the items have been discovered. Before a new team begins, be sure to replace all the items to their proper places. Time each team to determine the winner.

Here are some slogans and jingles to get you started:
- "Softens your hands while you do the dishes"— Ivory Soap
- "They're gr-r-reat!"— Kellogg's Corn Flakes
- "The San Francisco Treat"— Rice-A-Roni
- "Mmm, mmm, good"— Campbell's Soup

Blindfolds, Please!

Overview: Each person will wear a blindfold and make a snack for a friend according to that friend's directions. Warm up a meeting that will challenge your kids' memories and bring plenty of laughter.

Supplies: You'll need ingredients for the snack of your choice, bowls, utensils, serving plates or bowls, napkins, a blindfold, slips of paper, and pencils.

Preparation: Determine the snack, and set up a serving table with the necessary ingredients. Choose food items that can be separated into about six or eight different bowls such as those used to make ice cream sundaes, English muffin pizzas, nachos, potato skins, or a dinner salad. Be sure to place serving utensils in each bowl.

Time Involved: 30 to 60 minutes

Have each person write his or her name on a slip of paper, and place all the slips of paper in a bowl. Ask everyone to stand around the table and take a good look at the items on it. Leave one side of the table free for the first person to work freely. Draw a name out of the bowl, and have that person put on a blindfold. Choose another name, and ask that person what he or she would like on (or in) his or her snack. Once the second person has made a choice, the blindfolded person should make the requested snack.

After the first person is finished making the snack, have the second person put on the blindfold and choose a third name from the bowl. Continue until everyone has had the opportunity to make a snack. Cook the pizzas, nachos, or potato skins, and enjoy eating them together.

Pop and Obey

Overview: Kids will sit down on balloons and break them.

Supplies: You'll need balloons, slips of paper, a pencil, and chairs.

Preparation: Write assorted action movements on slips of paper, fold them lengthwise, and insert one into every balloon. Suggested actions are: "sing a song as loud as possible;" "run the length of the room twice;" "crawl around the room once;" "hop to five people on one foot and give them each a hug;" "whistle 'Row, Row, Row Your Boat'; " and so on. Blow up the balloons, making sure there are enough for each person to break at least one during the game.

Time Involved: 30 to 60 minutes

Divide the group into relay teams with no more than ten kids per team. Hand out one balloon to each person, and instruct kids to hold onto them. Have each team line up in a single file line behind a chair. One at a time, have kids place their balloons on the chair and attempt to break them. As soon as a balloon pops, the person should read the slip contained inside and then carry out its instructions. After the first person is done, the second person should begin. Continue until everyone on the team is finished, and have the first team to "pop and obey" sit down on the floor to signal its victory.

Calendar Charades

Overview: Kids will take turns selecting holidays to act out for the rest of the group.

Supplies: You'll need a large calendar with a page for each month, a red marker, a timer, and holiday-related prizes (optional).

Preparation: Beginning with the month of January, circle all the holidays with a red marker. Tear the pages of the calendar apart, and fold them into squares so that the months of the year are not revealed.

Time Involved: 30 to 60 minutes

Divide the group into teams of four to six. Instruct each team to select one calendar page. Give them five minutes to pick a holiday from their page and decide how they'll act it out. Have one team at a time act out its holiday while the others try to guess which holiday it is. You might want to help kids get started by having them think of things unique to each holiday such as Easter egg hunting, shooting off fireworks, and so on. The team whose holiday is guessed in the quickest time wins.

Depending upon the holiday that's closest, you can choose to hand out related gifts such as chocolate candy on Valentine's Day or small American flags on Independence Day.

Grocery-List Menus

Overview: Kids will look over prepared grocery lists and create their own meals on newsprint.

Supplies: You'll need paper, pens, newsprint, scissors, markers, tape, a long table, and a timer.

Preparation: Create several different grocery lists using a wide range of food items and including all the food groups. (You'll need one list for each group of kids.) Set up the table, cover it with newsprint, and tape the ends of the paper down. Cut several more paper strips of the same length, one for each team. Lay markers on the table. Depending upon your group size, one table may accommodate all teams simultaneously. If teams are large, have them take turns. Be sure to replace the paper for each new team.

Time Involved: 30 to 60 minutes

As kids arrive, divide them into teams of six or less. Hand out a grocery list to each team along with a pen for each member. Instruct each team to circle enough items on its list to create a complete meal including an appetizer, salad or soup, an entree, a beverage, and a dessert.

Next, have each team take a turn drawing a picture of its meal on the newsprint. While the team is drawing, have the other teams try to guess what each food item is. As soon as each team's meal has been identified, have the next team begin.

Be sure to have each team draw its meal as quickly as possible with multiple team members drawing simultaneously. The team whose menu is guessed in the shortest time wins.

Bubbles and Balloons

Overview: Kids will try to keep a balloon in the air until all their team members have completed a bubble-blowing obstacle course.

Supplies: You'll need balloons; liquid bubble-solution in assorted pans; bubble-blowing devices such as coat hangers, plastic wands, and so on; bubble gum; and a timer.

Preparation: Insert a piece of individually wrapped bubble gum inside each balloon and then blow the balloons up. Set up six or more stations around the room, each with a pan of liquid bubble-solution and a bubble-blowing device.

Time Involved: 20 to 30 minutes

As the group arrives, divide kids into teams of eight or less and give each person a balloon. The object of the game is for each person on the team to keep his or her balloon in the air while they run the obstacle course one at a time. The only time a person's balloon does not have to be in the air is when that person is running through the course.

Once a person has completed the run, he or she is to sit on the floor, pop his or her balloon, take out the gum, and begin chewing and blowing bubbles. As one person finishes the course, have the next person begin while the rest of the team members continue to keep their balloons in the air. The first team finished is the winner.

Maid for a Day

Overview: In a race to beat the clock, kids will take turns doing various household tasks as quickly as they can.

Supplies: You'll need a timer and various cleaning supplies to match the activities you choose.

Preparation: Decide what household chores you want the kids to do such as washing dishes, window cleaning, dusting, or sweeping. Set up a cleaning station for each chore.

Time Involved: 30 to 60 minutes

Divide kids into teams of four or less. Walk each team through the cleaning course explaining what is expected of them at each station. For example, at the first station, kids might run the vacuum cleaner around a circle of chairs. At the second station, they might fold a piece of laundry. At the next station, they might wash and dry a dish, and so forth. As one person finishes the first station and moves on to the second, the next person on the team should begin the relay. Be sure to "reset" each station as each team runs the course. Keep track of the course time for each team.

Christmas in July

Overview: Kids will select a star from a miniature Christmas tree and act out the "giving" deed written on it.

Supplies: You'll need miniature Christmas tree, assorted stars cut out of construction paper, a hole punch, scissors, ribbon, markers, and small gift boxes filled with treats (optional).

Preparation: After making the paper stars, write on them fast-paced or funny deeds that can be acted out. Examples might be: "sing 'Jingle Bells' at the top of your lungs," "ring a bell and announce that Jesus is born," "form a heavenly choir to sing 'Angels We Have Heard on High,' " and "feed a cookie to everyone in the room." Next, attach a piece of ribbon to each star and hang it on the Christmas tree.

Time Involved: 30 to 60 minutes

Variation

Wrap small gift boxes and fill them with goodies. Give one to each person to open after the game is finished.

Have group members take turns selecting a star from the tree and acting out the deed written on the back. The kids can either work alone or in groups. Continue until all the stars have been selected.

Ice Races

Overview: Kids will race down a hill on a block of ice. This game works best on a hot summer evening.

Supplies: You'll need a water hose, several twenty-five pound blocks of ice, and 6x50-foot rolls of plastic (the number of pieces of plastic and pieces of ice will depend on the size of your group).

Preparation: Purchase several twenty-five pound blocks of ice at a local icehouse. They will stay frozen in a cooler or in an air-conditioned building for a few hours. Spread the sections of plastic down a grassy slope and then wet the plastic so it is too slick to walk on. To make it even slicker, you can add dishwashing detergent also.

Time Involved: 30 minutes

Divide kids into teams of four players. Instruct each team to select one Rider and three Pushers. At the top of the slope, have the Rider for each team sit on the team's block of ice. As the race begins, the three Pushers should push the Rider down the plastic to the bottom of the slope. If a Rider falls off the ice, he or she must get back to the point where the fall occurred and continue on from that point.

Continue the race, eliminating the slower times, until you have a winning team.

Four-Corner Scramble

Overview: Kids will compete in a confusing massive group-race. It is great for large groups in a gym when you want to get everyone involved at once.

Supplies: None are needed.

Preparation: None is needed.

Time Involved: 30 minutes

Divide the group into four teams. Assign each team to one of the four corners of the room. Explain that the teams are going to race against each other in a corner-to-corner race. The object is for a team to get from its corner to the opposite diagonal corner as fast as it can. This activity is not just one race but several, each with a different twist.

Begin the game by having just a simple running race. Kids will soon discover that running in opposite directions will develop quite a traffic jam in the middle.

As the game progresses, use the following additional races:

- Have kids race leapfrog-style.
- Have kids race holding hands in pairs.
- Have kids run backward.
- Have members of the whole team lock arms and race.
- Have kids pair up and ballroom-dance to the other side.
- Have kids form a single file line with their hands on the peoples' hips in front of them.

In order to determine the winner of each race, have kids join hands and sit down when their whole team has reached their corner. Award points for first and second place in each race. The excitement will build with each event.

Water-Balloon-Attack Volleyball

Overview: Kids will play volleyball with the suspense of a water-balloon attack.

Supplies: You'll need a volleyball net, a volleyball, balloons, and water.

Preparation: Set up the volleyball net, and fill the balloons with water.

Time Involved: 30 to 40 minutes

Divide the group into two even teams and begin to play regular volleyball. Each time a team gets a point, give the team a water balloon. Explain that it may use be used to attack the other team at any time during the game. The object is to throw the balloon at the other team to distract team members and cause them to lose the point. Teams are allowed to stockpile balloons if they choose. Kids will soon discover that bluffing a throw at the other team can be just as distracting as actually throwing a balloon.

Be sure to keep score during the game. When it's over,

award the leftover balloons to the winners so they can really soak the others.

The Great Race

Overview: Kids will participate in a huge outdoor station-to-station relay race. This game works best when there are one hundred or more kids and you're trying to get everybody involved at once. The events for the race are designed to be wild, crazy, and fun; and they require little or no athletic skill.

Supplies: You'll need one folding chair, ten paper cups, water, a golf ball and a putter, a piece of paper, and a bag of one hundred jelly beans for each team; tape; and a timer.

Preparation: You'll need to designate where each event will be held and make an event list. Be sure to spread the stations around a field so that kids must run from one station to the next. Use tape to mark starting and finish lines where needed.

Time Involved: 30 minutes

Divide the group into teams, with at least forty kids on each one. Direct each team to select different kids to participate in each of the ten events so that everyone gets an opportunity to play. Begin by dispersing kids to the specific event areas where they'll participate. As the race begins, the first person should run from a starting line to the first event with the open bag of jelly beans. The person is to hand the bag of jelly beans to the kids doing that event. After the first activity is complete, one person should run to the next event with the bag of jelly beans. The kids there should complete their activity and run the jelly beans to the next activity area. Teams should continue in this manner until the bags of jelly beans have been raced around the field.

At the end of the race, count the jelly beans left in the bag and add one second to a team's time for each jelly bean that's missing. The object of the race is to finish it with as few jelly

272

beans lost as possible.

The following events will help you get started.

- Human Obstacle Course (Use people as obstacles.)
- Water Drink (A person drinks ten cups of water.)
- The Human Pyramid (Ten people form a pyramid.)
- Sink a Putt (A person makes a ten-foot putt into a hole.)
- Circle Sit-Down (Kids form a circle and sit on each other's knees for fifteen seconds.)
- Folding-Chair Race (The first person in line unfolds, sits in, and refolds a chair and then passes the chair down the line.)
- The Paper-Plane Flight (A person makes and throws a paper plane ten feet.)
- Over and Under With the Bag of Beans (Kids in a line pass the bag over and under using their hands.)
- Two Carry One (Two people carry a third who is holding the bag of jelly beans.)
- A Sprint to the Finish (Kids run a fifty-yard dash back to the starting line.)

Shoe Scramble

Overview: Kids will hunt from a pile of shoes for any two that fit. This game is simple but hilarious.

Supplies: You'll need as many old shoes as you can find laying around the house.

Preparation: None is needed.

Time Involved: 10 to 20 minutes

Divide kids into teams and station each team in a different corner of the room. Collect all the kids' shoes and throw them into a big pile in the center of the room. Mix up the shoes, and add some additional ones. Make the pile high and compressed, not spread out.

On your signal, have all the kids run toward the pile of

shoes. The object is for each person to find any two shoes that fit, put them on, and return to his or her corner of the room. When all the kids from a team have returned to their corner, have the team run a single lap around the building wearing their mismatched shoes.

The first team to complete the lap with the shoes actually on all members' feet should be declared the winner.

Wild Log-Ride

Overview: Kids will have fun running a challenging team relay.

Supplies: You'll need one "log" for each team and tape. Almost anything will work as a log, but each log should be similar to the others.

Possibilities for logs include real logs (about eight or ten feet in length), picnic-table benches, long pew cushions, or ladders.

Preparation: The key to this game is the logs. Use the tape to mark a starting line and a finish line, fifty to one hundred yards apart.

Time Involved: 10 to 15 minutes

Divide the group into teams of ten to twelve kids. Give each team a log. The object is for kids to use their hands to hold the log between their legs and race from the start to the finish line. If one of the kids falls down or if the log falls, the team must stop, pick up the log or the person, and proceed. The first team to cross the finish line intact is the winner. The key to making this game funny is to have the log packed with kids. The more kids on the log, the slower the race will go and the funnier it will be.

Variation

Have teams race forward for a set distance and then race backward toward the starting line.

The Off-the-Floor Challenge

Overview: Kids will use strategy and strength to see how many people they can successfully get off the floor. This game works best if group members are not that familiar with each other.

Supplies: You'll need one chair for each team, paper, a pencil, and a timer.

Preparation: None is needed.

Time Involved: 15 to 20 minutes

Leader TIP

Have teams race forward for a set distance and then race backward toward the starting line.

Divide the group into teams of ten people. Give each team an identical chair. Tell kids they are to work together in teams to get as many of their ten people as possible off the ground and onto the chair. Allow teams about ten to fifteen minutes to experiment with various formations and to practice getting people off the ground. When everyone is done practicing, hold the final competition.

In judging the competition, allow each team sixty seconds to build its human formation. Each team must stay with all of its members off the ground for sixty seconds. After the time is up, record the number of players that were suspended totally off the ground for the allotted time.

Part of the fun is watching the other team so if it's possible, judge one team at a time and let the others watch.

Triangle-Line Soccer

Overview: Kids will play a three-way game of line soccer. This game works best with kids who are somewhat athletic and enjoy physical games, although all kids can play.

Supplies: You'll need a soccer ball, three traffic cones, and a chalk field-liner (optional).

Preparation: If possible, use chalk to mark a triangle on a large athletic field. To do this, place three traffic cones in a triangle, all thirty feet from each other. Make sure the cones are equal distances from each other. Next, take your chalk field-liner and draw a chalk line between the three cones. If you don't have a chalk liner, be creative and use sand, towels, spray paint, flour or whatever else works. At the very least, mark the sides of the triangle using the cones.

Time Involved: 40 to 60 minutes

Divide the group into three equal teams. Assign each team to stand along one of the lines with equal distances between each person. Next, assign every person on all three teams a different number. (Each team should have the same numbers. For example, the kids on each team would be numbered from one to thirty.)

Start the game by placing the soccer ball in the center of the triangle. Call out a number, and have the kids with that number run into the triangle toward the soccer ball. There should be one person from each team in the center.

The object of the game is to advance the ball across either one of the two sides of the triangle without using any part of the hands or arms. The kids standing on the outside of the triangle are actively playing the game as goaltenders. Their job is to defend their team's side of the triangle. They are allowed to use any part of their bodies to stop the ball.

If one of the kids on the line catches the ball, he or she may throw or kick it toward one of the other goals. In order for a team to score, the ball must pass over the line and must not be more than waist-high when it crosses. Balls too high are retrieved and placed back into play.

Score the game by giving a team two points every time one of its members kicks a ball over an opposing line. The team whose line the ball crossed loses one point.

If the three kids in the middle fail to score quickly, call another number. After each goal, place the ball back in the middle and call a different number. It might be helpful to record which numbers have been called to allow everyone an opportunity to play.

Bag-of-Bones Race

Overview: Players will participate in a crazy over-the-head relay race. This game encourages teamwork as well as plenty of laughter.

Supplies: You'll need one old sleeping bag for each team.

Preparation: None is needed.

Time Involved: 15 to 30 minutes

To play the game, divide the group into fairly even teams of eight or more people. Have each team form a single file line facing in the same direction. Give each team a sleeping bag. Direct the first person in each line to get completely into the sleeping bag, with his or her head sticking out.

Begin the race by having the next two people in line hoist the person in the bag over their heads and pass him or her down the line.

When the person in the bag has been passed the entire length of the team, he or she should be lowered onto the ground. The person should then get out of the sleeping bag and crawl under everyone's legs back to the front of the line while carrying the sleeping bag.

Once he or she is back at the front of the line, the person should hand off the bag to the next person in line and then go to the end of the line. Continue the game until everyone on the team has been passed down the line and has crawled back.

If necessary, you can play the game by passing the person and the sleeping bag down the line at waist height. This may work better if the group is made up of younger players.

Skin the Snake

Overview: Kids will play a game guaranteed to bring any group together. If you have a large group of kids at a camp or retreat this game is a must.

Supplies: None are needed.

Preparation: Instruct kids to wear long pants for this game.

Time Involved: 30 minutes

Divide the kids into two large teams with up to one hundred kids per team. If necessary, form three teams. Line each team up in a single file line with persons facing the back of those in front of *them*. Have teams face the same direction with about twenty yards between them. Direct kids to each bend at the waist and reach forward with one hand while taking the other hand and reaching back between their legs to grasp the hand of the person behind them. (The first person in line will have no one to reach for.)

To begin, have the last person in line lay down backward on the ground while being careful not to let go of the hand in front of him or her. This action forces the whole line to move backward. As the line moves backward, each person in turn should lie on the ground directly in front of the previous player.

Once the last person is laying down, he or she should stand up and begin moving forward and pulling the person behind him or her up. The whole line will be doing the exact opposite of what they did to get on to the ground. The first team to get all the way back up wins. Holding hands the entire time is essential!

Write-On Pool Relay

Overview: Kids will get know each other in a hilarious pool race. This game is suited to a fairly large pool and a group of kids who have some swimming ability.

Supplies: You'll need one cheap T-shirt and one marker for each team.

Preparation: None is needed.

Time Involved: 15 to 20 minutes

Divide the group into teams of six to eight players. Give each team a T-shirt and a marker. Direct the teams to send kids to each end of the pool so there are at least three kids from each team on both sides.

Begin by instructing the first person from each team to put the T-shirt on over his or her bathing suit. Then, on the signal, have the first person from each team race to the other end of the pool holding the marker above the water. When the person reaches the other side, he or she should climb out, take off the wet T-shirt, and write his or her name on the arm of the next person in line. The next player then puts the T-shirt on and jumps into the pool. He or she should swim to the opposite end holding the marker above the water with the arm that has been written on.

When this person hands off the T-shirt, have him or her write his or her own name on the new person's arm as well as the previous person's name. The new person will then have two names written on his or her arm. Continue the race with each person putting on the T-shirt and receiving a growing list of names on his or her arm before jumping in and swimming with the marker to the other end of the pool.

When everyone has finished swimming across the pool, the last person should have the names of all the team members written on his or her arm. The first team to finish should be declared the winner.

Human Foosball

Overview: Kids will play a life-size beach game similar to the table game Foosball. This game offers a break from traditional beach games and is hilarious to watch and play.

Supplies: You'll need a soccer ball, shovels, and traffic cones for boundary markers.

Preparation: The playing area should be like a Foosball table with lines of alternating attackers and defenders up and down the field. Begin by marking goal areas that are five feet wide at each end of the playing area. Make the goal areas approximately one hundred feet apart. Next, mark eight parallel lines across the playing field, approximately ten feet apart.

Time Involved: 30 to 45 minutes

To play, divide kids into two teams. Station kids on the lines, alternating kids from opposing teams on every other line. Have one person stationed at each goal. Next, have each person dig a hole in the sand where he or she is standing. Each hole needs to be knee-deep and will take about ten minutes to dig.

After the holes have been dug, have the kids step into them and bury both legs up to the knees. They should now be stationed knee-deep in the sand. Make sure the kids from each team are facing toward the goal they are attacking. This means that they should be staring directly into the face of an opponent who is "planted" ten feet away.

The rules are simple. The game itself is like soccer, only the players use their fists to hit the ball. If they are buried correctly, their hands should just about touch the sand. The ball cannot be caught except by the person guarding the goal. It must not travel more than two feet off of the ground, and if it's hit higher than two feet, it should be given to the other team. A goal is scored whenever the ball passes across the goal at no more than two feet in the air. (A secret to keeping the ball down is to deflate it a bit.) If the goalkeeper catches the ball, he or she must put it back into play by hitting it from the ground with his or her fist.

Any individuals not playing the game can serve as ball re-trievers and can move the ball back into play whenever it gets stuck between players.

Hose Heads

Overview: Kids will attempt to put on nylon hose while blindfolded.

Supplies: You'll need a bag of clean, used nylon hose (one piece for each person), one blindfold for each team and a video camera (optional).

Preparation: Before playing, turn some nylon pieces halfway inside out, and tie loose shoelace-style knots in others.

Time Involved: 5 to 10 minutes

Have kids form pairs (preferably guys with girls). Congrat-ulate your kids on their recent promotions to Senior Nylon Testers. Distribute one length of nylon hose and a blindfold to each pair. Ask the girl in each pair to blindfold the guy.

Say: **The mark of truly superior nylon is how user-friendly it is. We'll test this by asking the blindfolded member of your team to be the one to actually put on the nylons over his clothes. You may remove your shoes, but that's all.** Pause while anyone who wants to re-move his or her shoes does so.

Continue: **The member of your team who is not blindfolded will give instructions if your nylons should be inside out...or knotted...or tangled up in any other way. This person may not touch the nylons but can only give advice.**

Speed is important, of course, but so is *style*. Finish-ing first is your goal, but the important thing is just

to finish!

Dump the rest of the nylons on the floor between the teams. Say: **When I say "one," you blindfolded Testers slowly come up and take a nylon piece. When I say "two," go back to your partners. When I say "three," let the testing begin!**

Add extra fun by pulling out a video camera as the guys struggle to put the nylons on. Keep the video camera out of sight until the guys are blindfolded.

Unidentified Fictional Objects

Overview: Kids will work as a team to complete a fairy tale.

Supplies: You'll need pens, paper plates, and a timer.

Preparation: None is needed.

Time Involved: 10 minutes

Form teams of up to seven players each, and have members of each team form a circle. Give each person a paper plate and a pen.

Say: **Around the rim of the plate you're holding, write "Once upon a time, a beautiful princess..."** Pause while kids write.

Say: **When I give you the signal, toss your plate across the circle to someone else and prepare to have one tossed to you. You'll have twenty-three seconds to write the next line of the story and then you'll toss the plate again and continue the story that's written on the plate that you catch. We'll keep going until we finish the story. You must write quickly! Ready?**

Keep the plates and pens moving. Just prior to giving the command for the fifth switch, say: **This is the final part of** the story. Begin by writing: "And they all lived," and then finish the sentence any way you want after you receive a new plate.** Give kids a moment to finish and then say: **Toss the plates!**

Ask kids to take turns reading their fairy tales aloud.

Muddy Obstacle Course

Overview: Kids will go through an obstacle course filled with mud.

Supplies: You'll need eight tires, a large quantity of mud, dirt, water, sand, opaque balloons, baseball caps, thumbtacks, plastic tarps, a working garden hose, heavy tape, large trash bags, one-gallon plastic bags, and old towels.

Preparation: Follow the instructions for each of the following obstacles:

- Mud Mayhem—Make a "popping hat" by pushing a thumbtack through a baseball cap so that the point is facing out of the top of the hat and secure it in place with heavy tape. You'll need one hat per team. Fill balloons with water and one balloon for each team with watered-down mud. Give each team a trash bag filled with water balloons and one balloon that has mud in it.
- Gross Tire-Walk—Mix mud to a fairly thick consistency. Line up eight tires in two rows. Line tires with trash bags, and fill two tires with mud, two with water, two with sand, and two with dirt.
- Mud-Pie Carry—Lay mud pies sealed in one-gallon plastic bags at a starting line.
- Marsh Plunge—Spread mud along the length of tarps, and mark a finish line at one end.

Time Involved: 15 minutes

Divide kids into teams of five. Have each team select members to do each of the following:

- One to do the Mud-Pie Carry
- Two to perform the Mud Mayhem
- One to do the Gross Tire-Walk
- One to do the Marsh Plunge

Each team must complete the course as follows. The first person must place a mud pie between his or her knees and carry it to the second event without dropping it. As soon as that person tags the person in the popping hat, the Mud Mayhem begins.

This phase of the activity begins as the person in the popping hat sits down. The other teammate selected for this event begins to remove balloons from the garbage bag and pop them on the teammate's hat until they discover the one that has mud inside. When they make the discovery, the person in the popping hat is to jump up and run to the person waiting at the Gross Tire-Walk who then must walk through all the tires without missing one. After completing this phase, that person is to run to the person waiting at the Marsh Plunge. This person must make a running slide down the Marsh Plunge on his or her belly. If the final person fails to cross the finish line, he or she must go back and plunge again. The winning team gets to hose off first!

Newspaper Delivery

Overview: Kids will work as a team to build a newspaper and deliver it.

Supplies: You'll need one Sunday edition of the paper for each team.

Preparation: Take the sections of the paper apart and place them all over the building in good hiding spots. For instance, you might hide the front page under a chair, the sports section in the gym, and the classifieds in an office by the phone.

Time Involved: 20 minutes

Divide kids into teams. Tell them the object of the game is to assemble a Sunday paper with all the sections in correct order and to be the first team to deliver it to you complete. So they know what they are searching for, you might tell them either how many sections they need to find or give them the front page section with the table of contents.

Balloon-Egg Game

Overview: Kids will pop their "eggs" and divide into teams determined by the colors inside.

Supplies: You'll need three-inch colored squares of paper (one color for each team with an equal number of squares for each person on a team), a white balloon for every player, and a children's wading pool or another large container.

Preparation: Place a colored square of paper inside each balloon. Be sure to create the same number of balloons with each color so your teams will be evenly divided. Blow up and tie all the balloons. Place them in a "nest," such as a children's wading pool, in the center of the play area.

Time Involved: 5 minutes

Say: **We have a bunch of eggs in the room that need to be hatched. The way that they get hatched is for each of you to run to the center of the room, grab an egg, and sit on it until it pops. Inside the egg, you'll find a slip of colored paper. Your job is to find the other hatchlings with the same color. To do this, you must run around the room saying "bawk, bawk, bawk" and the color of your paper until you find all the hatchlings that have the same color. For instance, if your paper is red, run around saying "bawk, bawk, bawk, red" until you find the other people saying the same thing. Ready? Set? Go!**

Indoor Ice Arena

Overview: Kids will enjoy the fun of the ice arena even if there is no ice rink in town or it is the middle of summer.

Supplies: You'll need two pieces of wax paper per person, masking tape, a bamboo pole for limbo, and a music source.

Preparation: Using masking tape, mark off a large carpeted room like an ice rink. If you really want to get into it, use wooden boxes to create advertisements with sponsor names printed on them.

Time Involved: 10 minutes

Have the kids take off their shoes and wrap wax paper around their stocking feet. Secure the wax paper with masking tape around the ankles. Explain that the object of this activity is to ice-skate with the wax paper on their feet.

Call for various activities over the course of the game such as, "all skate," "guys only," "girls only," "couples only," "hokey pokey," "limbo." Make sure you have rink-music to play, especially for the hokey pokey and limbo.

Toilet Basketball

Overview: Kids will play a variation of basketball.

Supplies: You'll need one free-standing toilet for each half court, several rolls of toilet paper, and colored masking tape.

Preparation: If you will only be playing on a half court, set the toilet at the goal line and tape off the floor like a basketball court. For a full court, place a toilet at each goal and tape the floor accordingly.

Time Involved: 15 minutes

Divide your group into two teams. The object is to score a basket by tossing the roll of toilet paper into the toilet. The game begins at center court. Players can only be in motion when they do not have the toilet paper in their possession. Those holding the toilet paper must stop and either pass or shoot. No physical contact is allowed.

The team with the highest score at the end of fifteen minutes wins.

Silly String Wars

Overview: Kids will get wild when they are handed cans of Silly String.

Supplies: You'll need a can of Silly String for each person, flashlights, and glow-in-the-dark wristbands in two colors.

Preparation: None is needed.

Time Involved: 30 minutes

Either supply a can of Silly String for each player or have each person bring a can as an admission fee for the event. Divide the group into two teams. Give each member of one team one color of glow-in-the-dark wristbands and each member of the opposing team the other color of wristbands.

The object of this game is for one team to "string" every member of the other team. Each person must ration his or her can and should not shoot frivolously. Prior to the game, establish boundaries and capture areas. Every person should begin the game with a flashlight and a can of string.

When a person gets "strung," he or she must go to the other team's capture area. After one team has captured all the kids on the opposing team, the game ends. The winning team gets to blast the losers with all of the leftover Silly String!

Water Noodle Hockey

Overview: Hockey never looked quite like this! Kids will love this modified water polo.

Supplies: You'll need foam plates, five-foot water noodles (two per person plus six extra to make goals), and plastic ties.

Preparation: Make a goal by using plastic ties to connect three water noodles into a goal box shaped like a three-sided square. You'll need one goal for each end.

Time Involved: 20 to 60 minutes

Divide kids into two teams. The object is for each person to mount one water noodle and use his or her second one as a hockey stick and an oar. Players are to pass the foam-plate puck across the water to the opponent's goal. The first team to score three goals wins.

Nut Night Skits

Overview: This activity will help you see the hidden creativity in your kids as they prepare a skit using a bag of unrelated items.

Supplies: You'll need one bag with ten unusual items in it for each team.

Preparation: Prepare the bags containing the chosen items. Make sure each bag has ten items and that all of the bags have the same ten items.

Time Involved: 60 minutes

Divide the group into teams of five or six players each. Give each team a bag. Say: **Inside each bag are ten items. Some of them are fairly normal and some are quite unusual.**

The object of this activity is for your team to create a skit using every article in the bag. We will come back together in half an hour to perform these skits.

Hot Slime

Overview: This activity is like the game Hot Potato, but with a nineties twist. Kids will also become more familiar with new Christian music and artists.

Supplies: You'll need toy slime, a cassette or CD player, and cassette tapes or CDs of Christian music.

Preparation: Make a music tape with fifteen- to twenty-second clips from different Christian artists. Place a pause between each clip.

Time Involved: 5 minutes

Begin by having kids form a circle. Tell them they need to pass the slime around the circle to each other until the music ends. When it stops, have the person caught holding the slime try to name the musical artist or the song.

Cherry Bobbing

Overview: Do you need a change this Halloween? Kids will bob for cherries in a pan of cherry gelatin.

Supplies: You'll need lots of maraschino cherries and lots of cherry gelatin, a large washtub, and towels.

Preparation: Prepare the cherry gelatin as directed on the package. Once it has set, pour it into the washtub and mix it with the cherries.

Time Involved: 10 minutes

The object of this game is to give everyone an opportunity to go face-first into the tub of gelatin and come up with a cherry. No hands are allowed in the gelatin, and kids with long hair should pull their hair back and secure it with rubber bands.

Pasta Bowl

Overview: Your kids will not only experience pasta like never before, but they will learn it has many different names!

Supplies: You'll need a variety of pastas, including spaghetti, macaroni, fettucine, tortellini, fusilli, pasta shells, and mostaccioli; a pasta bowl; whipped cream; spoons; pots of water; plastic tarps; and tape.

Preparation: Cover the floor with plastic tarps, and prepare the stations as follows:

- Mostaccioli Roll: Place raw mostaccioli on the floor, and mark off a race lane with tape.
- Pasta Shell Shot Put: Cook pasta shells according to the directions on the package. Place these at the station with a container of whipped cream and a spoon.
- Speed Slurp: Cook spaghetti, fettucine, and macaroni according to the directions on the individual packages and place at the station in separate piles or bowls.
- Fusilli-Tortellini Team-Up: Place raw fusilli and tortellini at this station with a pot of water across the room from it.
- Finish Line: Place a large pasta bowl at the finish line.

Time Involved: 25 minutes

Divide your group into equal teams. If you don't have large enough teams to have one person at each station, send a player who has already completed an event to the next available station. The stations are as follows:

1. Mostaccioli Roll—At the word "go," the first person on each team must roll a piece of raw mostaccioli down a raceway

with his or her nose to the person waiting at the second station.

2. Pasta Shell Shot-Put—When the second person is tagged by the first person, that person begins filling a pasta shell with whipped cream. Once it is stuffed, it must be thrown to the next station where the third person must catch it. If the shell is dropped, another one must be filled and thrown.

3. Speed Slurp—After catching the shell, the third person must take one strand of cooked spaghetti out of a bowl by placing one end between his or her lips and slurping the entire strand into his or her mouth. The player must do the same with a strand of cooked fettucine and finally with a piece of cooked macaroni. The person should then run to the fourth station to be a tortellini stringer for the next player.

4. Fusilli-Tortellini Team-Up: The fourth person holds a piece of raw fusilli onto which the third player is to string ten raw tortellini rounds. Once the "string" is complete, it must be carried very carefully to a pot of water across the room and dumped. If either the fusilli is broken or the tortellini is dropped, the two must go back and start over stringing ten pieces of tortellini. After making their deposit into the pot of water, they must run to the finish line and deposit their fusilli in the pasta bowl.

Other events can be added as well. This event is also fun as part of a spaghetti dinner for families, especially when some of the adults get involved also.

Mall Madness

Overview: Kids will have fun, while being reminded of the materialistic society we live in.

Supplies: You'll need the "Mall Madness Expense Sheet" handout (p. 292), pens or pencils, and a calculator.

Preparation: Make one photocopy of the "Mall Madness Expense Sheet" handout (p. 292) for each team.

Time Involved: 60 minutes

Have your group meet in the food court of a local shopping mall. Divide them into teams of three or four, and give each team a copy of the handout and a pen or pencil. Say: **I will give you one hour to find the most expensive things in this mall. You must record the prices and have each clerk who quotes a price initial your sheet. You cannot change an answer to a more expensive one once you have written a price down. When we meet back here in one hour, we will total each team's expense sheet. The team with the highest total wins.**

Have a calculator on hand when the kids return, as these totals will probably be astronomical!

After you have shared these totals, have ice cream and talk about different reasons why people might spend money on such items. For a fun conclusion to your "mall madness," ask:

● **If you had unlimited wealth, which item would you choose to purchase? Why?**

Mall Madness
EXPENSE SHEET

- The most expensive piece of jewelry
  $ _____   _____
- The most expensive piece of candy
  $ _____   _____
- The most expensive shirt
  $ _____   _____
- The most expensive pair of shoes
  $ _____   _____
- The most expensive "service" available in the mall (for example, a haircut, a tanning session, a visit to a doctor's office, a visit to an eye doctor's office, or a manicure)
  $ _____   _____
- The most expensive coat
  $ _____   _____
- The most expensive drug that is over the counter
  $ _____   _____
- The most expensive wedding dress
  $ _____   _____
- The most expensive book
  $ _____   _____
- The most expensive video game
  $ _____   _____
- The most expensive camera
  $ _____   _____
- The most expensive vitamin
  $ _____   _____
- The most expensive pair of glasses
  $ _____   _____
- The most expensive painting
  $ _____   _____
- The most expensive pair of tennis shoes
  $ _____   _____

Tikes and Bikes

Overview: This event is a great outdoor event for older kids to begin to building relationships with the younger kids of the church.

Supplies: You'll need paper, pencils, balloons, water, string or twine, a stopwatch, and tricycles or bicycles.

Preparation: Put traffic cones around the race area in a parking lot.

Time Involved: 50 minutes

Tell kids in advance that they can only attend this event if they pay the entry fee—bringing along a younger child (a sibling, a younger church member, or a child in the neighborhood). Each younger person must bring a tricycle or a bicycle.

Each pair (a teenager with a younger partner) will compete against other pairs in a series of bike races. The object is for the young children to compete in events using their bikes or trikes while the teenagers use the same pieces of equipment for their events.

Events for Tikes (the little kids)
● The Indy 500: This is an oval-shaped track that the younger kids must complete five laps around. Be sure to record their individual times on separate team sheets.
● The Downhill: Locate a small hill, and have the kids race down to a finish line at the bottom. Again, record their individual times.

Events for the Teenagers (the big kids)
● The Backyard Dash: This is a 100-yard dash in a straight line; where the riders must ride backwards. Record each individual time on the correct team sheet.
● The Figure-Eight: This race is run as a figure-eight pattern. Each teenager must do five laps around the course. Record each time.

Total up the time for each pair. The fastest pair wins.

Take advantage of this event and close with a brief discussion on "winning the race—God's race."

Tied-Up Volleyball

Overview: This game is much like a game of volleyball, only the members of the entire team are connected and must move together.

Supplies: You'll need a volleyball, a volleyball net, and ropes.

Preparation: Set up the volleyball net.

Time Involved: 30 to 45 minutes

Divide your group into two teams. Have members of one team stand next to each other. Tie each person's wrist to the wrist of the person standing next to him or her. When this task is accomplished, the team members should be able to raise their hands in coordination with the person next in line. Do the same to the other team. Play the game like you would play a regular volleyball game, except the entire team will need to be involved in every shot. To make the game easier, try using a large beach ball instead of a volleyball.

Cemetery Crawl

Overview: Kids will to get to know some local history, begin a study on death and dying, and have some good Halloween fun.

Supplies: You'll need flashlights, paper, and pencils.

Preparation: Go to the cemetery in advance and find some interesting tombstones for the kids to discover. Record the information with a point value for each piece. Make a copy of the information for every team.

Time Involved: 60 minutes

Have kids meet at the chapel of a local cemetery after dark. Divide into teams. Make sure each team has a copy of the handout, a pencil, and a flashlight. Give kids forty-five minutes to find the tombstones, record the information, and return to the chapel. Award points for the correct answers.

Examples of items to include on your handout:
- The oldest tombstone—50 points
- The newest grave—50 points
- The biggest tombstone—50 points
- A military person—10 points for each one listed
- The person who lived to be the oldest—50 points
- The names of a couple buried side by side under a grove of trees—100 points
- The person who died on—(you come up with a list of dates and point values)

(Make up a list of approximately twenty items.)

The Wave

Overview: Kids will move rapidly from one chair to another in this fast-paced game.

Supplies: You'll need one sturdy chair for each person.

Preparation: Set the chairs in a tight circle.

Time Involved: 15 to 30 minutes

Begin by having each person sit in a chair. Designate a person to be "It." Have the person who is "It" leave his or her chair and stand in the center of the circle. As soon as "It" leaves his or her chair, the person to the right of the empty chair must move to sit in the chair. This will create a clockwise motion in the circle as each person moves to his or her left to sit in a vacant chair. "It" must try to sit in one of the chairs being rapidly vacated and occupied.

When "It" sits in a chair, the displaced person becomes the new "It" and must begin searching for an empty chair. There are no timeouts. You can add to the confusion and laughter by changing the direction from clockwise to counter-clockwise.

Canned-Food Cleanup

Overview: Kids can play this broom hockey game in conjunction with a canned food drive.

Supplies: You'll need canned food from a variety of food groups, a box, and one broom for each team.

Preparation: Place all the collected food along one wall. At the far side of the activity area, place one box on its side for each team.

Time Involved: 10 minutes

Begin by having the kids form equal teams. Have members of each team form a single file line. Explain that each team is to form multiple "balanced meals" using the food placed along the wall. Each person is to choose only one item at a time, sweep it into the team's box, and return the broom to the next person in the relay line. This next person will choose the next item and repeat the process. Play continues until all the cans are in boxes.

Afterward, gather kids together and have them actually lay out their balanced meals. Award one point for each acceptable meal. Don't miss this opportunity to discuss the importance of bringing more than corn and green beans for a food drive!

Gummy-Worm Relay

Overview: Kids will stick together in this sweet relay.

Supplies: You'll need one gummy worm and two toothpicks for each pair and masking tape.

Preparation: Mark a starting line and goal line with tape.

Time Involved: 5 minutes

Have kids form pairs. Give each pair two toothpicks and a gummy worm. Have both partners attach their toothpicks to opposite ends of the gummy worm and then grasp the toothpicks with their mouths. Have each pair stand on the starting line and grasp hands.

On your cue, each pair must head toward the goal line. If a pair's gummy worm falls off either of the toothpicks, the pair must stop and reattach it. The winning pair is the one who crosses the finish line first with its worm still attached to both toothpicks.

Ice-Log Relay

Overview: Kids will pass an ice log in this "cool your heels" relay.

Supplies: You'll need snack-size resealable plastic bags and water.

Preparation: Freeze water in the plastic bags ahead of time. (You'll need at least one for each team.)

Time Involved: 5 to 10 minutes

Start by forming equal-sized teams. Have members of each team lie on their backs,

Variations

● Have same-gender teams stand side by side and pass the ice logs armpit-to-armpit.
● Have kids stand front to back and pass the ice log between their elbows.
● Playing this game in a swimming pool is also lots of fun!

head to foot in a straight line. Remove the ice logs from the plastic bags. The person at the front of each line must grasp the ice log between his or her feet, lift feet up over head, and pass the ice log to the next person. The second person in line must grasp the ice with his or her feet and pass it to the next person in line in the same manner. The last person must drop the ice log on the ground behind his or her head.

Midget Fluff-Hockey

Overview: Kids will use rolled-up newspaper sticks and fluffy balls for a kinder and gentler version of hockey.

Supplies: You'll need newspaper, masking tape, a bag of polyester filling, and knee pads (optional).

Preparation: Roll the newspaper into long sticks, and wrap each with enough masking tape to secure it. Remove the polyester filling from the bag, shape half of it into a ball, and wrap it with tape. Mark a goal at each end of the playing area as well as a center line.

Time Involved: 10 to 30 minutes

Form two teams. Inform kids that they must play the game on their knees. Provide each player with a rolled-up newspaper stick. Choose a goalie from each team, and have the remaining kids spread out on either side of the center line.

Begin the game by tossing the "fluff puck" high into the air at the center line. Points are scored by getting the "fluff puck" past the opposing team's goalie and into the goal. At the midpoint of the game, call a timeout and choose a new goalie for each team. The team with the most points at the end of a designated time is declared the winner. Each of the winning team's players can sign the "fluff

Variation

You can make the game more challenging by binding kids' ankles with masking tape so that they can only take "baby steps" on their knees.

puck" with a black permanent marker so that it can be prominently displayed in your church trophy case!

Featherweight Relay

Overview: Kids will pass a square of toilet paper with their own air power in this more-challenging-than-it-sounds relay.

Supplies: You'll need a drinking straw for each person, a roll of toilet paper, and masking tape.

Preparation: Mark the starting and finish lines with masking tape.

Time Involved: 5 to 10 minutes

Form teams of equal numbers. Designate a starting line and a finish line. Have each team space its kids across the playing field from the starting line to the finish line. Have kids place the straws in their mouths.

Tear off two squares of toilet paper, and give one to each team's first person. The first person must suck on the straw to hold the square with the other end. On your cue, have the first person run to the second person. The second person must then receive the square by sucking on his or her straw. If the square does not make the pass, it is the carrier's responsibility to pick it up and try to transfer it again. As soon as the second person has the square, he or she should carry it to the next person on the team. The person at the end of the line must then return the square to the first person, so that every team member has the opportunity to be the carrier.

Take this opportunity to discuss the idea of carrying burdens by asking:

● **What were your first thoughts about passing something so light?**

● **What, if anything, changed your initial perception?**

● **How is this like or unlike carrying an emotional burden?**

● **Which do you think would be more difficult to carry: several unconnected squares of tissue or a ten-pound book?**

● **What do you think happens to people when they are carrying a lot of fairly light emotional burdens?**

Read Psalm 55:22. Say: **It is our privilege as Christians to cast our cares on God, whether our burden is small or great. It's not the weight of the burden that matters, it's trying to carry it ourselves that slows us down.**

Mummy Relay

Overview: Kids will do a mummy-roll race in this relay that really keeps them all wrapped up.

Supplies: You'll need a bedsheet for each team.

Preparation: None is needed.

Time Involved: 5 to 10 minutes

Form multiple groups of equal size. On each team, have kids number off one and two. Send the Ones to one side of the activity area and the Twos to the opposite side with each half of the team facing the other half.

Lay a bedsheet in front of each half of the Ones. On your cue, have the first person on each team lay down on the sheet and roll himself or herself up (kids will need to grasp the fabric in their fists to keep it together). The person must then roll all the way across the area to his or her teammates on the opposite side. The person wrapped in the sheet must then get untangled and lay the sheet out for the next person.

Continue the game until each person on the team has traveled to the opposite side of the playing area.

Woolly, Woolly

Overview: Kids will pull the wool everywhere except over their eyes in this fast-paced action game.

Supplies: You'll need four rolls of two-inch masking tape or duct tape and multiple bags of cotton balls.

Preparation: Mark off a line with tape in each corner of the playing area.

Time Involved: 10 minutes

Form four teams of equal size. Have each team select a person to be the Woolly. Each team needs to wrap its Woolly's arms to his or her body with tape sticky-side out. Each Woolly must then go to a corner and stand behind the tape line. The rest of each team goes to the center of the play area where the cotton balls have been placed.

The object of the game is for each team to cover its Woolly with as many cotton balls as it can in two minutes. Team members do not have to proceed in any particular order, but each player may carry only one cotton ball at a time. Any two people who bump into each other must be seated where they collide, and they can no longer carry cotton.

At the end of two minutes, bring each Woolly to the center of the playing area and count the cotton balls on each one.

Sparkler Tag

Overview: Kids will shoot fizzling targets in this everyone-for-himself game.

Supplies: You'll need effervescent antacid tablets, string, scissors, water guns, buckets of water, and a whistle (optional). Kids can bring their own water guns, but be sure to standardize the type to keep the game fair.

Preparation: Drill holes in the centers of the tablets, and cut a thirty-inch string for each player. Place buckets of water in various places around the edges of your playing area.

Time Involved: 10 to 20 minutes

Give each of the kids an antacid tablet, a piece of string, and a water gun. Tell them to thread the tablets onto their strings and tie them around their necks or waists where they will be visible. The tablets become the targets for all other kids to aim at.

Give kids thirty seconds to scatter around the area you have defined and then blow a whistle or shout a command for them to begin the game. The object is for kids to try to defend their tablets while shooting at other players.

A person becomes a refill helper when his or her tablet gets squirted enough to fall off its string. The helper takes a position at a water bucket and refills water guns so that the remaining kids can continue playing. The person who can protect his or her tablet the longest is the winner.

Defender Tag

Overview: Kids will defend each other in this fast-paced game of small-group Tag.

Supplies: None are needed.

Preparation: None is needed.

Time Involved: 10 to 20 minutes

Form your group into teams of four players each. Have each team select one person to be "It," one person to be the Protected, and two to be the Defenders. Make sure the teams have enough space between them so they won't bump into each other.

Instruct the Defenders and the Protected on each team to all hold hands. On your cue, each "It" needs to try to tag the Protected person of the group while the trio spins and dodges to keep him or her from getting tagged. As soon as "It" tags the Protected person, he or she becomes a Defender, the Protected person becomes "It," and one of the Defenders becomes the Protected person.

This game can be played until all the kids are exhausted or until everyone gets a turn—whichever comes first!

Hoop Tag

Overview: Kids will enjoy this small-group Tag game which requires quick reflexes and hand-eye coordination.

Supplies: You'll need a Hula Hoop.

Preparation: None is needed.

Time Involved: 5 to 15 minutes

Have one of the kids stand on the inside of the hoop and the rest of them around the outside of the hoop. Instruct the outside kids to each hold onto the hoop with one hand. The person on the inside is "It." He or she will try to tap the hand of one of the Holders. The Holders must quickly switch hands to keep from getting tagged.

The rules are as follows:

- the holders must each have one hand on the hoop at all times,
- the person who is "It" cannot tag a hand that has been lifted from the hoop, and
- whenever a person is tagged, he or she becomes "It."

Jerusalem Journey

Overview: Kids will try to gain an advantage in this Tag game through the artful use of alliteration.

Supplies: None are needed.

Preparation: None is needed.

Time Involved: 5 to 20 minutes

Select one person to be the Traveler. The rest of the group needs to stand around the Traveler, either holding his or her fingers or touching his or her back.

The Traveler first chooses and announces his or her destination, such as Jerusalem. Then the Traveler says "I went to J...J...J...Jericho" or "I went to J...J...J...Joplin" or any other location that begins with a J. When the Traveler finally says "I went to J...J...J...Jerusalem," all the kids should scatter and run to avoid being tagged by the Traveler. The first person tagged becomes the new Traveler.

If anyone is fooled by the Traveler's other journeys and lets go prematurely, that person automatically becomes the new Traveler.

Each new Traveler can choose a different destination and distract the kids accordingly. However, make sure the ultimate destination is announced before the game begins.

Ghana Jump

Overview: In this traditional children's game from Ghana, kids will enjoy the challenge of second-guessing their opponents.

Supplies: None are needed.

Preparation: None is needed.

Time Involved: 5 to 10 minutes

Have kids stand in a semicircle an arm's distance away from each other, facing inward. Choose one person to be the Challenger. He or she will stand facing one of the kids in the semicircle.

The Challenger and the chosen opponent will jump up and clap their hands to each other's. Then they will both jump up and land with their legs apart and clap their own hands together. Then they simultaneously jump, landing with their feet together and hands at their sides. Finally, they both jump and thrust forward whatever foot they choose, while at the same time they stick out their opposite hands in an attempt to clap each other's outstretched hands. If the Challenger and his or her opponent land with opposite feet extended, the Challenger moves on to the next person to repeat the same jump routine. If both the Challenger and the opponent land with the same foot extended, the Challenger must take the place of the first person who then continues the game by going on around the circle.

> **Leader TIP**
>
> Have all the kids practice the jump sequence several times with partners before you begin the game.

Baby Steps

Overview: Kids will run a relay race while trying to keep on infant-sized shoes.

Supplies: You'll need two pairs of baby shoes (the smaller, the better) and tape.

Preparation: Determine and mark both a starting line and a finish line.

Time Involved: 10 to 15 minutes

Form two equal teams. Have members of each team stand in a single file line at the starting line. Say: **Remember what it was like to be really small? Maturity is a great thing. It's tough to be a little kid. I wouldn't want to be in those shoes again for all the money in the world!** Show kids the shoes, and continue: **These probably won't even cover your big toe! But the object of the game we are going to play is to find a way to keep them on during this relay race. You are allowed to get to the finish line and back in any matter you want to, but you have to keep these shoes on your feet as you go.**

Have everyone remove their shoes and socks. Kids may choose to run while trying to keep the shoes on, crawl like babies, or wear both shoes on the same foot. Let kids be creative!

This is a great game to play if you are equipping your group to minister to a group of children. After the relay, hold a short discussion by asking:

- **What do you remember about being a little child?**
- **What things made you feel respected?**
- **What things made you feel bad?**
- **What did you think of teenagers when you were very young?**
- **How will those memories help you in your relationships with children?**

Say: **As you remember your childhood feelings, try to think of ways to connect with children that are kind, respectful, and Christlike.**

Ice Treasure

Overview: Kids will take turns trying to find a hidden treasure in this outdoor game that's great for a winter retreat.

Supplies: You'll need an ice cube and lots of snow.

Preparation: None is needed.

Time Involved: 5 to 10 minutes

Have kids form a circle, and choose one of them to stand in the middle.

Have each person make a snowball. Give one of the kids the ice cube to hide inside his or her snowball. When all the snowballs have been made, instruct the person in the center to close his or her eyes and count to fifty (twenty-five will be adequate for a small group). While the person in the middle is counting, have the kids in the circle pass their snowballs around. However, instruct them not to throw them! After the count is complete, allow the person in the center three chances to guess who is holding the snowball containing the ice cube.

Each time the person in the middle makes a guess, the person who is holding the snowball must crush it to reveal whether the ice cube is inside. If the player in the center guesses correctly, the person holding the ice cube must trade places with the person in the middle.

Construct new snowballs for Round Two.

Stepping Out

Overview: Kids will take turns stepping out and over each other in this wacky race.

Supplies: You'll need two yardsticks (three-foot pieces of rope can be substituted) and tape.

Preparation: Designate a starting line and a finish line.

Time Involved: 5 to 10 minutes

Variation

• You can make this game more challenging by adding obstacles for the racers to step over or maneuver around.
• If you have enough yardsticks or rope pieces, you can run the relay with all pairs racing at the same time.

Have each person pick a partner and then form two teams with an equal number of pairs. Have the pairs line up one behind the other in their teams.

Give the first pair in each team a yardstick. Instruct the partners to each hold one side of the yardstick and take turns stepping over it as they move toward the finish line. As they race toward the finish line and back again, they must not lose their grip on the stick. The stick should be given to the next pair on the team to repeat the process. Continue the relay until all the kids have completed it.

Jumping Jacks

Variation

You can make this relay more interesting by including some obstacles along the route such as old tires or cushions. Kids with physical disabilities may participate by walking around the obstacles or by rolling in wheelchairs through the course.

Overview: In this unique relay race, kids will have an opportunity to work together for the good of the team.

Supplies: You'll need tape.

Preparation: Mark a starting line and a finish line.

Time Involved: 5 to 10 minutes

Begin by dividing kids into two equal teams, and have members of each team line up single file.

Say: **This is a relay race that requires lots of hopping. When I give the signal, have one person from each team hop to the finish line and back.**

Next, have that person tag two people on his or her team who then must lock arms and hop together to the finish line and back. These two must then tag the next three kids from their team, who are to lock arms and hop down and back. Continue this process until the entire team locks arms together and hops down and back. If any arms become unlocked during the race, those people must return to the starting line and start again. The first team to get everyone down and back with locked arms will be the winner.

Four-Post Relay

Overview: Kids will see which individual or team can complete the circuit in the fastest time.

Supplies: You'll need a large ball of twine, four wooden stakes that are at least 5 1/2 feet long, a hammer, and a stopwatch.

Preparation: Secure the stakes in the ground, one on each corner of an imaginary square. Each stake should protrude at least five feet above the ground, and the stakes should be at least fifty feet apart.

Time Involved: 15 minutes or more

Begin the game by dividing the group into two teams (or you may have kids play individually if you have a small group). Secure one end of the twine on the first stake. On your signal, have a person from the first team run around the posts one time with the twine ball, allowing it to unwrap and make a giant square. He or she must then hand the twine ball off to the next person, who will proceed to run around the posts with the twine. Keep track of each team's time.

Invisible Basketball

Overview: Kids will work together to defeat a make-believe basketball teams playing this Hoosier state favorite.

Supplies: You'll need basketball goals, a basketball, and tape.

Preparation: Use tape to mark five spots on the basketball court from which your team must shoot at the basket.

Time Involved: 20 to 30 minutes

Explain the game by saying: **The object of this activity is for our group to compete against an invisible basketball team. We must work together to score. Whenever someone from our team makes a basket, we get two points. If we miss a shot, our invisible opponents get three points. The first team to score twenty-one points wins.**

Crab-Walk Hoop Soccer

Overview: Kids will play a variation on soccer while crab-walking.

Supplies: You'll need any kind of ball, tape, two chairs, and two buckets or small trash cans.

Preparation: Tape a 12x6-foot rectangle at each end of your activity area and a line to indicate the center court. Place a chair in each goal area.

Time Involved: 20 to 40 minutes

Form two teams, and ask for two volunteers from each team. One of the volunteers will be the Hoop and one will be the Hooper. Other team members are crab-walkers. Ask the Hoop to stand on the chair in the goal area with a bucket held at his or her waist, and ask the Hooper to kneel in the goal area. The Hoop and Hooper from the same team share the same goal.

Crab-walkers must assume a crab-walking position (sitting on their behinds with their feet and hands flat on the floor) and scatter around on their side of the court. Ask one crab-walker from each team to meet you at center court. Begin the game by dropping the ball. Play should begin when it hits the floor.

The objective of the crab-walkers is to kick the ball to their Hooper, who must stay on his or her knees and use his or her hands to make a basket. The Hoop is allowed to move the bucket but is not allowed to bend his or her knees or come off the chair. Crab-walkers must always maintain the crab-walking position, and they can't enter the goal area. The Hoopers are not allowed to move outside the goal area. If they desire, have players rotate positions after each point. Continue the play until one team scores five baskets.

If you have a large group, consider adding an extra Hooper for every five additional players. With more players, you might want to consider increasing the play area and goal size.

Which Way Relay

Overview: Kids will map out their crazy travel plans with this geography relay.

Supplies: You'll need a map with lots of cities, landmarks, or points of interest on it; masking tape; index cards; a pen; and highlighters.

Preparation: Make two large photocopies of the map, and tape them to a wall at least ten feet apart. (You can copy the map onto smaller sizes of paper and then tape them together.) Use a highlighter to mark the same starting point on each map. For example, you might use the city where you live or the capital. Next, choose a variety of cities, landmarks, and points of interest from the map. Write each one on an index card. Use some locations that are easy to find and others that are hard to find. Duplicate the cards so that you'll have two identical sets. Make at least one card for every person plus several extras for each team. Shuffle each set of cards separately. Make a third copy of the map and circle the places you've selected so you'll have a key if necessary. Be sure to clear away any furniture so the kids can run from one end of the room to the other.

Time Involved: 10 to 15 minutes

Form two groups, and tell kids that they're going on a road trip! Before they leave, they'll need to make an itinerary of the trip as all good planners do. Have each group stand at the wall opposite its map. Place the prepared deck of index cards and a highlighter marker on the floor in front of each team.

When you say "go," the first person from each team must select the top card in the set and run to the map. He or she then must locate the destination written on the card and highlight a route to it from the starting point. The person should then run back to the team and give the marker to the next person in line who will draw another card and continue the game in the same manner. Each team is to continue until its set of cards is gone. After all the destinations have been found, have the next person in line run to the map and mark the route from the last destination back to the starting point.

> **Leader TIP**
>
> If your map doesn't have roads on it or if you want the game to move more quickly, have kids draw a straight line from one destination to another. You can also allow teams to help their team members by yelling out the locations.

If a person can't find the destination written on the card, he or she may run back and select another one. Kids must keep in mind, however, that someone else will eventually have to find that destination.

Sponge-Paint Tag

Overview: Kids will create autographed shirts either during or at the end of a retreat or a workcamp project. This is best played on a warm, sunny day when kids can be washed off with a water hose for cleanup.

Supplies: You'll need one sponge and one T-shirt for each person, bowls, scissors, permanent markers, and several colors of nontoxic paint. (You can use tempera paint, fabric paint, or fabric dye. However, it's best to use something that won't fade when it's washed.)

Preparation: Set up bowls of paint in the corners of your activity area. If you use a thick fabric paint, you may want to dilute it in water. Provide a different color of paint for each team.

Time Involved: 10 to 15 minutes

Prepare your kids for this messy game by having them wear old clothes to the activity. Give each person a T-shirt and a sponge, and have kids put the shirts on. You can have them wear their T-shirts over their old shirts for extra protection from paint.

Have kids each cut a shape from the sponge that symbolizes who he or she is. For example, one person might cut out his or her initial and another person might cut out a musical note if he or she likes music.

Next, form four teams, and tell them the object of the game is to get their team to tag as many people as possible by running to their assigned bowl of paint, dipping the sponges lightly into it, and stamping them on other people's T-shirts. Tell kids they will receive one point for each person they tag, but they'll lose a point whenever they deliberately tag someone's arm, leg, or face. They can tag anyone regardless of whether he or she is on their team, but they only get a point for tagging someone once. If they tag everyone before the end of the round, have them try to tag people again just for fun.

Tell kids they can tag more than one person before returning to the bowl of paint, but if they have too much paint on their sponges, their symbols won't show up very well. Give kids one minute to tag as many others as possible.

After one minute, call time, and gather everyone together. While you're allowing the paint to dry on the shirts, have the kids tally their points. Close the activity by passing out markers and letting kids sign each other's works of art.

Socket Ball

Overview: Kids will play a combination of basketball and soccer.

Supplies: You'll need a basketball or a playground ball and two portable net-style goals or four traffic cones.

Preparation: Set a goal up at the boundary line under each basket on a basketball court. If you're using cones, set up a goal by centering two cones under each basket approximately five feet apart.

Time Involved: 30 to 60 minutes

Explain to your kids that Socket Ball is simply basketball and soccer combined! Form two teams, and have each team designate a goalie. Tell the kids they can score either baskets or goals—they will be awarded two points per basket and one point per goal. They can score goals or baskets with either their hands or their feet.

Start the game with a tip-off. Allow kids to dribble the ball either with their hands or their feet. They can also pass the ball with either their hands or feet. Out-of-bounds balls can either be kicked in or thrown in.

The goalie is only allowed to defend the goal, although he or she can block shots like anyone else.

If you're using traffic cones as goals, designate an imaginary line about waist-high as the crossbar of each goal. When a goalie catches a shot, the ball can either be kicked or thrown back into play.

Rule violations result in either a free kick or a free pass for the other team at the point of violation. Inform your players of these additional rules:

- No drop kicks
- No pushing or holding
- No traveling: any time a person moves with the ball, he or she must dribble the ball
- No tripping

Balloon Blowout

Overview: Kids will compete to see who can create the largest balloon bouquets.

Supplies: You'll need numerous multicolored balloons, string, and scissors.

Preparation: Hide the deflated balloons around a large area. Cut a three-foot length of string for each team.

Time Involved: 20 to 30 minutes

Divide your group into teams of two or more students, and give each team a piece of string. Have each team scatter out and pick a spot that will be its home base. When you signal the start of the game, have kids disperse and search for balloons while leaving their string at their home bases. They may bring back only one balloon at a time.

Once a person has found a balloon, he or she must take it back to home base, blow it up, tie it, and secure it to the string. The person then continues to search for other balloons and continues the process. The team with the largest balloon bouquet at the end of the allotted time wins.

To prolong the game, you can stipulate that each team retrieve only balloons of a certain color or that the bouquets contain certain numbers of yellow, red, or green balloons.

Balance Talents

Overview: Kids will compete to see which partners can balance the longest on one leg while tossing an object back and forth.

Supplies: You'll need identical objects such as beanbags, apples, oranges, eggs, or toilet paper rolls (one for each pair) and masking tape.

Preparation: Using masking tape, establish a line at one end of a room or field. Establish another line that is parallel to the first and six feet away. Place another parallel line three feet farther away, and continue in this manner across the room.

Time Involved: 10 to 60 minutes

Divide kids into pairs of two. Form two lines with the partners in each pair facing each other and standing on the lines that are six feet apart. Have kids scatter out at least an arm's length from each other. Instruct them to each hold one foot up and grasp the ankle. (Let kids choose which leg they'd prefer to balance on.) Allow them a few minutes to practice balancing on one foot. Give an object to one person in each pair. The object of the activity is for the two to toss the object back and forth while each balancing on one foot.

Once the teammates have tossed and caught the object once without either partner losing balance or touching a foot down, have kids each move back to the next line. A team should be disqualified if either partner loses balance. (You might want to have several referees on hand to help you watch.) The partners that end up standing the farthest apart win the game.

Thread the Needle

Overview: Kids will use a square dance type of maneuver to make one team from two.

Supplies: You'll need the "Thread the Needle" handout (p. 319).

Preparation: None is needed.

Time Involved: 10 to 60 minutes

Divide the class into two teams of equal size, and designate the teams Team A and Team B. Have members of each team stand side by side, and have teams stand on opposite sides of a large area facing each other. Kids on a team should stand far enough apart so they can stretch their arms and grasp the wrists of their teammates on either side.

Pick someone in the middle of the line on Team A to be the lead person, and designate the two people on the ends as end persons. Designate only two end persons for Team B. Take all five designated players aside and, using the diagram, explain the maneuver to them. Next, give the five players one minute to explain the maneuver to their respective teams without using the diagram. (This won't be easy, but here's a tip: Their teammates need only keep following the line in front of them—the five designated persons will do the rest.)

When you signal the start of the game, have the teams start walking toward each other. If they're doing the maneuver correctly, the lead person on Team A will pull ahead of his or her teammates like the point of an arrow. The members of Team B, however, will be advancing slowly in a straight line, keeping their arms outstretched and grasping each other's wrists.

Before the two teams reach one another, the lead person on Team A should duck underneath the outstretched arms of any two kids on Team B. His or her teammates (the "thread") should follow behind him or her through the "eye of the needle."

Meanwhile, Team B continues to advance, except now the

end persons on Team B will begin to curl around in order to grasp the wrists of the end persons on Team A. Eventually they will get pulled through the needle as well. If this maneuver goes as planned, the kids will create a loop with everyone connected.

If kids were unsuccessful in their first attempt, have them try again. The second time around, designate a new lead person and new end persons. Also, be sure to let Team A be the thread and let Team B be the needle. If your group is having difficulty, show them the diagram and walk them through the maneuver. Once they have been successful, have everyone form a large circle, drop arms, and give themselves a hand.

At the end of the activity, you can talk about the importance of communication in a group effort. You might also want to consider discussing how followers (in this case, the end persons) are just as critical to teamwork as leaders are.

To prolong the game, challenge everyone to complete the maneuver in less and less time. If the class is large enough, form two groups at each end of the activity area and have them compete to see which one can complete the maneuver first.

Thread the Needle

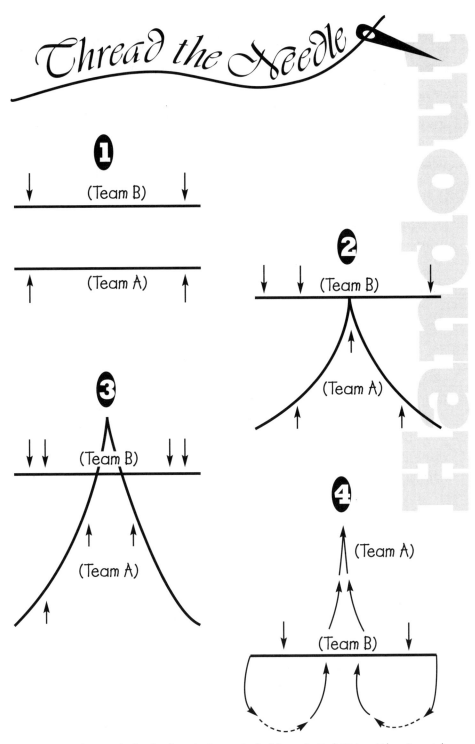

Spud Missiles

Overview: Kids will try to hit a moving target with potatoes.

Supplies: You'll need a bag of potatoes (at least one potato for each person), an object sharp enough to carve names or initials on the potatoes, masking tape or string, a rubber bucket with a handle, a rope with which to suspend the bucket from a ceiling beam or a tree limb, and a ladder.

Preparation: Using the rope and ladder, suspend the bucket from a beam or a tree limb. Use masking tape or string to "draw" a line about fifteen feet from the bucket.

Time Involved: 20 to 60 minutes

Dump the sack of potatoes on the floor or ground. Have each person select a potato and carve his or her initials in it. (If two kids have the same initials, have one of them carve his or her first name instead.) Have kids stand side by side behind the line.

Explain that you're going to grab the bucket, pull it toward you, and let it go so that it starts swinging. The object of the game is for each person to get his or her potato in the bucket while observing the following two rules:

● A person must launch the spud using an underarm toss.

● A person may not launch the spud until the bucket is swinging away.

Anyone violating either rule will be disqualified. To claim victory, a person's potato must be in the bucket when it stops swinging.

You can swing the bucket repeatedly for as long as you want the game to continue. You can modify the game by shuffling kids around or by drawing the line farther away from the bucket. You can also adjust the bucket to hang at various heights.

Fishers of Men

Overview: Kids will try to keep their "fish" (water balloons) from being scooped up in a swimming pool.

Supplies: You'll need fifty or more balloons (half should be red and the other half should be blue), water, buckets, and two pool nets.

Preparation: Fill fifty balloons with water, and put them into separate buckets for each team.

Time Involved: 10 to 20 minutes

Divide your group into two equal teams, the Red team and the Blue team. Pick one person from each team to be the Enemy. Instruct everyone to get into the pool except for the Enemies and then throw all the balloons into the water. The Enemies are to remain outside the pool and should each be given one of the nets. Their job is to scoop out as many water balloons as possible.

They cannot scoop the balloons, or fish, until the balloons are floating on the surface. It is each team's responsibility to keep pushing the team's water balloons under the water. At the end of two minutes, the team with the most fish left in the water wins. Allow other players to be Enemies and play the game for as long as the balloons hold up.

Travels in Time

Overview: Kids will use teamwork to dress their team up with the items in suitcases and then solve an interesting Bible mystery.

Supplies: You'll need three suitcases; a supply of clothes, ties, hats, and other accessories (enough for each person to have at least one item); a Bible; a baby bottle or a rattle; a Father's Day card; and tape.

Preparation: Mark a starting line with tape. You'll need to

Leader TIP

You may want to use items from your church's lost-and-found. Be sure to include funny items such as high-heeled shoes, silly hats and gloves, jewelry, and out-dated ties. The kids will get a kick at how everyone looks!

divide the clothing equally into the three suitcases. In one suitcase, include the Bible; in the second suitcase, place the baby item; and in the third suitcase, place the Father's Day card. Put the suitcases at a designated spot about thirty feet from the starting line.

Time Involved: 10 minutes

Form three teams. Say: **Each team has been chosen to go on a Bible mystery trip. In the Bible, there are many stories of people who went on journeys. Each of them was obeying God, and they traveled because they were told to do so.**

Leader TIP

The Father's Day card relates to Abraham (father of many nations); the baby item belongs to Joseph and Mary for baby Jesus when they traveled to Egypt; and the Bible belongs to Paul representing one of his mission-ary journeys.

Explain that the kids on each team will need to run to a designated suitcase, open it, and put the clothing on. Each person must put at least one article of clothing on. When everyone on the team is dressed, kids must close the suitcase and run back to the starting line.

Their next objective is to determine which Bible family or person each team represents and try to guess the journey they're on. Allow kids to use their Bibles for this part. When kids are finished, be sure to take pictures of your funny-looking travelers.

Banzai Bowling

Overview: Kids will have fun participating in a church bowling tournament.

Supplies: You'll need tape, potatoes, footballs, large candles, plastic soda bottles, pens, bowling score cards (optional), and prizes (optional).

Preparation: Set up several "bowling alleys" on any hard surface that is easily cleaned. For each alley, you'll need twelve soda bottles and a "ball" (use a potato, a football, or a candle). You can change the object you use as the ball for each new round. Use tape to mark the lanes.

Time Involved: 30 minutes

Begin by dividing your group into teams of four or five players each. The object is for the kids to throw or roll objects at soda bottles. Create your own scoring system, or use the standard bowling system. Give prizes to the winning team.

Telephone Charades

Overview: Kids will pass messages using only body language.

Supplies: None are needed.

Preparation: None is needed.

Time Involved: 20 minutes per team

Divide your group into two teams. Begin by instructing the first team to go into a room out of earshot. Have the second team go into another room and begin thinking of an action they want the kids on the first team to act out. Ideas can include such actions as a fish dying, a goose flying through the air, someone riding a bull, and so forth. (The best action ideas make use of the whole body and can be easily summed up in about three words.)

Next, bring one person from the first team into the second team's room. Tell the person from the first team the action he or she is to act out. Summon a person from the second team, and have the first person, without saying anything, act out the action. When the action is complete, have the first team member sit and summon a third person from the first team. Have the second person act out the action in front of the third person. Continue this sequence without using any verbal communication. When the last person from the first team enters the room, have him or her watch the action and then guess what it is supposed to be. If the last person guesses correctly, give the team a point. (It will add interest to the game to have the first person act out the action again so the entire team can see how close the last person was to the original action.)

After the first round, have the teams reverse roles and continue playing.

Are You Wearing Purple Socks?

Overview: Kids will get to know each other in a chaotic fashion.

Supplies: You'll need chairs.

Preparation: None is needed.

Time Involved: 20 to 30 minutes

Form a large circle with enough chairs so that everyone but one person has a place to sit. Pick one person to stand in the middle, and ask everyone else to take a seat. The object of the game is for the person in the middle to pick a seated person and ask him or her a question. For example, a question might be, "Are you wearing purple socks?" The response determines what the whole group will do. If the answer to the question is "yes," everyone must get up and move two chairs in either direction. When all the kids are on the move, the middle person will have an opportunity to get into a seat.

Leader TIP

Only one person may be in a chair at a time.

If the person answering the question responds "no," he or she is required to add a second part to the question, such as "but I know some people here today didn't brush their teeth this morning," or "but someone here has visited Europe before." If the second part of this statement is true about some of the seated kids, they must stand up and try to find other chairs. The person left standing without a chair is the one who must remain in the middle and ask the next yes or no question.

Lost Toothpick

Overview: Kids will try to find a toothpick in a swimming pool.

Supplies: You'll need toothpicks.

Preparation: None is needed.

Time Involved: 30 to 45 minutes

While all the kids are in the pool, have them turn and face a wall and close their eyes. Take a toothpick, jump into the pool, and place it somewhere on the bottom. On your command, have kids get out of the pool and wait until the toothpick has had a chance to rise to the surface. Have kids carefully watch for it. (The approximate surfacing time should be one minute.) Whoever sees it should jump in and retrieve it as quickly as possible. The person who retrieves the toothpick gets to hide it for the next round.

A floating toothpick is hard to see and grab, especially when kids all make waves and start splashing. Most of them will end up in the pool fighting for it, which makes for lots of laughs.

Everybody's "It"– Three-Legged Tag

Overview: Pairs of connected kids will try to tag other pairs without being tagged themselves.

Supplies: You'll need rope or bandannas.

Preparation: None is needed.

Time Involved: 30 minutes

This activity is a simple twist on the game of Freeze Tag. Have kids choose partners and tie their legs together as they would in a three-legged race. When everyone is tied together, explain that in this game everyone is "It." If a pair gets tagged, it is frozen in place and can't move. The last pair to remain untagged wins.

You may also want to try other three-legged tag games.

Competitive Improv

Overview: Kids will act out random scenarios.

Supplies: You'll need weird clothes and hats, a pen, white paper, and red and green paper.

Preparation: Using the categories "people," "places," and "dilemmas," write out several examples of each on small pieces of paper. Examples for each category include: people—doctors, pilots, mothers, neighbors, or shoeshine people; places—an elevator, a supermarket, a movie theater, or an aerobics class; dilemmas—asking someone on a date while you're nervous, getting teeth removed while you're fearful, or you're a man mistaken for a woman. Next, put each slip of paper into a different hat. Find a place you can designate as a stage, and put the clothes and funny hats on it.

Time Involved: 1 hour

Give every person a red sheet of paper and a green sheet of paper. Ask for eight volunteers and divide them into two teams, Red and Green. Have each team pick two pieces of paper from each of the three categories. Allow each team five minutes to think of its improv using one item from each category.

As the teams are preparing, have the rest of the group help you decide on voting criteria such as the best use of props, the funniest improv, the most creative improv, the most believable improv, and so on. Give each team three minutes to act out its improv, using two players at a time. After the teams are both done, ask the group to vote using the criteria they chose.

Continue by having another two kids from each team act out the next category. Continue the activity as before until all the team members have had an opportunity to perform. Once the first two teams are finished, play a second round by choosing new teams.

Blind Relays

Overview: In this relay kids will have to trust the directions of their teammates.

Supplies: You'll need blindfolds and several traffic cones.

Preparation: Determine a starting line, and place one traffic cone twenty-five feet from it.

Time Involved: 20 minutes

The object of the game is for each blindfolded person to run from the starting line around the cone and back. Begin by forming your group into two equal teams, and have each team form a single file line behind the starting line. As each person takes a turn at running around the cone, the rest of his or her teammates are allowed to help by shouting verbal instructions.

When you give a start command, have the first blindfolded

person in each line run around the cone and return to touch the second person on his or her team. Continue the relay until every person has had an opportunity to try. The first team to successfully finish wins.

After the first successful relay, add some additional cones along the course to make it more challenging and race again!

Guess Who

Overview: Kids will try to guess the leader. This is a good game to boost kids' energy between times of prolonged sitting.

Supplies: None are needed.

Preparation: None is needed.

Time Involved: 15 minutes

Choose one person to leave the room. When he or she has exited, choose another person to be the leader. The object is for everyone to stand up and follow the actions of the leader while trying not to let the first person know who the leader is. Instruct kids not to look at the leader but to catch what he or she is doing out of the corners of their eyes. The leader should change actions about every fifteen seconds. Typical actions would be such things as finger-snapping, clapping, patting someone on the back, jumping up and down, turning around, and so on. Start the game after you have asked the first person to come back into the room.

You can continue this activity as many times as you like using new guessers and leaders.

Speed Twister

Overview: Kids will play a speedy game of Twister that adds a fun dynamic to this classic game.

Supplies: You'll need a Twister spinner, four Twister boards (or newsprint; a paper plate; and red, blue, green, and yellow markers), paper, and a pen.

Preparation: No preparation is necessary unless you choose to make the Twister boards yourself. To make, cut six-foot lengths of white newsprint. Using a paper plate to trace, create a row of eight red circles, a row of eight blue circles, a row of eight green circles, and a row of eight yellow circles. (The kids will enjoy the game more if you play some age-appropriate music in the background.)

Time Involved: 30 minutes

Divide your group into four teams. Have kids from each team stand next to an assigned Twister board. Explain that you will call out four spins at a time. Since each Twister circle can only be occupied by one person, kids will need to make a mad dash to the circles. Kids who do not end up on the circles are out. Those who are successful in completing all four commands are allowed to stay in the game while four more spins are announced. Continue until only one winner remains on each board. You can then take the four winners and have a championship round between them.

Variation

You can add to the excitement and challenge by taping all four Twister boards together and letting larger groups play together on the same board.

To begin the game, secretly rotate the spinner four times in a row and write down the spin sequence. For example, you might write "right hand yellow" "left hand yellow," "right foot green," and "right foot red." When you're ready, call out all four spins at once and let the game begin.

Giant Stand-Up

Overview: Kids will work together to accomplish a fun task.

Supplies: None are needed.

Preparation: None is needed.

Time Involved: 15 minutes

Start this activity by having kids pair off and sit on the ground, back-to-back. Instruct them to link arms with their partners and then stand up. (They'll need to lean against each other to accomplish this.)

For the next part of the game, instruct kids to face their partners and form two longer parallel lines. Have the lines turn back-to-back, sit on the ground, and link arms with the people to their right and left. The object is to have both lines stand up together. Kids will need to push against their partners' backs to successfully do this. Have them begin on your command to start.

Emphasize that the group needs to work together. If they don't successfully stand up, have kids continue trying until they are successful. Most groups succeed by the second time.

The Great Paper Race

Overview: Kids will see how many sheets of paper they can wad up and transport to the other end of their activity area. This is a great way to recycle paper that has already been used.

Supplies: You'll need 8½x11-inch paper (you can used recycled paper for this event), manila folders, and masking tape.

Preparation: Tape a starting line and a finish line at either end of your activity area.

Time Involved: 10 minutes

Divide your group into teams of four to five players. Give each team a pile of paper (use the same number of sheets for each team) and a manila folder.

Give the following instructions: **When the game starts, your team will wad up sheets of paper. Have**

one team member begin to stack
the paper wads on the manila
folder. Once the manila folder is
stacked full, one person from the
team should carry it to the finish
line. The person carrying the folder
cannot touch the paper wads at any
time. He or she can only touch the
folder. When that person crosses the
finish line, he or she needs to dump
the paper into a pile and quickly return to the rest of the team.
Continue the process of stacking and
carrying until all of your paper is used up.
Whatever paper drops off during the transport must
be left and can't be retrieved.

Variations

- Add an obstacle course of chairs for kids to maneuver through as the paper is being carried to the finish line.
- Deduct a point for every paper wad that falls on the floor before it gets across the boundary line.
- Set a time limit for the game.

Keep track of which team finished first. After teams are all
done, total up the number of paper wads in each team's pile.
Award one point for each paper wad. Then award bonus points
for the position each team finished in. For example, you might
award twenty points to the team in first place, ten points to the
team in second place, and so on.

Duck-Feet Race

Overview: Kids will put on "duck feet" and run a race.

Supplies: You'll need two sheets of 8x14-inch cardboard,
scissors, two heavy rubber bands for each team, and extra cardboard and rubber bands.

Preparation: Make duck feet by cutting small one-inch
slits in the long sides of the cardboard pieces, running each
rubber band around the cardboard, and hooking it through
the slits or notches (see diagram on page 332).

Time Involved: 5 to 10 minutes

Duck Feet Race

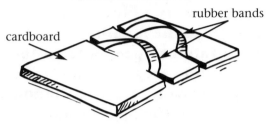

cardboard

rubber bands

332

Variation

If a team's rubber band breaks or one of the pieces of cardboard becomes torn beyond use, provide a replacement and allow them to continue the relay. If a person's duck feet come off during the race, he or she must go back to the starting line and begin again.

Variation

● Cut the cardboard to actually look like duck feet.
● Provide the teams with cardboard, rubber bands, and markers, and ask them to make and decorate their own duck feet for the race.
● Create an obstacle course with chairs for the teams to run through.
● Use chairs to mark off an oval track, and have the teams run around it.

Divide the group into two or more teams. Identify starting and finish lines. Give each team a set of duck feet. Explain that the first person on each team is to attach a pair of duck feet to his or her shoes. On the command to start, that person is to either run or walk out to the finish line and back. The next player should quickly put the duck feet on and do the same thing.